HAUNTED
BY ATROCITY

MAKING THE MODERN SOUTH

David Goldfield, Series Editor

HAUNTED BY ATROCITY

Civil War Prisons in American Memory

BENJAMIN G. CLOYD

Louisiana State University Press
Baton Rouge

Published by Louisiana State University Press
Copyright © 2010 by Louisiana State University Press
All rights reserved
Manufactured in the United States of America
Louisiana Paperback Edition, 2016

DESIGNER: Michelle A. Neustrom
TYPEFACE: Adobe Caslon Pro

LIBRARY OF CONGRESS CATALOGING-IN-PUBLICATION DATA

Cloyd, Benjamin G., 1976–
    Haunted by atrocity : Civil War prisons in American memory / Benjamin G. Cloyd.
      p. cm. — (Making the modern south)
    Includes bibliographical references and index.
    ISBN 978-0-8071-3641-6 (cloth : alk. paper) 1. United States—History—Civil War,
1861–1865—Prisoners and prisons. 2. United States—History—Civil War, 1861–1865—Atrocities.
3. Military prisons—United States—History—19th century. 4. Military prisons—Confederate States of America—History. 5. Prisoners of war—United States—History—19th century.
6. Prisoners of War—Confederate States of America. 7. Memory—Social aspects—United
States—History—19th century. I. Title.
    E615.C58 2010
    973.7'71—dc22
    978-0-8071-3738-3 (pdf)

                                                                           2009044597
    ISBN 978-0-8071-6400-6 (pbk. : alk. paper)—ISBN 978-0-8071-3738-3 (pdf)—
    ISBN 978-0-8071-4629-3 (epub)—ISBN 978-0-8071-4630-9 (mobi)

The paper in this book meets the guidelines for permanence and durability of the Committee on
    Production Guidelines for Book Longevity of the Council on Library Resources. ⊗

 For Katie

CONTENTS

ILLUSTRATIONS

Following page 110

ACKNOWLEDGMENTS

It is gratifying that a book about the power of remembrance should inspire such warm memories of my own past.

A few individuals are responsible for the origins of this project. My oldest debt is owed to my parents, Gregory Cloyd and Eileen Kennedy, and my brother Liam, for providing constant encouragement in ways both seen and unseen. When I was an undergraduate at Notre Dame, Father Robert Kerby's spellbinding courses on the Civil War so transfixed me that I decided to pursue graduate school. Even so, I continue to hold him in the highest esteem.

This book would not be possible without the influence of Gaines Foster. Although it has now been several years since I left Louisiana State University, he remains a superb mentor who always manages to be both gracious and pointed in his wisdom. His patience in commenting on the different incarnations of this work will not be forgotten. Other LSU comrades have shaped me and this project as well. Charles Shindo revealed the powerful hold of consumption on the American mind. Matt Reonas offered—as he always has—keen insight and enduring friendship, and I am additionally indebted to him for inspiring the book's final title. Court Carney made a variety of intangible but vital contributions, which should surprise no one who has had the good fortune of his company over the years. During my tenure at Hinds Community College, I have been inspired by the supportive example of my colleagues: Martha Wilkins, Loyce Miles, Sheila Hailey, Eric Bobo, Bill Simpson, Mickey Roth, Cam Beech, Chris Waldrip, Mike Lee, Eric and Lisa Pridmore, and Ben Fatherree. With reliable good cheer, James Kennedy obtained countless volumes for me via interlibrary loan. Stephen Wedding read the manuscript and insisted on clarity—readers of this book owe him almost as much as I do.

Several institutions and individuals facilitated the enjoyable task of collecting research materials with tremendous professional and personal courtesy. Well-deserved thanks go to the staffs of Andersonville National Historic Site, the Georgia State Archives, the Library of Congress, Middleton Library at LSU, the National Archives, the Southern Historical Collection at the University of North Carolina, Chapel Hill, and the United States Army Military History Institute for indulging me in my curiosity. In particular, I would like to express my gratitude to Dale Couch and Greg Jarrell at the Georgia State Archives, Richard Sommers of the United States Army Military History Institute, and Superintendent Fred Boyles at Andersonville National Historic Site for their interest in and support for my investigations. And Sean and Megan Lumley, now my old (sadly) but always dear friends, kindly shared their home with me to enable my research.

Throughout the publishing process, it has been a pleasure to work with the staff at LSU Press. I am grateful that Rand Dotson expertly shepherded the manuscript to existence while gracefully balancing our friendship with his editorial responsibilities. W. Fitzhugh Brundage offered excellent suggestions for the book's improvement which I have tried to incorporate. David Goldfield commented—perceptively, to no surprise—both on my ideas at an American Historical Association panel in 2007 and on the manuscript, and I am honored by his faith in and commitment to this project. All of the above individuals deserve credit for the merits of this work. Any blame for its failings, of course, belongs to me.

My deepest obligation is to Katie Cassady, source of an ever-growing body of wonderful memories, who, along with our traveling circus of Doc, Parker, and Ella, reminds me of the importance of perspective. She deserves a book about a far happier subject than this one.

HAUNTED
BY ATROCITY

Introduction

F ew stories are as grim as those of the mishandling of wartime captives throughout history. Regardless of civilization or era, armed conflict traditionally results in the misery of those unfortunate enough to endure detainment. The experience of the United States confirms this pattern. There exists, however, a distinct dividing line in American military history as it pertains to prisoners of war. Soldiers captured during conflicts such as the American Revolution and War of 1812 certainly suffered during their imprisonment.[1] During the revolutionary struggle, the British held perhaps as many as 32,000 American patriots captive. Infamous British prison ships such as the *Jersey* claimed thousands of American casualties.[2] But even a war as vicious as the American Revolution provided little indication of what awaited prisoners during the Civil War.

Between 1861 and 1865, as a central element of what historian Charles Royster called "the scale of destruction," the Union and Confederacy engaged in an unprecedented imprisonment of combatants.[3] Of the approximately 410,000 soldiers held prisoner in the Civil War, 56,000 died in confinement. That figure accounted for nearly one-tenth of the 620,000 men who perished in the conflict. But the numbers only hint at the depth of the catastrophe. Both the Lincoln and Davis administrations consistently emphasized the pragmatic needs of the war effort over humanitarian concerns for prisoner welfare. In both the Union and the Confederacy, political maneuvering and ideological expediency determined the fate of each side's captives. Even in the midst of a war defined by its destructiveness, the extent of the agony that occurred within Civil War prison camps enraged and shocked Americans, North and South. According to scholar David Blight, "No wartime experience . . . caused deeper emotions, recriminations, and lasting invective than that of prisons."[4] The extraordinary suffering sparked a lasting debate over the intertwined issues of the meaning of and the responsibility for the tragedy of Civil War prisons.

To avoid false pretenses, two issues that define the purpose and scope of this book need clarification. This is not, nor is it intended to be, a comprehensive description of events that occurred between 1861 and 1865 in the numerous military prison camps of the Civil War. This is instead an account of how multiple generations of Americans, angered, dismayed, and perplexed by the treatment of Civil War prisoners of war, engaged in an ongoing search to find meaning in the tragedy experienced by those captives.

Of the unfortunate soldiers confined in Civil War prisons, none received more attention than the Union captives who endured Andersonville, the infamous Confederate prison in Georgia. Andersonville became and remains the dominant symbol of prison cruelty during the Civil War. Several factors ensure Andersonville's singular reputation despite the persistent misery that occurred in other prison camps. Thirteen thousand Union soldiers died there, making Andersonville the deadliest of all Civil War prisons. In 1865, the camp's commander, Henry Wirz, was executed for war crimes against Union prisoners. During the postwar decades scores of Andersonville survivors published embellished memoirs rehashing their wartime experiences. And while most of the other prison sites disappeared into oblivion, Andersonville, due to the consistent northern fascination with the prison, has been preserved. Today at Andersonville National Historic Site, visitors will find Andersonville National Cemetery, the old prison grounds, and the National Prisoner of War Museum. Much of this narrative focuses naturally therefore on Andersonville, and it would not be unfair to change the subtitle of the book to "Andersonville in American Memory." Yet I stand by my chosen title. For all the sectional bitterness provoked by Andersonville, and despite its central role in the prison controversy, this is ultimately the larger story of how reunited Americans endeavored to learn from their shared failure.

From 1861 to the early twenty-first century, as they contested, commemorated, and commercialized the story of Civil War prisons, Americans sought answers to the question of how such horrors could be possible in a civilized society. Out of that national discourse, an important pattern emerged, one that illuminates the essence of the malleable, complicated relationship that exists between past and present, or, in a word, memory.[5] The concept of memory can seem deceptively simple, but why we remember—the empowerment derived, the identity defined, the wallets fattened, and the myriad emotions unleashed—is anything but. Americans were and remain strangely compelled to recall the brutality of Civil War prisons.[6] The attempt to remember Civil War prisons, although certainly motivated by the desire to honor the dead, persisted mostly to assuage confusion over the senseless nature of the tragedy. Americans of each generation explored the prison controversy and shaped the interpretation of its history in response to their own contemporary political, social, cultural, and financial needs. As they did so, the inevitable selectivity of memory encouraged them to externalize the evils done in Civil War prisons as the fault of others. The consistent refusal to confront the reality of the prison atrocities nourished the cherished myth of American exceptionalism. That statement is intended partly as criticism but even more as recognition of how the retelling of the tale of Civil War prisons provides evidence of the nebulous relationship between memory and history. What is remembered depends on who is recollecting, and the transient nature of memory ensures that the effort to remember naturally distorts the perception of the past. Only a more thorough and honest understanding of why this was (and is) so can offer hope that we might yet find the answers, so persistently elusive, that we will continue to seek in response to our eternal questions about what the Civil War, and its prisons in particular, truly means.

Finally, because this is a study of memory—which by its nature requires careful attention to the identity of those quoted within these pages—I have honored the individuality of past voices by retaining, in all cases, their modifications of traditional grammar.

"Our Souls Are Filled with Unutterable Anguish"

ATROCITY AND THE ORIGINS OF DIVISIVE MEMORY,
1861–1865

A s the mutual bloodletting of the Union and Confederacy commenced in 1861, the relatively innocuous question of the fate of
prisoners of war was of little concern. The excitement over the opportunity to claim prisoners in battle prevented much forethought about
what to do with them once captured. The only fear seemed to be that captured soldiers would not unswervingly demonstrate patriotism during detainment. On June 19, 1861, the *Charleston Mercury* denounced a band of
captured Confederate soldiers who swore allegiance to the Union. This dis-
honorable act of taking the oath represented a forfeiture of their "Southern
citizenship" and a betrayal of the Confederacy. "The United States Government had the right to hold them as prisoners of war," the *Mercury* editor
declared, because "they were not the first, and will not be the last, of mankind who will be subject to imprisonment. It is the fate and the fortune
of war." In a final blast, the paper warned Confederate troops that "war is
bloody reality, not butterfly sporting. The sooner men understand this the
better."[1] As long as optimism for a quick resolution of the crisis persisted,
such reminders of the "bloody reality" of war could be excused as necessary.
The expected brief duration of the conflict promised at worst a short, if intense, period of suffering or imprisonment that any honorable soldier could
withstand. But it would take years, not months, to clarify the true meaning
of "bloody reality." As the war escalated into a shocking cycle of violence,
no other group came to experience the destructive nature of the clash like
prisoners of war did.

The story of Civil War prisons reflects the larger pattern of the conflict.
Just as few in 1861 predicted the slaughters of Antietam or Shiloh, no one
anticipated the capture of large numbers of prisoners at a time or foresaw

the need for the preparation of prison camps. In the unlikely event of prisoner accumulation, contemporary military convention held that upon capture "a prisoner was subject to immediate exchange or release on parole to await exchange at some later date."[2] Immediate exchange allowed capturing armies to avoid the burden of feeding and sheltering hordes of prisoners by swapping captives after a battle. When paroled, a captured soldier swore not to fight or aid the enemy in any way and would then be released. The parole oath precluded the soldier from active duty until declared officially exchanged at a later date. In the early stages of the war, when exchanges were intermittent and before the recognition of how precious the commodity of manpower would become, many paroled soldiers were simply discharged from the army. Both exchange and parole restored the captives to freedom, and once exchanged, soldiers soon returned to the front lines. Although a third fate, imprisonment, potentially awaited captured soldiers, the chances of being held in large-scale prisoner camps seemed far-fetched during the first summer of the war. Unfortunately for the eventual hundreds of thousands of captives, the unprecedented scale and complexity of the conflict made it impossible to divorce the issue of exchanging prisoners of war from the fundamental questions that provoked the war itself.

According to President Abraham Lincoln's interpretation, secession from the Union was theoretically impossible, a perspective that made all Confederates traitors and their army an insurgent force. In practice, his position proved unfeasible since all captured Confederates technically would face trial and potentially execution for treason. Confederate President Jefferson Davis's threats of retaliatory executions against captive Union soldiers further indicated the danger of Lincoln's stance. With reluctance, both Lincoln and Davis realized the necessity for some concessions on the prisoner issue. As a result, the Union, as historian William Hesseltine pointed out, "held captive men of the South and treated them as prisoners of war, rather than as traitors, but they refused to admit that their captives were other than traitors."[3] Given this conflicting position and Lincoln's desire to avoid legitimizing the Confederacy's existence, the exchange of prisoners proceeded tenuously. In a cautious attempt to skirt any official recognition of the Confederacy, the Lincoln administration accepted only a piecemeal, informal process of prisoner exchange despite the Confederacy's desire to standardize the process.[4] From the outset of the war, both the Lincoln and Davis administrations viewed prisoners of war as a problem of political expediency. The lack of humanitarian concern for the war's captives foreshadowed the disasters to come.

During 1861, the small numbers of prisoners taken allowed opposing generals to negotiate limited exchanges while evading the political question of official recognition of the Confederacy. Despite these special exchanges, prisoners accumulated behind enemy lines.[5] In December 1861, the United States Congress came under increasing pressure from prisoner families and the press and consented to "inaugurate systemic measures for the exchange of prisoners in the present rebellion," since "exchange does not involve a recognition of the rebels as a government."[6] The practical impact of the congressional resolution was minimal, although it eased the public demands for the swapping of prisoners. It allowed exchange, but it did nothing to organize the process. Special exchanges continued, according to Hesseltine, as Union commanders still made exchange arrangements "on their own responsibility" rather than as part of a "general system."[7]

Placing the burden of exchange on the shoulders of individual commanders consistently delayed the process by creating a vast amount of paperwork. Preoccupied with preparations for battle, military officers found themselves distracted by requests for mercy forwarded to them from congressmen. Exchanges not only had to be cleared by superiors on both sides but also required investigation to insure that both parties complied with the terms. The resulting bureaucratic headaches increased after General Ulysses Grant's capture of some 15,000 Confederates at Fort Donelson in February 1862.[8] Although the Union enjoyed the upper hand in exchange negotiations since it held the majority of the prisoners, its advantage turned pyrrhic during the spring and summer as the inconvenient pressure of caring for their southern captives intensified. Prisoner exchanges all but ceased as the Confederacy, still seeking acknowledgment of its legitimacy, insisted on the implementation of a formal cartel and refused the Union's sporadic requests for special exchanges. Renewed public sympathy for faster repatriation also spurred the Lincoln administration to compromise with the Confederacy, which, like the Union, strained to meet the demands of the now thousands of prisoners confined in Richmond. Shiloh and the Peninsular Campaign further burdened both sides with unwanted prisoners, and they returned to the bargaining table.[9]

On July 22, 1862, Union general John A. Dix and Confederate general D. H. Hill concluded several days of negotiations with the establishment of

the Dix-Hill cartel, an agreement intended to bring efficiency to the practice of exchange. The cartel called for two agents to oversee a streamlined
process and established official exchange locations at Dutch Gap, Virginia,
on the James River, and at Vicksburg, Mississippi. At these two sites, prisoners would be exchanged according to their rank. Excess captives were to
be paroled within ten days of their capture, relieving both sides of the need
to imprison solders while they awaited official exchange. The cartel's intended permanence, based on the mutual agreement that "misunderstanding shall not interrupt the release of prisoners on parole," implied that exchange would continue on a consistent basis. The wording of the cartel
consciously avoided any mention of Confederate sovereignty.[10] During the
cartel's operation, the accumulation of prisoners gradually dissipated, although the prisons never fully emptied, and the issue of prisoner exchange
appeared resolved. The successful implementation of the cartel represented
an exception to the common experience of prisoners during the war. For an
all-too-brief period, the harmony of shared political convenience improved
conditions for Civil War POWs. New concerns soon emerged, however, to
reaffirm the provisional and insincere nature of the Union and Confederacy's commitment to prisoners of war.

As the war entered 1863, both sides grew dissatisfied with the exchange
cartel. Two issues in particular destroyed the supposedly permanent exchange process. A debate arose over the validity and terms of paroles issued
to thousands of prisoners. Both the Union and the Confederacy struggled
with the assimilation of paroled troops into their armies. Many soldiers resisted a return to the line of fire, insisting that their paroles exempted them
from service until their exchange became official. Neither the armies of
the North nor, even more critically, those of the South, however, could afford to lose the services of these men indefinitely. Instead of going home to
await their official exchange, paroled soldiers were sent by their respective
armies to parole camps. Although these bases effectively kept paroled soldiers in the service so that when officially exchanged these troops could return to the front lines, the existence of parole camps also created problems.
The camps not only occupied valuable space that could have been used for
housing actual prisoners, but they also further strained the resources of the
Union and Confederacy. Paroled soldiers required an expensive investment
in food and supplies while they awaited official exchange and a return to
active duty. Both sides also increasingly found that soldiers happily turned

capture and parole to their advantage as a risky but viable method of escaping the front lines. Immediate parole on the battlefield became an especially attractive option for many commanders, as it placed the burden of caring for POWs back on the other side.[11] The issue came to a head in September 1863, when Robert Ould, the Confederate commissioner of exchange, declared the paroled prisoners from Vicksburg exchanged in an attempt to bolster western Confederate forces while also relieving the pressure of sustaining idle troops. The Union indignantly denounced the exchange as invalid, and once again the swapping of prisoners slowed to a crawl.[12] Given the escalating costs and demands of the war by 1863, it is understandable, while not commendable, that both the Union and Confederacy valued financial gain and military expediency more than prisoners' lives. For those captives still awaiting exchange, however, these policy choices ensured a period of indefinite suffering.

A second issue, one inseparable from the larger cause and theme of the Civil War, also contributed to the destruction of the supposedly permanent exchange process in 1863. Slavery, or more precisely, the steps taken by the Lincoln administration to destroy the institution, also affected the fate of prisoners of war. Even as Lincoln considered the ramifications of emancipation during the second half of 1862, the Union began to organize regiments of African American soldiers. By the end of the war, nearly 200,000 black troops, most former slaves, served in the armed forces of the North. Their commitment changed the nature of the war. The Confederacy, outraged by the Union's affront to white supremacy and the encouragement of slave resistance, increasingly adopted a "black flag" policy toward these African American troops. Perhaps no other aspect of the war reveals the reprehensible nature of Confederate racism more than these repeated slaughters. The "black flag" meant that when units of different races clashed, both sides soon learned to expect a fight to the death. No-quarter combat, most famously symbolized by the Confederate massacre of black soldiers at Fort Pillow in 1864, eliminated surrender as an option for African Americans in battle.[13] Should a black soldier be fortunate enough to survive capture without being massacred, the official Confederate policy toward captured African American soldiers denied them the status of a POW, including the right of exchange, and insisted that they be executed or returned to slavery. It remains unclear how many African Americans suffered one of these fates. Relatively few black captives, perhaps no more than 1,200, ever made it to a Confederate prison camp.[14] As the experience of "the Negro Squad," a group of African American prisoners at Andersonville, attests, once imprisoned, white and black captives underwent a further difference in treatment with the coercion of blacks into labor around the prison grounds.[15] An irony existed in the conjoined issues of race and the tragedy of Civil War prisons. Although few African Americans experienced the inside of a Confederate prison, Civil War prisons were, in part, symbols of emancipation. What is clear is that, given the hazards African Americans faced in their service to the Union, their loyal devotion should be seen as all the more impressive.

Until mid-1863, the effect of the status of African American soldiers on the exchange cartel was less controversial than the parole issue, since black units rarely received the opportunity to fight and thus the Confederacy captured relatively few black troops. But by September 1863, the Union, buoyed by the victories at Gettysburg and Vicksburg, hardened its stance and demanded the exchange of black soldiers on identical terms with that of white prisoners. This position reflected the recent changes in the Union's moral justification for the war and the emerging centrality of the cause of racial equality. For this logical yet unprecedented commitment to protecting the status of African American POWs, the Lincoln administration deserves considerable credit, although its motives were not entirely altruistic. The policy placed the Confederacy on the defensive, by now a familiar posture, and the Davis regime refused to budge. The Confederacy insisted that the process of exchange exclude not only African American prisoners but also captured white officers of black regiments, whom the Davis administration reserved the right to try on charges of inciting slave rebellion.[16] The linking of exchanging prisoners with the fundamental questions of slavery and racial equality meant, according to Robert Garlick Hill Kean, a Confederate War department official, that "the question has no solution."[17] Cessation of the cartel followed, as by the end of 1863 both the Union and Confederacy refused to engage in exchange. This "misunderstanding," despite the promise of the Dix-Hill cartel, could reach resolution only through the conclusion of the war itself. Once again, the future became tenuous for thousands of prisoners of war as the larger causes and meanings of the conflict overshadowed concerns about the impact on their lives.

From the perspective of the Lincoln administration, the end of the cartel made sense for an additional reason, one even more pragmatic than the protection of the rights of African American soldiers. By late 1863 recognition grew that exchanging soldiers with the manpower-starved Confederacy hurt the Union war effort by returning seasoned soldiers to southern armies. Put bluntly, exchange favored the shrinking Confederacy by prolonging its ability to wage war. Thus it was no coincidence that, in December 1863, Secretary of War Edwin Stanton appointed a new commissioner of exchange, General Benjamin Butler. At the time, "Beast" Butler, vilified for his behavior in New Orleans earlier in the war, was perhaps the most detested Union figure in the Confederacy. Although Butler personally desired a resumption of the cartel process, the appointment of someone with his reputation signaled the Union's willingness to forgo exchange. The South interpreted Butler's selection as an affront, and in defense of their honor, many Confederate exchange officers refused to deal with Butler, thus eliminating any chance of compromise.[18] A few months later, General Grant summarized the feeling of the Union brass: "It is hard on our men held in Southern prisons not to exchange them, but it is humanity to those left in our ranks to fight our battles." The Union officially remained open to exchange, as long as the Confederacy included African American soldiers, but leaders like Grant recognized that the North benefited from the absence of a working exchange policy. "We have got to fight," Grant observed, "until the military power of the South is exhausted, and if we release or exchange prisoners captured it simply becomes a war of extermination."[19]

Not intended for public consumption, Grant's comments reflected the moral inconsistency of the Union concerning prisoner exchange. The admirable decision to insist on proper treatment of African American prisoners by the Confederacy loses some of its luster when placed in the context of the manipulative appointment of Butler as well as when appreciating the more tangible military rewards that motivated Union leaders. Suspicion persists that under different circumstances the principle of racial equality might have well been abandoned had it not been so convenient. Only in early 1865, with the outcome essentially certain, did the crumbling Confederacy consent to an inclusive policy of exchange with the Union, and the prisons emptied as the war concluded. The turbulent process of negotiating the exchange of prisoners of war reveals an unflattering truth about the destructive character of the Civil War. Victory in the all-consuming struggle resulted in part from the prioritization of some lives over others. Consistently, and consciously, the leaders of both the Union and Confederacy emphasized the demands of the war effort over humanitarian principle.

The troubling nature of that choice only deepens with the recognition that war leaders on both sides knew about the brutal conditions endured by captured soldiers, especially by the latter stages of the war. The grim statistics—30,000 Union prisoners perished in Confederate prisons, while 26,000 Confederates died in Union prisons—testifies to a shared failure of both the Union and Confederacy to care appropriately for prisoners of war.

Although the reasons for the disaster varied on each side, in both cases the appalling mortality resulted in part from the ineffective organization of the respective prison systems. From the outset of the war, the Confederacy channeled most of its prisoners through Richmond, a natural focal point given the strategic importance of northern Virginia. Although sizable prisons eventually existed in additional locations, among them Florence and Columbia, South Carolina, Tuscaloosa, Alabama, and Salisbury, North Carolina, until the breakdown of the cartel in 1863 the vast majority of the Union prisoners remained in the Richmond area awaiting exchange. The actions of the Davis administration indicated that oversight of the prisons ranked as a low priority. Rather than appoint a specific officer to oversee the captives, in the summer of 1861, the Confederacy placed the prisoners under the jurisdiction of Brigadier General John Winder, the provost marshal general of Richmond. Although his father, General William Henry Winder, negotiated an exchange cartel with the British during the War of 1812, John Winder possessed no particular experience with, or talent for, prison management. By 1862, Winder's responsibilities in Richmond included everything from returning deserters to discharging unfit soldiers. These duties prevented him from concentrating his attention on the needs of the growing numbers of Union prisoners.[20] Eight thousand captives at the two main Richmond prisons—Libby Prison, where Union officers were housed, and Belle Isle, for Union enlistees—faced increasingly dire conditions before the implementation of the Dix-Hill cartel effectively relieved the overcrowding during the summer of 1862.

Despite the near crisis and the possibility that exchange might fail again at some point, the Davis administration tellingly continued to demonstrate apathy toward the problem of caring for prisoners of war. Because the majority of captives fell under Winder's jurisdiction and no single commander supervised all Confederate prisons, by default he retained the most authority over the prisons. Yet he found his power challenged by both field commanders and prison officials in other departments of the Confederacy, who often issued orders conflicting with those given by Winder.[21] In the absence of coordinated leadership, plans for the construction of additional prison facilities occurred only out of desperation. When the cartel broke down in late 1863, the Richmond prisons once again overflowed. Only then did the Confederacy act, hastily establishing a large stockade at the small railroad depot of Anderson Station, Georgia, and reassigning Winder to its oversight. The reactive pattern of delayed Confederate attention to the obvious need for housing its prisoners began the misery that ultimately resulted in the infamous prison of Andersonville.

Finally, in late 1864, three years into the conflict, it occurred to the Davis administration that a semblance of bureaucratic organization might reduce the haphazard (mis)functioning of the Confederate prison system. On November 21, Adjutant General Samuel Cooper installed Winder as the first Confederate commissary general of prisoners, a position that unified his authority over all the prisons of the Confederacy. One line in the order confirming Winder's appointment was especially telling: "Department, army and other commanders are required not to interfere with the prisoners, the prison guard, or the administration of the prisons."[22] Although this was seemingly redundant, the muddled organizational state of Confederate prisons required such a statement. The sad irony of the belated appointment was that the war was almost over and the vast majority of prison deaths had already occurred. Throughout the conflict, a leadership void existed at the top of the Confederate prison system. Without direction, little incentive inspired subordinate officers to take responsibility for the deteriorating conditions experienced by Union prisoners. Some sympathy for the Confederacy's slow reaction to the need for a well-defined prison system is legitimate. The onset of war created a variety of unforeseen challenges besides the problem of housing prisoners, and today's inseparable combination of central government and bureaucracy did not fully or naturally exist in the Civil War era. But it remains inexcusable, even sinister, that, despite the momentum of the war against it, the Confederacy never bothered to address the exigencies of prisoners of war.

While it too had flaws, the Union's prison bureaucracy was much more organized than the Confederacy's. In October 1861, Secretary of War Simon Cameron recognized the need for a department to handle prisoners of war. Cameron selected Colonel William Hoffman for the task, and Hoffman filled the post of commissary general of prisoners for the duration of the conflict. With authority over all matters pertaining to prisoners,

Hoffman quickly issued orders in the hopes of establishing a well-defined prison bureaucracy. He devised a strict accounting system for prisoner transfers, illnesses, and deaths, which would organize the previously chaotic camps. Prisoners would be divided into messes, enabling the government to care more easily for and keep track of them. Under Hoffman's administrative plan, prisoners were to receive standardized rations and necessary articles of clothing.[23]

The establishment of a prison bureaucracy, however, did not translate immediately into efficient management of Union prisons. General Henry Halleck, the Union chief of staff, inexplicably failed to announce Hoffman's appointment to the army until April 1862. Halleck's tardiness undermined Hoffman's ability to organize the scattered camps into a cohesive system at a time when the lack of exchange placed severe demands on Union resources. Although Hoffman planned the construction of a new prison for Confederate officers at Johnson's Island, located on Lake Erie in Ohio, the design allowed space for only 1,280 men. The camp reached completion in late February 1862, but Grant's 15,000 Fort Donelson captives immediately placed Johnson's Island and other existing facilities on the verge of obsolescence. All over the North, Confederate prisoners crowded into what had previously been training camps. The overabundance of captives passed only with the establishment of the exchange cartel that summer. Meanwhile, Hoffman grew increasingly frustrated with the lack of respect for his position.[24] On September 19, 1863, he complained to Secretary of War Edwin Stanton about his compromised authority over area commanders, many of whom countermanded his orders:

> It would facilitate the management of the affairs of prisoners of War, and lead to a more direct responsibility if the commanders of stations where prisoners are held could be placed under the immediate control of the Commissary General of Prisoners. By the interposition of an intermediate commander the responsibility is weakened, and correspondence passing through him is necessarily much delayed, and through frequent change of commanders it is impossible to establish a uniform and permanent system of administration.[25]

Hoffman naturally hoped to augment his power over the prison camps, but his letter also underscored the disordered state of affairs he faced and testified to his belief that only the creation of a properly structured bureaucracy (run by him) could adequately organize the chaos. Despite these obstacles, by January 1864 Hoffman succeeded in consolidating the prison bureaucracy through the implementation of an elaborate record-keeping system. Every month, at each camp, detailed rolls of prisoner arrivals, transfers, deaths, and prison expenditures were logged and forwarded to Hoffman's Washington office for scrutiny. Although not a seamless process, and in sharp contrast to the Confederate camps nominally headed by Winder, Union prisons became better organized during the war. Organization, unfortunately, did not equate to a significant improvement in the quality of prisoner treatment.

The comparatively superior structure of the Union's prison bureaucracy was undeniable. Yet it was also undeniable that casualties in Union prisons multiplied throughout the war. As in the Confederacy, the end of exchange meant the burden of thousands of prisoners, which in turn strained the resources and available prison space of the Union. But the established Union prison system, not encumbered by the type of collapse occurring in the South, should have avoided the high casualty rates of its Confederate counterpart. It did not. At Elmira, the New York camp generally considered the worst Union prison, the 24-percent mortality rate rivaled the 29-percent figure compiled at Andersonville, and almost doubled the average casualty rates of all prisoners during the Civil War.[26] During the war, 12 percent of Confederates held in Union prison camps died, compared to 15.5 percent of the Union soldiers imprisoned in Confederate prisons. The prevalence of diseases such as smallpox and dysentery, as historian James Gillispie convincingly argues, was the overwhelming (and unavoidable) killer of prisoners, even in the more stable Union prison system.[27] The inability to treat such diseases explains much of the suffering in Civil War prisons, but the impersonal nature of the misery inflicted does not excuse or explain the willingness of both sides to abandon prisoners to their fate. The striking consistency of the prison experience in both the Union and Confederacy suggested that disease ravaged the prisoners and mismanagement heightened their anguish. But the existence of these horrors resulted from deliberately cruel choices made during a war defined by callous destruction.

The prisoners themselves certainly thought so. A sense of fury dominated what Walt Whitman called "the scrawl'd, worn slips of paper" on which Confederate and Union prisoners documented their trials.[28] The sentiments scribbled in prison diaries testified to the horrors experienced by

Civil War prisoners and represented firsthand attempts not only to understand the existence of such misery but also to determine who bore responsibility for the suffering. Numerous Confederate captives chronicled the hardships they experienced in the North. Captain William Speer, imprisoned at Johnson's Island, Ohio during 1862, stated that "the horrows of the prison are so grate . . . if everybody could Know & feel as I do I think there would be nomore Jales built." Only the hope of exchange sustained Speer, who held President Lincoln responsible for the suffering. "I do believe," Speer announced, "if Abraham Keeps me in here much longer that I will be a good lawyer as to asking questions & finding out the truth of all the reports."[29] Speer's initial suspicion that something sinister existed in the Union policy toward Confederate captives made him one of the first to blame the Union administration for the harsh prison system. In an 1863 diary entry, Confederate soldier James E. Hall, held at Point Lookout, Maryland, lamented that there was "nothing that a man can eat. The crackers are as hard as flint stone, and full of worms. I don't believe God ever intended for one man to pen another up and keep him in this manner. We ought to have enough to eat, anyhow." Hall reserved his hostility for the two men he held responsible for the sad state of affairs at Point Lookout, Abraham Lincoln and Jefferson Davis. "Dam Old Abe and old Jeff Davis," he wrote; "dam the day I 'listed."[30] Hall's inclusion of Davis as a target of his frustration showed a sophisticated comprehension of the situation—prisoners of war were essentially pawns in the political maneuvering over exchange and as a group susceptible like no other to the bitterness of the increasingly violent conflict. The anger Speer and Hall directed at the two presidents, the personifications of the Union and Confederate governments, reflected a belief that powerful leaders could easily control government and bureaucracy if they so desired. These prisoners thus understood their suffering as caused by heartless, intentional policy choices.

Other Confederate prisoners chronicled the litany of suffering. Sergeant Bartlett Yancey Malone, another inhabitant of Point Lookout, described the shooting of a fellow prisoner in the head by a Yankee guard. The captive's crime, according to Malone, was "peepen threw the cracks of the planken."[31] At Fort Delaware, Private Joseph Purvis denounced this "wretched place" and expressed fear that the smallpox, "Colra," or yellow fever might catch him as it had many of his companions.[32] Robert Bingham, who passed through Fort Norfolk and Fort Delaware before reaching Johnson's Island, summed up the growing Confederate resentment against their experience in Union prisons. "The Yankee nation is the most infamously mean race that blights God's green earth," Bingham declared. Not only was "there no honor, no truth, no faith, no honesty among them," but Bingham insisted, "they delight to insult and annoy defenseless captives."[33] By the last months of the war, a sense of despondency prevailed. Writing from Elmira, L. Leon described the bustling trade in dead rats among the prisoners along with the "frightful" smallpox outbreak that he claimed killed at least twenty men a day.[34] Joseph Kern, at Point Lookout, told the grim tale of one man freezing to death in the early months of 1865 when a tent mate refused to share a blanket with him.[35] On January 22, 1865, John Dooley, imprisoned on Johnson's Island, finally received the news dreamed of for months. Although he rejoiced at the impending exchange, Dooley remained depressed about his surroundings. "There is continual suffering among the prisoners," he wrote, and "many go to the slop barrels and garbage piles to gather from the refuse a handful of revolting food. Such is the infamous government we have to deal with, and now I do not wonder if we be overcome in the end."[36] Amid the tales of deprivation and illness the diarists perceived a consistent sense, regardless of prison, of conscious Union cruelty that threatened their already precarious survival.

As strongly as the Confederate prisoners resented their treatment, Union prisoners at least matched, if not surpassed, the southern complaints. Like their Confederate counterparts, Union soldiers alleged intent to their suffering. The 1862 diary of Second Lieutenant Luther Jackson, captured at Shiloh and held in Montgomery, reflected the complexity of the nightmare in which prisoners found themselves ensnared. "This people are so mean in their revenges," Jackson wrote; "how different from the treatment their prisoners get from us." Jackson believed in the singular brutality of the Confederacy toward its prisoners. But for all the southern cruelty, it became increasingly difficult for Jackson to justify the innocence of his own government. Less than a month before his death, Jackson declared, "Ah! Uncle Sam! You don't do right in not having prisoners exchanged sooner." "If they care so little for us," he continued, a few days later, "they had better disband their forces."[37] George Comstock, imprisoned at Libby and Belle Isle, acknowledged that "some are cursing the Government for not doing more for us." Comstock, however, refused to attack the Union administration and remained hopeful despite his deteriorating health. "It is a stiff battle now against insanity," he stated during the summer of 1863, "we are so hungry." He also directed his anger at the Confederate guards, whom he sarcastically referred to as "noble southerners . . . pacing to and fro, and keenly watching for an excuse to shoot." "It is horrible," Comstock insisted, days before his exchange, "that men should be treated this way."[38] Captain Samuel Fiske, writing under the pseudonym Dunn Browne, also implicated the corrupt Confederate guards at Libby Prison as the main source of prisoner difficulty. "I have been among Italian brigands, and Greek pirates, and Bedouin Arabs," he declared, but "for making a clean thing of the robbing business, commend me to the Confederate States of America, so styled. They descend to the minutiae of the profession in a way that should be instructive to all novices in the art."[39] Corporal Newell Burch decried the "awful, awful suffering" in Richmond and described how prisoners died from smallpox only to be replaced by more prisoners.[40] Another inhabitant of Belle Isle, J. Osborn Coburn, found the conditions so appalling that he asked his diary, "Why does a just God permit them to continue evil doing?" Treated as a "beast" by the Confederacy, Coburn believed that "a terrible retribution awaited" the South. Although he retained faith in his "benevolent government," by winter 1863, Coburn's prospects seemed grim. "We are literally freezing and starving," he despaired; "surely our country will not permit much longer. We must have something done or all shall perish in a little while."[41] But for all the detailed accounts of the miseries of Belle Isle and other Confederate prisons, the new prison stockade at Andersonville in 1864 soon replaced Richmond as the ultimate symbol of southern savagery.

Although horrifying accounts of prisons such as Libby, Macon, and Columbia chronicled the suffering encountered there by Union prisoners during the last months of the war, from 1864 on Andersonville represented the nadir of the Confederate treatment of their captives.[42] As Lieutenant Thomas Galwey noted in his diary, the prospect of ending up at Andersonville held such terror that it "nerved many a man to one more effort to escape capture."[43] Despite their best efforts, however, well over 40,000 men found themselves crammed into the Georgia prison during its existence. There, according to Private John Sawyer Patch, "one could see sights & sounds that would make his blood run cold."[44] Sergeant Henry W. Tisdale described the chaos during the summer months, when Andersonville's population peaked. "The prison is one mess of human beings," he wrote, and the disorganization and overcrowding manifested itself in the pollution of the stream, the lone source of drinking water, with human excrement. The water, Tisdale noted, "is never cleaned up and is a good deal of the time one seething mass of maggots."[45] According to Private Charlie Mosher, "the fleas, lice and maggots are holding high carnival in here." Mosher related the appearance of one unfortunate prisoner "with not only the lice and fleas feeding on him, but out of every aperture of his body the maggots were crawling."[46] Given these circumstances it is possible to wonder not why 13,000 prisoners died at Andersonville, but how the others did not.

Many Andersonville diarists spent their time puzzling over who exactly bore the responsibility for their grim situation. Sergeant Charles Ross suspected that the deteriorating conditions, particularly the disease and absence of food, were not accidental. The Confederacy, he thought, intended "to starve us clear down to skeletons and then kill us outright."[47] Charles Lee, like Coburn at Belle Isle, mused that "it does seem as though the curse of God would rest upon a Government which treats their prisoners in this way."[48] Mosher blamed the brutality on the commonly vilified Captain Henry Wirz, commandant of Andersonville Prison, and the Confederate guards. The use of dogs to capture Union escapees particularly galled Mosher. To him the practice indicted not just Wirz, but southern society as a whole. Mosher bitterly wrote, "It must have taken years of education for men who claim to be civilized and Christianized to have reached this high state of trying to capture prisoners of war with blood hounds. None but a slaveholding people could or would do such things."[49] Although Wirz proved a popular target for Union criticism, many diarists reserved their venom for other Confederate officials. Francis Shaw referred to himself and his fellow prisoners as the unwilling "subjects of Old Jeff," yet another indication that captives associated their suffering with policy choices, in this case, made by Davis.[50]

But just as Union prisoners believed that their government would free them, they felt rejected as the months passed without exchange. In the eyes of Amos Stearns, the Union abandoned him to a miserable fate. "Day after day passes," he worried, "and nothing is done about taking us out of this bull pen. Can it be that our government does not care for men who have served it faithfully for most three years?"[51] George Read exclaimed, "If our government allows us to remain here . . . don't talk to me of patriotism after this," and he angrily declared that "somebody will, must receive an awful punishment for this. No human thing could be guilty of placing men in such a situation. I trust the ones that are to blame for it will receive a hard and just punishment."[52] Resentment toward the Union's refusal to exchange showed as well—some prisoners bitterly complained of the injustice imposed on them in order to protect the rights of African Americans. Inhabitants of Andersonville such as Private William Tritt, who focused his anger on "Old Abe and the niggers," and Private M. J. Umsted, who lamented, "all for the Sons of Africa," revealed a frequent belief among Union prisoners that the Lincoln administration, not the Confederacy, represented the main obstacle to a resumption of exchange.[53] It defied many prisoners' racial logic and tested their loyalty that, as white men, they should have to endure captivity for the cause of African American freedom. The circulation among Andersonville prisoners of an anonymous poem, "They Have Left Us Here to Die," aptly reflected the reality that while Union captives hated and blamed their Confederate hosts for their misery, they were not oblivious to the fact that their plight resulted in part from the actions of their own side.[54]

As the accounts of atrocity accumulated, they cemented the realization, on both sides, that something terrible occurred in the prisons of the Civil War and thus began the complicated process of interpreting that horror. These early records, written in environments of extreme stress, represented the first efforts to assess responsibility for the suffering. What the diarists revealed was a world of deprivation and cruelty, and they maintained strong but, importantly, distinctly varied opinions about who they felt deserved blame. In the minds of various Civil War captives, Abraham Lincoln, Jefferson Davis, Henry Wirz, prison guards, the government, the Union, the Confederacy, African Americans, and many other agents all merited and received condemnation. Taken in total, the portrayal conveyed in these wartime accounts of the prisoner experience is one of sophistication. The prisoners, while intensely critical of their opposition, did not absolve their particular side or own leaders of responsibility. They recognized their unfortunate role in an increasingly destructive, all-or-nothing struggle and that their fate rested on the resolution of the issues essential to the war itself. Their testimony shows the essential brutality of the Civil War and the willingness of both sides to act with calculation and cruelty. But of course a complete understanding did not exist during the war itself. Prisoners struggled to comprehend their predicament as individuals, and so each emphasized different factors as they constructed their reasons for blame. This lack of consensus on the issue of responsibility set the tone for the prison controversy—from the beginning, discussion of Civil War prisons took place in an environment of recrimination, confusion, and discord.

As Union and Confederate citizens realized the implications of the prisoner accounts trickling out of the camps, this tragedy within a tragedy inflamed public opinion. The prolonged controversy over the establishment and collapse of the exchange cartel sparked greater resentment against the opposition as both sides complained about the poor treatment of their captured soldiers. As early as December 23, 1861, the *New York Herald* described the conditions Union prisoners experienced in Richmond as "the most brutal and savage known to modern civilization." The *Herald* editor justified his assessment with descriptions of half-naked, starving prisoners. Not only did the captives suffer from a lack of care and medicine, the writer claimed; they also served as targets for the rifle practice of the Confederate guards. Although the accuracy of the *Herald*'s information may be questioned, the article revealed the anger aroused by the prisoner-of-war issue and its effectiveness as propaganda. By invoking the suffering of prisoners, and at times exaggerating the harsh conditions that they encountered, both sides further stoked already heated emotions. Their antipathy and revulsion for each other proved both intense and durable. Throughout the rest of the war, claims of deliberate atrocity continued to arise as the Union and Confederacy fought, not just to achieve victory, but to establish their moral superiority over their opponent. That desire fueled the *Herald* editor's assertion that "the rights of honorable warfare, not to mention those of Christian civilization and tender heartedness, are not . . . regarded" in the Confederacy, as our "brethren of the South act towards their brethren of the North with a barbarity" not witnessed since "ancient times."[55] Not to be outdone, an increasingly outraged *Harper's Weekly* described the "revolting" treatment and "sickening inhumanity" of "the filth" and "poison" Union captives endured.[56] By characterizing each other as not just un-Christian, but purposefully barbaric, both Union and Confederate citizens interpreted the prisoner-of-war controversy during the conflict as motivation to support the sacrifices of their imprisoned troops and reason to celebrate the relative virtue of their causes.

From 1862 onward, the initial acrimony over the treatment of prisoners exploded into outrage as former captives began publishing accounts of their sufferings. Although the earliest memoirs, such as the *Journal of Alfred Ely,* which appeared before the Dix-Hill cartel in 1862, contained little resentment toward the Confederacy or Union, they made clear that the life of a prisoner on either side was not an enviable one.[57] More importantly, these early testimonials heightened the public visibility of the camps at a time when prison casualties began to rise. By 1863, the publication of prison accounts, diaries, and letters reflected and fed the growing obsession with the prison conditions on both sides.[58] Readers in the North, vicariously experiencing the conflict, could not help but feel sorry for Union captain J. J. Geer, who described how he "lay wounded and languishing in the loathsome jails of a merciless enemy."[59] Along with that sympathy a rising fury emerged, both North and South, against the fact that their opponent would not only tolerate but even encourage such brutality.

The unpublished diaries and letters of the Union and Confederate public, particularly women, reflected the heightening bitterness surrounding the prisons. In addition to the anger, writings from the home front showed that the families of captives suffered as well. An 1864 extract from the diary of Elizabeth Van Lew, of Richmond, depicted the terrible suffering at Belle Isle. "It may be brave to meet death on the battlefield," wrote Van Lew, "but months and weeks and days of dying, a forgotten, uncared for unit of a mighty nation! Surely this is the test of bravery and patriotism!"[60] By the fall of 1864, other writers described the fearful results of that test. Iowa soldier J. B. Ritner, in a letter to his wife, told her, "the most pitiful sight I have seen during the war is that of our soldiers coming back from the southern prisons . . . so wasted away with hunger that they looked like mere skeletons."[61] In November 1864, Jane Stuart Woolsey, a Union nurse, wrote a letter in which she quoted a Surgeon Smith on the condition of the returning Union prison survivors: "They are too low, too utterly wrecked to have hope. . . . These living skeletons and puling idiots are worse than any sight to see on the battlefield." Woolsey continued, outraged that the prisoners "have been subjected to every cruelty, every infamy of cruelty, we can conceive of." Although a nurse who witnessed the plight of Confederate prisoners at Point Lookout, Woolsey insisted that she "knew what the contrast is" between the Union and Confederate prison systems.[62] Woolsey believed not only that Confederate brutality was intentional but that the Union prison system operated far more humanely.

Southern women refuted Woolsey's belief in Union exceptionalism. Of the Yankee treatment of prisoners, Lizzie Hardin stated in her diary that "when men who have been confined in separate prisons, many of them hundreds of miles apart, come home at different times and by different routes, and all agree that they were so badly supplied with food as to be forced to eat rats and dogs, I believe it must be the truth."[63] Sarah Morgan described the pain of hoping for the return of a captured soldier, only to learn of his death in prison. "We have deceived ourselves," Morgan wrote; "we readily listened to the assertions of our friends that Johnson's Island was the healthiest place in the world."[64] More fortunate news awaited Floride Clemson, John C. Calhoun's granddaughter. At the end of the war, she recounted the return of her brother, Calhoun Clemson, from Johnson's Island. He seemed "graver," Floride Clemson wrote, and she attributed his somber nature to Calhoun's experiences as a prisoner. In her diary Clemson claimed that Calhoun said "they retaliated upon him in prison." Despite the physical suffering, for poor Calhoun "the loss of hope was the most terrible thing."[65] Although both sides remained convinced of the purposeful nature of the suffering, the diaries and letters from the home front clearly demonstrated the poignant toll that the prisons took not only on the captives but also on their families.

By 1864, in recognition of the emotional attachment to the prisoner controversy, both the Union and Confederate press devoted extensive coverage to the prison camps. The steady publication of articles, pictures, cartoons, prisoner testimony, and even government reports on the problem further inflamed public opinion. In an August 1864 letter to a North Carolina editor, Confederate officer Thomas J. Green, held at Johnson's Island, called on the newsman to "agitate, agitate, agitate the subject" of the poor conditions of the prison camps and especially the failure to exchange the thousands of suffering captives.[66] Green need not have worried that the issue of prisoner treatment and exchange needed more exposure. If he had had access to southern newspapers, he would have been pleased to see that agitation over the treatment of prisoners continued to grow. A few months earlier, a *Charleston Mercury* editorial denounced the "Northern bastiles where our gallant Confederate soldiers pine in wretchedness, to which death is a relief, and where they are plied with cruelty."[67] A letter to the *Macon Daily Telegraph* editor, published June 11, 1864, and signed simply "Rebel," revealed a complete lack of sympathy for the suffering that Yankee prisoners encountered in nearby Andersonville. "Rebel" claimed that he and his fellow Confederate prisoners, who in 1863 experienced the hardships of Camp Douglas,

Chicago, endured a mortality rate that "was some 3 1/3 times greater than
. . . in the Yankee prison (Andersonville)," and "yet the Yankees said that
the 'prison was too healthy for damned rebels.'"[68] Given the destruction the
war brought to the Confederacy, especially by late 1864, the plight of Yankee
prisoners aroused little sympathy in Dixie. Louis Manigault, the secretary
to Major Joseph Jones, a Confederate surgeon sent to inspect Andersonville
Prison in the fall of 1864, displayed the cold reality of the situation when he
wrote his wife that "I examined about 30 dead Yankees, a fearful sight. They
have however caused us such suffering . . . that I feel no pity for them, and
behold a dead Yankee in a far different light from a dead Confederate killed
in fighting for all that is dear to him."[69] From Manigault's perspective, imprisoned Union soldiers deserved their fate.

During the same period, the Union refused to yield the moral high
ground in the prisoner debate. The 1864 appearance of composer George
Root's "Tramp! Tramp! Tramp!; or, The Prisoner's Hope," followed by 1865's
"Starved in Prison," reminded the northern public of the importance of
fighting to save the thousands of Union prisoners who anxiously awaited a
return to freedom.[70] The popularity of prison-related songs showed that the
appeal of the prison controversy to the public's interest could generate profits as well as patriotism. Root's success also foreshadowed the flood of doc-
uments throughout the last years of the war that blamed the Confederacy
for the dying captives. In January 1864, *Harper's Weekly* expressed outrage
at the way the South continued to mistreat Union prisoners. "They do not
massacre their prisoners outright," the editor admitted, but instead "drag
them away to starve in loathsome dungeons." Refusing to accept the deteriorating conditions encountered in Confederate prisons as an excuse, the
author contended, "If the rebels can not treat prisoners honorably they have
no right to take them."[71] The writer also mentioned the possibility of retaliation against Confederate captives held in Northern prisons as a means of
encouraging the Confederacy to make caring for its prisoners a higher priority. The anger the prisoner issue provoked deepened as, in the absence of
exchange, more and more prisoners died over the course of 1864. The press
continued to ignite public sentiment. In November 1864, a *New York Herald*
article, titled, "Our Suffering Prisoners," summarized northern antipathy
toward the South. How, it asked, could "a community boasting of Christianity and enlightenment . . . be guilty of so many barbarities as have been
perpetuated by the rebels towards their Union prisoners."[72] To supplement

the angry editorials, photographs and other illustrations appeared as well.

Most photographs or cartoons published during the war years depicted the toll that prison life took on the health and strength of young soldiers. In the North, the circulation of the shocking images of emaciated troops, who had been hale and hearty when they left home, often conveyed the harsh reality of prison life better than any article could. Beginning in 1863, a series of illustrations appeared in *Harper's Weekly* confirming the rumors of prison evils taking place in the Confederacy. That December, one of the early drawings showed a ragged group of Union prisoners at Belle Isle, in Richmond. Most of them sat or lay prone on the ground, half naked, without the strength or desire to move. Two other prisoners stood, weakly, clutching each other for support. The gloomy scene revealed a world of brutality and deliberate cruelty as the northern soldiers helplessly awaited their fate. On the front page of the March 5, 1864, edition, a picture of tottering prison escapees, held upright only with the help of Union soldiers, suggested that even these brave, determined individuals—the strongest—barely survived the hell of prison in Dixie. More images in December 1864 and January 1865 followed, focusing northern attention on the pitiful health of the recently exchanged survivors of southern prisons.[73]

When illustrations of Union prisons occasionally appeared, as in the April 15, 1865, issue of *Harper's Weekly,* they depicted a much more benign existence. A panoramic drawing of Elmira Prison, in New York, complete with an American flag waving in the breeze, presented a stark contrast to the claustrophobic, graphic images that northern artists offered of the suffering individuals in the South. When a picture focused on Confederate prisoners, as in one rendering of Fort Lafayette, in New York, they sat peacefully inside a comfortable barracks room reading and playing games.[74] The much cozier image fit the popular opinion in the North, fed by the press, that Confederate prisoners lived in luxury while their counterparts starved and died.[75] The sharp contrast indicated the deepening fury of the Civil War. It also showed a stubborn refusal in the North, fueled by the influence of such propaganda, to confront the reality of the evil done in the name of its cause. The anger over the seemingly singularly brutal treatment of northern soldiers in southern prisons, fed by the constant publication of charges and images of atrocity, increased the bitterness and sense of moral outrage that fueled the destruction of the Confederacy during the latter stages of the war.

A dualistic, highly partisan perception of Civil War prisons thus emerged during the conflict. Both the citizens and press of the Union and Confederacy embraced a one-sided presentation of the prison controversy that prejudiced public discussion of the tragic conditions. In an environment of heightened patriotism, the desire to believe the best about your country—and by extension yourself—encouraged then, as now, a tendency to focus on the behavior of the opponent rather than self-scrutiny.[76] The illusory nature of the public's understanding, in contrast to the more balanced reality described by the prisoners themselves, revealed another aspect of the Civil War's destructive essence—the reality of the war and the justifications of its purpose became indistinguishable. The irony of the accusations hurled by both sides against each other was that instead of ameliorating the suffering of prisoners, it fostered an environment in which the expectation of mistreatment grew, which made the worsening conditions of the prisons a self-fulfilling prophecy.

The vitriolic reaction to the prison tragedy by private citizens requires context, however. As in response to the exchange question, both the Union and Confederate governments manipulated the emotional issue of Civil War prisons for political gain during the last two years of the war. In May 1864, the U.S. House of Representatives released a report, complete with images of emaciated captives, detailing the brutal treatment Union prisoners experienced in the Confederacy. "The evidence proves," asserted the House, "a determination on the part of the rebel authorities, deliberately and persistently practiced," to "subject" soldiers to "a system of treatment" so horrible that the survivors "present literally the appearance of living skeletons . . . maimed for life."[77] Similar conclusions appeared in a subsequent publication by the United States Sanitary Commission, which not only attacked the Confederate prison system but praised the humane Union prison facilities.[78] Seizing the opportunity to fan the flames of patriotism and vindicate the superior morality of the northern cause, the Union government publicized its officially sanctioned version of the truth about Civil War prisons. The connection between the distortions of Union propaganda, the northern press, and the beliefs of devoted northerners like Jane Woolsey is unmistakable.

It was also calculated. The sweeping denunciations of the Confederacy by the Union certainly rang hollow with the men unfortunate enough to find themselves in the prisons so often discussed in the newspapers back home. Union prisoners wondered why the government, despite its haste to blame the Confederacy for the deplorable circumstances imposed on northern captives, seemed unwilling to take action on behalf of the Federals suffering in southern prisons. In August 1864, a small group of Andersonville prisoners, temporarily released by the Confederate authorities, arrived in Washington, D.C., to inform the government of the terrible conditions and casualties that the soldiers experienced in the Georgia prison camp. "One of the sad effects ... of this terrible war," the preamble to the prisoners' presentation stated, "has been to deaden our sympathies. . . . Does the misfortune of being taken prisoner make us less the object of interest and value to our Government?"[79] The answer to the Andersonville captives' question depended on perspective. Although Union prisoners felt abandoned by their government, which consistently demonstrated indifference toward the problems experienced by prisoners of war, they possessed immense "value" to the Union war cause. Unfortunately for Union prisoners, the Lincoln administration calculated their "value" differently. The reality of the prisoners' worth was shown by the actions of General Sherman, who, as he marched through Georgia, made no serious effort to free the Andersonville prisoners.[80] Sherman's actions confirmed the absence of humanitarian morality, except when convenient, in the Union war effort. The propaganda "value" of northern captives as martyrs, accompanied by a barrage of inflammatory rhetoric and images, outweighed the "value" of their lives.

Even during the final months of the war, as exchange resumed and the prison camps slowly emptied, the excoriation of the Confederacy and its prisons persisted. With victory at hand, northerners continued to equate superiority on the battlefield with moral superiority. On January 29, 1865, Senator Charles Sumner of Massachusetts, no stranger to attacking the ethical failings of southern society, gave a speech criticizing the congressionally proposed policy of retaliating against rebel prisoners in response to the brutal treatment accorded to Union prisoners. "We should do nothing by which our country shall forfeit that great place which belongs to it in the vanguard of nations," Sumner pleaded, even as he admitted that "when we read the stories of their atrocities ... when the whole scene in all its horror is before us ... our souls are filled with unutterable anguish."[81] Although Sumner rejected the idea of retaliation in northern prisons, his speech, reprinted and circulated, nevertheless confirmed the guilt of the Confederacy and the innocence of the Union in the debate over responsibility for the prison atrocities.

Despite Sumner's magnanimous stance, refusing to trade an eye for an eye in response to the South's provocation, the Union government's actions toward captive Confederates demonstrated that, claims of innocence aside, a policy of de facto retaliation already existed. Inspired by the information published in the House of Representatives report concerning the brutal treatment of northern prisoners, during the spring of 1864 Union secretary of war Edwin Stanton approved a series of reductions in the rations given to Confederate prisoners held in the North in order to match those issued to Union prisoners in the South.[82] The ruthless nature of Stanton's reprisal offers further evidence of the destructive scale of the Civil War. Stanton's policy, although perhaps a response to the racial atrocities of Fort Pillow, was certainly motivated by bitterness and an artificial sense of moral superiority.[83] While it gained the Union a small military advantage in terms of cutting costs on prisoner care, it also contributed to the deaths of southern prisoners. The fact that President Lincoln remained silent despite clear knowledge of the impact of these actions also confirmed the brutal pragmatism that defined the Union leadership's approach to the conflict.[84] But the most telling aspect of the policy of retaliation concerns the lack of protest, or even interest, it inspired in the North. Despite all the attention devoted to the inhumanity of the Confederacy, in the last stages of the war northerners displayed a hardened apathy toward the suffering endured by imprisoned Confederates.

Refusing to accept the Union version of the prisoner-of-war controversy, the Confederacy stuck to its rhetorical guns even as the real ones fell silent. On March 3, 1865, the Davis administration released its own report describing the prison situation. What made the testimony "important," the Confederate Congressional Committee stated, were the "persistent efforts lately made by the Government of the United States . . . to asperse the honor of the Confederate authorities and to charge them with deliberate and willful cruelty to prisoners of war." These "efforts," according to the report, "are designed to inflame the evil passions of the North; to keep up the war spirit among their own people." Not content with that insight, the committee continued by asserting that "in nearly all the prison stations of the North . . . our men have suffered from insufficient food, and have been subjected to ignominious, cruel, and barbarous practices, of which there is no parallel in anything that has occurred in the South." As for the collapse of the exchange cartel, the Confederate document acknowledged that "the policy of seducing negro slaves" and "arming" them against the South "gave rise to a few cases in which questions of crime under the internal laws of the Southern States appeared." Despite the disagreement over the status of African American troops, however, the Congressional Committee declared that that issue "ought never to have interrupted the general exchange." Unfortunately for the Confederacy, "the fortunes of war threw the larger number" to the Union, which, in keeping with its strategy of attrition against the South, "refused further exchanges." Therefore, "the responsibility of refusing to exchange prisoners of war rests with the Government of the United States," and so too did the blame for every resulting "sigh of captivity" and "groan of suffering."[85]

The final paragraphs of the committee's report offered a defense of the Confederate prison system. Admitting that "privation, suffering, and mortality, to an extent much to be regretted, did prevail" in places like Andersonville, Salisbury, and the Richmond prisons, the committee insisted that it was "not the result of neglect" or "design, on the part of the Confederate government." Instead, the report cited "haste in preparation; crowded quarters, prepared only for a smaller number; want of transportation, and scarcity of food" as the causes of the suffering, all of which "resulted from the pressure of the war and the barbarous manner in which it has been conducted by our enemies."[86] J. B. Jones, a Confederate War Department clerk, confirmed these sentiments in his diary. Upon hearing about the shocking mortality at Andersonville, Jones summed up the Confederate quandary, writing "that climate is fatal to them; but the government cannot feed them here, and the enemy won't exchange." According to Jones and the Confederate committee, the "savage warfare" of the Union, including such practices as the blockade, the confiscation and destruction of food and medicines, and the incineration of homes, crops, and tools, prevented the proper treatment of Union prisoners by the Confederacy.[87] Resting their case, the Confederate leaders declared that the Union was "desolating our country, in violation of the usages of civilized warfare," while simultaneously refusing "to exchange prisoners" and had "forced us to keep 50,000 of their men in captivity." The hypocritical Union then dared "to attribute to us the sufferings and privations caused by their own acts. We cannot doubt that in the view of civilization we shall stand acquitted, while they must be condemned."[88]

The Confederate report, like its Union counterpart, qualifies as a propaganda masterpiece. Leaving aside the accurate description of the Union's political manipulation of the prison controversy and the admission that Union prisoners suffered greatly in the Confederacy, the bulk of the document represented a distortion of reality. Instead of accepting responsibility, Confederate leaders chose to hide behind the excuse that somehow losing the war justified the mistreatment of their Union captives. This position ignored the consistent effort to politicize the status of prisoners of war, as the Confederacy did throughout the conflict. The delusional statements about African American soldiers in the Civil War minimized the centrality of racial equality as a legitimate cause of the war and stood as an unapologetic defense of the Confederacy's amoral "black flag" conduct. The report also concealed the fact that Confederate leaders such as Secretary of War James Seddon preferred to ignore the growing misery. Even worse were the actions of Commissary General of Subsistence Lucius Northrop, who, on his own authority, intentionally inflicted unnecessary suffering on Union prisoners by withholding rations and other supplies that, even in the last months of the war, existed and could have lessened the misery of Union captives. And like his foil Lincoln, President Davis, never shy in his efforts to centralize the Confederate war effort, clearly knew about the brutal conditions imposed upon prisoners held by the Confederacy yet chose to look the other way.[89] In retrospect, these canards issued by the Davis administration, like the Confederacy itself, fail to convince. But the truth of 1865 was that what remained to southerners, doomed to defeat, was their honor, and the arguments outlined in the report provided ammunition for future defenders of the Confederacy's handling of prisoners.

No aspect of the Civil War revealed its cold inhumanity more than the treatment of prisoners by both the Union and the Confederacy. The reason for the perpetration of atrocity toward Civil War prisoners was clear—it furthered the war aims of both participants—and the responsibility lay on both sides. The appalling death rates of Civil War prisoners resulted from a culture bent on destruction, and both North and South insisted on wreaking that devastation even on its unarmed captives. Unfortunately for prisoners, the reality that they were placeholders for the fundamental issues of the war—racial equality, Confederate sovereignty, moral superiority—ensured their suffering. Their status as prisoners, dependent on the mercies of their captors, offered little protection in a confrontation characterized by consumptive wrath. The most frightening aspect of the entire prison tragedy was the sanctimonious outrage generated in response to their opponent's

atrocities even as Americans, North and South, accepted, with unquestion-
ing swiftness, their own brutality. War, regrettably, especially a fratricidal
conflict like the Civil War, by its nature clouds judgment and lures people
into actions that appear essential, but of course are not.

A further injustice endured long after 1865. Throughout the Civil War
both governments consistently manipulated the prison trauma for political
gain. Using Civil War prisons as fodder for propaganda benefited the war
effort in that it lessened criticism of the refusal to exchange and focused the
building anger over the treatment of prisoners on the actions of the enemy.
In doing so, the emotional controversy, driven by inherent confusion about
who was exactly to blame for prison casualties and by lingering guilt about
the 56,000 dead prisoners, escalated into a rhetorical war within the larger
conflict. Vindicating the Union or Confederate treatment of prisoners became an opportunity to prove the justice of each side's cause and a means to
assert moral superiority over a depraved, uncivilized enemy. Patriotic northerners and southerners ignored their own failings and decried those of their
opponents instead. But the end of the war did not mean the end of the illusion. The reality of unleashing destruction, of course, is that the bitter feelings last. The painful controversy remained raw precisely because of the frequent and remarkable employment of each section's divisive memories of
Civil War prisons in cajoling both a devotion to cause and justification for
violence. The hardened animosities created and intentionally nurtured during the war would prove surprisingly durable in the reunited nation.

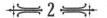

"Remember Andersonville"

RECRIMINATION DURING RECONSTRUCTION, 1865–1877

In May 1865, amid the excitement of the transition from war to peace, Union troops arrested a Confederate officer, Captain Henry Wirz, the camp commandant of Andersonville Prison, and transported him to Washington. There the wrath of the enraged northern citizenry awaited him. During the operation of Andersonville, approximately 13,000 Union soldiers out of the 45,000 unfortunate souls housed there died. Those statistics meant that the Georgia prison camp, both in the percentage of fatalities and in sheer numbers, distinguished itself as the deadliest Civil War prison. But the scale of the casualties represented only one of the reasons for the focus on Wirz. Northern anger over the Confederacy's prisons continued to build and needed an outlet for its release. At the war's conclusion, the Committee on the Conduct of the War further inflamed public opinion when it published a sweeping denunciation of the Confederacy's amoral prosecution of the Civil War, a report that included over twenty pages of statements about the suffering occurring in Confederate prisons.[1] With Wirz already in custody, such accounts of the terrible prison conditions in the northern press added to the grief and resentment over Lincoln's assassination. These emotions made Wirz a natural target in the charged postwar environment. Over the next few months, the question of Wirz's fate made headlines across America. His trial and the nature of the proceedings helped assure that the bitter memories of the treatment of prisoners of war remained as strong throughout Reconstruction as during the Civil War itself.[2]

Beginning with Wirz's arrest in May, the American public seemed riveted to the events surrounding his trial, which commenced in August and ended in October. The northern press avidly covered the story and railed against the crimes that Wirz, supposedly at the behest of the Confederate government, conspired to commit against the Union prisoners. According to northern popular opinion, the callous brutality demonstrated at Andersonville by Wirz and his co-conspirators typified the barbaric nature of the rebellious South. The animosity directed toward Wirz grew so vociferous as the trial approached that many declared him not just guilty, but an inhuman monster. A July 1865 *New York Times* editorial demanded that "some expiation must be exacted for the most infernal crime of the century."[3] In an August edition of *Harper's Weekly* an editor judged, "of his guilt there can be no doubt," even though the trial was still in its initial stages.[4] A series of illustrations depicting the Andersonville atrocities, including one of Wirz stomping on a prisoner, appeared in *Harper's* in September.[5] These engravings hardened northern sentiment against the yet-to-be-convicted Confederate officer. In October, another *Times* article compared the "diabolical and fiendish" Wirz to a "tiger sporting with its helpless prey."[6] Such biased press coverage indicated the climate of hatred that Wirz's presence incited in the North during 1865. One reflection of that anger exists in the diary of Abram Parmenter, a member of the Veterans Reserve Corps stationed in Washington, D.C., during the Wirz trial. On August 25, Parmenter was outraged by "some astounding facts brought to light—in regard to the brutal and inhuman treatment of prisoners." The next day, Parmenter described the trial as "a sickening tale of suffering." When the Wirz defense commenced on September 27, Parmenter dismissed it as "rather feble."[7] The anti-Wirz hysteria, demonstrated by the press and confirmed by public opinion, meant that long before the trial concluded, northerners like Parmenter were already convinced of Wirz's guilt.

The public vitriol directed at Wirz encouraged the inflammatory rhetoric used by the prosecution during the legal proceedings. The trial commenced on August 21 before a military tribunal. The federal government— represented by its lead attorney, Colonel Norton Parker Chipman—initially hoped to prove the existence of a massive conspiracy to murder brutally Union prisoners by the thousands among Jefferson Davis, Robert E. Lee, John Winder, Wirz, and other leading Confederate officials.[8] Along with the charge of conspiracy, Wirz stood accused of over a dozen murders of Andersonville prisoners. Although Secretary of War Edwin Stanton halted the proceedings and forced the overzealous Chipman to remove the names of the Confederate leaders specifically charged in the conspiracy with Wirz, the firm northern belief in the reality of the plot never wavered. Since the fate of Davis still remained undecided, Stanton and the federal government balked at implicating the ex-Confederate president in the Wirz matter. When the trial resumed on August 23, Wirz faced two revised charges. The first charge stated that Wirz conspired with unknown others "to impair and injure the health and destroy the lives of large numbers of federal prisoners." The second accused Wirz of thirteen separate murders of unknown Union prisoners at Andersonville.[9] As scholars have pointed out, the language of the ten pages of charges, with repeated references to Wirz as "malicious," "evil," "cruel," and "wicked," set the tone for the prosecution's portrayal of Wirz throughout the trial.[10] By demonizing Wirz, Chipman and the government desired not only to pin responsibility for the prison atrocities on the shoulders of individuals like Wirz but also to remind posterity of the inherently corrupt and evil nature of the Confederate South.

Throughout the proceedings, the prosecution continued to rail against the inhuman cruelty of Wirz. "Mortal man," Chipman declared, "has never been called to answer before a legal tribunal to a catalogue of crime like this." But despite his insistence that Wirz bore responsibility for the "long black catalogue of crimes, these tortures unparalleled," Chipman saved much of his venom for the Confederacy itself. "With what detestation," he stated, "must civilized nations regard that government whose conduct has been such as characterized this pretended confederacy." The "treasonable conspiracy" of the South against the Union prisoners of war resulted not from "retaliation, punishment, nor ignorance of the law," Chipman explained; rather "it was the intrinsic wickedness of a few desperate leaders, seconded by mercenary and heartless monsters, of whom the prisoner before you is a fair type." Chipman further argued that individuals such as Wirz, Winder, and implicitly Davis and others deliberately worsened the already difficult conditions for the Union prisoners. The deaths of Union captives occurred because of the cruelty of these "diabolical" men in charge of the Confederate prison system, men representative of a "murderous" rebellion. Throughout the trial, the prosecution presented Andersonville as a moral outrage perpetuated by one fiendish individual in the service of a fiendish cause. Judge Joseph Holt, the judge advocate general in charge of the proceedings, spoke for many in his closing statement: "This work of death seems to have been a saturnalia of enjoyment for the prisoner, who amid these savage orgies evidenced such exultation and mingled with them such nameless blasphemy and ribald jest, as at times to exhibit him rather as a demon than a man." The toleration of such cruelty in the Confederacy naturally correlated to the inherently barbaric nature of the treasonous South. The consistent juxtaposition of Wirz's individual crimes with the general accusations of endemic Confederate brutality sufficed to explain the prison casualties in the minds of many in the North.[11]

In looking for someone to declare culpable for the horrors of Civil War prisons, the U.S. government found a perfect target in Wirz. He proved to be a malleable symbol of the Civil War prison controversy at a time when confusion abounded concerning what actually happened at Andersonville and other prison camps. In reality, Wirz was no mass murderer but simply an ineffective and callous officer placed in a position of authority in a Confederate prison system defined by those same characteristics. The natural result of that unfortunate combination, in an era of relative medical primitivism, meant death on a massive scale. But descriptions of Wirz as a "monster" motivated by inhuman malice made political sense because it offered the angry northern public a demonic figure on which to focus their outrage. And the relatively innocuous official status of Wirz, as a mere captain, allowed the government to place responsibility for the prison debacle on the Confederacy without further stirring up the emotions of southerners, as a trial of Jefferson Davis might have done. Wirz's background as a Swiss immigrant also facilitated the campaign against him because he lacked the credentials and connections of other Confederate leaders. In a nativist political culture, it was far more politically expedient to blame a lone, expendable immigrant than to put Davis, a former U.S. senator and secretary of war, on trial for Andersonville.[12] And even though Wirz received the blame, Chipman and Judge Holt never missed an opportunity to remind the public that Wirz represented the "spirit" of "murderous cruelty and baseness" that characterized "the inner and real life of the rebellion, and the hellish criminality and brutality of the traitors who maintained it."[13] Although the prosecution tried him as an individual, Wirz became the personification of southern brutality—evidence of the debased and dehumanized character of traitors. Even though the fate of Wirz alone hung in the balance, the trial process accomplished the goals of political leaders such as Stanton. The proceedings reinforced northern convictions concerning Civil War prisons by explaining the suffering at Andersonville and other Confederate prisons as singularly cruel, unlike the supposedly humane Union prisons.

Other prejudices worked against Wirz as well. Though a legitimate legal process, military law differed from the more exacting standards of civil law. Military justice, according to historian Gayla Koerting, allowed for the inclusion of "circumstantial evidence" in the trial record, unlike a traditional court of law. The resulting predisposition against Wirz by the tribunal was deemed acceptable because the officers prosecuting Wirz were "men of honor" who could be relied upon to rule appropriately.[14] Other scholars have suggested that regardless of the honor at stake, the "intimate 'old boy' relationship that existed between the prosecution and the members of the military commission" cast serious doubt on the "intellectual integrity" of the military tribunal.[15] These inherent flaws in the nature of military justice, especially given the emotional intensity created by the constant commotion over the prisoner-of-war issue, doomed Wirz even before the trial and obscured significant flaws in the government's prosecution of the case. Of the 160 witnesses who testified, 145 stated that they never saw Wirz kill a prisoner; moreover, those who insisted that Wirz committed murder failed to name any of the victims.[16]

The trial culminated in an inevitable verdict of guilty, and Wirz received a death sentence. He rebuffed last-minute efforts to convince him to declare Davis the architect of the Andersonville conspiracy in exchange for clemency.[17] On November 10, 1865, spectators assembled around the gallows hurled cries of "remember Andersonville" at Wirz.[18] The chant grew louder as he ascended the steps. The trap door opened, and with the cheers of an exultant crowd ringing in his ears, Wirz joined many of his former wards in death. Wirz became the only ex-Confederate officer executed for conspiring against POWs during the Civil War.

In the midst of the northern celebration over Wirz's death, a few lonely southerners such as Robert Kean, now a former Confederate War Department official, took offense at the trial, insisting that it represented a mockery of justice. "The real object," Kean wrote in his diary, "is to make a case against Davis and Seddon, or at least blacken them." Kean perceived the proceedings as a smokescreen designed to divert northern attention from the real culprit behind the prison suffering, Edwin Stanton. "That official," Kean argued, "preferred for thousands to perish miserably, in the effort to [have federal prisoners] eat Confederate corn from the Confederate armies." "The perfidy by which the cartel was abrogated was a settled policy to starve the Confederacy," Kean continued, "though thousands of their own men starved and rotted with scurvy."[19] As for the charge of conspiracy, former Confederate doctor Randolph Stevenson made a simple yet compelling argument: "Captain Wirz could not conspire alone."[20] No other Confederate official went to trial for the Andersonville crimes, although had he not died shortly before the end of the war, General Winder, as the Confederate commissary general of prisons, would probably have faced charges. Wirz himself recognized that in his case, justice reflected popular opinion: "I know how hard it is for one, helpless and unfriended as I am, to control against the prejudices produced by popular culture and long continued misrepresentation."[21] In defeat, however, the similarly one-sided nature of these defensive southern arguments, which conveniently minimized the racism and intent that lay behind the conditions in Confederate prisons, barely registered. Northerners ignored these protests and continued rejoicing over their revenge.

On the day of the execution, Abram Parmenter recorded his disappointment at arriving too late to see Wirz hang, but the demise of the "Andersonville wholesale murderer" comforted him. The execution of Wirz, Parmenter commented further, seemed an appropriate fate "to satisfy the just claims of the law, and an outraged people."[22] A few days after Wirz's burial, a *Harper's Weekly* editor wrote, "There are crimes against God and man which ought not to be forgotten, and these for which Wirz suffered . . . are of them."[23] Even with Wirz dead, the palpable righteousness of the northern public lingered.

The public excoriation and death sentence imposed on Wirz by the government satisfied a northern citizenry willing to overlook the warped sense of justice behind the process. It also made for exciting headlines and robust newspaper sales figures. By the end of 1865, northerners viewed Andersonville and Henry Wirz as the primary symbols of Confederate atrocity.[24] This was not coincidence—the Wirz trial represented the logical continuation of the wartime pattern in which the government manipulated the emotional controversy of Civil War prisons for political gain. The desired object, not the message, changed after Appomattox. Instead of rousing a people to war, the one-sided vilification of Henry Wirz, and by extension the Confederate prison system, now justified the proper outcome of the conflict. It was an appealing vision, especially to a people still celebrating their dearly earned triumph. Nor was it technically incorrect, as the Confederacy had indeed inflicted intentional suffering on its prisoners, although the process of singling out Wirz now seems a product of convenience. Victory gave the North what Robert Penn Warren once called a "Treasury of Virtue," a sense of moral reassurance, out of which its citizens could easily condemn the sufferings at Andersonville and other southern prisons rather than admit the failures of Union prison camps.[25] Blaming Wirz and his fellow unnamed Confederates as uniquely responsible for the tragedy at Andersonville excused any acknowledgment of the tortured morality of the exchange process, bureaucratic dysfunction, or retaliatory behavior present in the Union prison system and signified an attempt to remember not only the 56,000 prisoner deaths but the Civil War itself in a positive light.

Northern satisfaction soon proved temporary and problematic. Exultations over Wirz's execution camouflaged but could not undo the truth that the Union, and not just the Confederacy, bore responsibility for the deliberate brutality that took place in Civil War prisons. Celebration could not last forever, and the task of integrating the former Confederacy back into the United States loomed. Many considerations complicated the process of Reconstruction, not least among them the difficulty of achieving a true sense of forgiveness between North and South. The combination of wartime prison atrocities with their repeated emotional manipulation created a powerful and singular memory that confirmed northern virtue, defied attempts to redefine the prisons as part of a just conflict, and distracted attention from the important questions of racial equality raised during the war. Nor would that memory, with its assurance of northern moral superiority, allow the reconciliation of the sectional bitterness that remained. "Prison horror," according to historian David Blight, "and the hatreds it fostered in both sections, infested social memories of the war during Reconstruction years as nothing else did."[26] Throughout the 1860s and 1870s, the persistent northern anger over Civil War prisons delayed the spirit of national reconciliation and obstructed the acceptance of an inclusive reunification.

From the very beginning of Reconstruction, the northern memory of Civil War prisons helped shape the contemporary political environment and became a significant issue in national politics. Thaddeus Stevens, a leader of the anti-Johnson wing of the Republican party and a driving force behind congressional Reconstruction, justified his unrealized desire for the confiscation and redistribution of Confederate property on the ground that ex-Confederates merited punishment for the barbarities at Andersonville and other places.[27] In the 1866 *Report of the Joint Committee on Reconstruction,*

Stevens and his congressional allies denounced President Johnson's lenient policy of Reconstruction. Reminding Johnson and his supporters that the ex-Confederate states waged war "with the most determined and malignant spirit, killing in battle, and otherwise, large numbers of loyal people," the committee declared presidential Reconstruction an insufficient penance for the South. In case the oblique reference to the deaths of thousands of Union soldiers in Confederate prisons went unnoticed, the committee included several pages of testimony from Dorence Atwater, a former inmate of Andersonville who compiled a roster of the dead and detailed the brutal conditions at Andersonville and other southern camps.[28]

During the late 1860s, inflammatory rhetoric and images about Civil War prisons appeared in the northern press. These outcries were sparked initially by the question of what should be done with Jefferson Davis, who still awaited trial or release from prison. On June 30, 1866, cartoonist Thomas Nast, in *Harper's Weekly,* contrasted the brutality and suffering of Andersonville with the relative luxury that Davis enjoyed at Fortress Monroe, Virginia. The public, an accompanying editorial maintained, should remember that Davis "is the same man who could see from his house in Richmond the island upon which Union prisoners were slowly starved and frozen, and who knew that thousands of his fellow-men imprisoned at Andersonville were pitilessly tortured into idiocy and death."[29] The ongoing animosity directed at Davis over his responsibility for the Confederate prison system may have delayed his discharge from prison, although he, unlike Wirz, escaped formal charges. And in late 1867, in response to southern irritation with the passage of the Reconstruction Acts, *Harper's Weekly* ridiculed the South for protesting against northern "tyranny," pointing out that not only had the southern cause failed but also "there was no fame garnered at Salisbury: nor is Andersonville very bright and shining with classic glory."[30] Although the prison controversy never became the central focus in the debate over Reconstruction, the Radical Republicans' use of the prison issue justified a stronger policy and convinced the public to support Congress as it successfully wrested control of the process away from Andrew Johnson. Once again, invocation of the traditional one-sided portrayal of Civil War prisons successfully served the desires of northern politicians. Throughout Reconstruction, discussion of the prison camps would consistently be used to justify the cemented relationship between northern morality and the Republican political agenda.

Nothing symbolized the claims of Republican politicians as effectively as the existence of the corpses of thousands of dead prisoners. In a culture still reeling from the impact of inconceivable death, a strong fascination with the physical remains of the dead persisted. The popularity of the 1866 exhibit "Andersonville Relics," displayed at the National Fair in Washington, encouraged *Harper's Weekly* to predict that "whatever relates to the Andersonville dead is not likely soon to become void of interest, at least not to the loyal North."[31] And so, in the immediate aftermath of the war, the Johnson administration created an official program under the auspices of the Quartermaster's Department to properly identify and bury the Union dead. By the end of 1867, among the national cemeteries created were four former Confederate prison sites: Andersonville, Danville, Florence, and Salisbury. Other victims of Confederate prisons were interred in the nearest national cemeteries. Meanwhile, the northern graves of perished Confederate prisoners lay all but forgotten.[32] The priority placed on honoring the Union dead while ignoring their Confederate counterparts reflected the hardened intent of a North determined to honor its self-confirming memory of the prisons. Captain and Assistant Quartermaster James M. Moore, charged in 1865 with marking the graves of Union soldiers at Andersonville, revealed this sentiment when he reported that "nothing has been destroyed; as our exhausted, emaciated, and enfeebled soldiers left it, so it stands to-day, as a monument to an inhumanity unparalleled in the annals of war."[33]

Although the presence of the dead inspired much of the lingering acrimony over Civil War prisons, an even greater source of recrimination came from the publication of numerous Union veterans' prison narratives, a practice that remained common well into the early twentieth century. The frequent rehashing of the trauma, along with the animosity with which most former prisoners wrote, encouraged hostile memories of the prison camps. In many ways the postwar accounts, which took the form of memoirs, unsurprisingly resembled the wartime prisoner testimony. What separated the postwar accounts from their predecessors, especially after the Wirz trial, was the strident, amplified rhetoric. The competition and popularity of the memoirs encouraged the polemical nature of the accounts. Between 1865 and 1867, dozens of prison memoirs appeared, and the need to distinguish one's product through sensationalism and vitriol became irresistible.[34] This impulse led to titles such as *Martyria* and *Life and Death in Rebel Prisons* along with declarations like those of Joseph Ferguson, whose exaggerated account stated, "It is past question that the Confederate authorities did deliberately, and with thoughts of murder in their hearts, perpetuate the awful enormity of torturing to death sixty or seventy thousand helpless but brave men; slain by a refined process of cruelty."[35] Statements like these served the needs of the individual prison survivors in that it allowed them to share their experiences and turn a profit. Such declarations also catered to the appetite of the northern public for reminders of the moral justice of the Union cause at a time when white southerners were engaging in race riots, creating black codes to restrict the rights of the newly freed slaves, and forming the infamous Ku Klux Klan to terrorize African Americans. Authors like Ferguson knew that the northern public expected an attitude of outrage and denunciation toward the brutal, treasonous, and unrepentant South, and they willingly gave their audience reassurance of Yankee superiority over Confederate baseness.

Another distinctive feature of the early postwar northern prison narratives involved the cessation of blame directed at the U. S. government for refusing to exchange prisoners for much of the war. Men like William Burson instead argued that "the rebels knew just how to demoralize the Union prisoners and make them useless to the Federal Government, and adopted this means to accomplish their hellish purpose."[36] From Burson's perspective of hindsight, Union leaders deserved credit for avoiding this Confederate ruse. Alfred Richardson, imprisoned at Salisbury, North Carolina, praised the "credulity and trustfulness of our Government towards the enemy" in sending private shipments of supplies to Union prisoners, which the Rebels "openly confiscated." Richardson lodged his only criticism of Union policy against Edwin Stanton's "cold-blooded theory" that "returned prisoners were infinitely more valuable to the Rebels than to us." Although this policy contributed to his hardship, Richardson seemed accepting of the correctness of the Union's calculation, especially in the aftermath of victory. Along with the vindication of Union policy came Richardson's attack against the camp commandant at Salisbury, Confederate major John H. Gee. Gee, claimed Richardson in an attack reminiscent of the accusations leveled at Wirz, insisted on giving the prisoners quarter rations even though the commissary warehouse, as well as the surrounding regions, enjoyed ample supplies of corn and pork.[37] Like Richardson, other survivors singled out the men they held personally responsible for their suffering. Warren Goss, an Andersonville prisoner, blamed the harsh conditions on "the inflexible Winder," while Josiah Brownell expressed his disdain for Wirz, saying of him "a more brutal coward I never saw."[38] In 1867, J. F. Brock swore that defenders of the Confederate prison system, and, in particular, "Jeff Davis and Benj. Hill are both liars."[39] Readers of these memoirs, most of whom were already familiar with the old conspiracy arguments, saw no reason to doubt the words of these heroes, and so the belief that deliberate brutality occurred only in Confederate prisons became even more ingrained in the North. The consistent appearance of similarly styled prison memoirs in the decades to come preserved a memory of Civil War prisons that rejected the prospect of reconciliation on the logical grounds that former Confederate supporters, capable of such atrocity, deserved continued contempt.

Although outnumbered, ex-Confederate prison survivors resisted the one-sided charges of their Union counterparts. In their own late 1860s memoirs, Confederate veterans of Union prisons not only refuted the northern arguments but also made their own accusations. Decimus Barziza, held at Johnson's Island, ridiculed the "alleged" brutality supposedly taking place in southern prisons and insisted that the "horrible treatment" at prisons like Fort Delaware and Point Lookout occurred with the purpose of forcing Confederate prisoners to swear an oath of allegiance to the Union or face "starvation, cold, and ill-treatment."[40] A. M. Keiley felt impelled to write his own prison account as a response to the North, which "is not only writing the story of the late war, but the character of its late enemies." In doing so, Keiley compared his experience at Point Lookout and Elmira with those of the Andersonville prisoners. Keiley believed that Union major E. L. Sanger, the head of the Medical Department at Elmira, acting on the instructions of Edwin Stanton, refused to supply the prison with the medicine prisoners needed. An indignant Keiley wondered how the North could "studiously ignore" the evidence of its own brutality while condemning Wirz, "who was not the monster whom that scandalous tribunal declared him."[41] As bitter as he felt about the treatment he received in the North, the one-sidedness with which northerners attacked the Confederate prison record angered Keiley the most. Other southerners perceived the northern hypocrisy as well. L. M. Lewis, in the preface to W. A. Wash's prison account, hoped that "if we would have a just verdict from the grand juries of coming generations," northern prisons such as "Alton Penitentiary, Camp Douglas, Camp Chase, Rock Island and Elmira" should "be placed by the side of the exaggerations about Libby, Belle Isle, Tyler and Andersonville."[42] As they reminded readers of the inconsistencies in the Yankee interpretation of the prison controversy, Barziza, Keiley, Lewis, and Wash reinforced southern frustrations not just with the war, but with a reunion dominated by northern memory.

The persistent bitterness of the prison narratives on both sides ensured that the emotions stirred up by Civil War prisons retained their relevance as the first postwar presidential election loomed in 1868. As part of its strategy, the Republican Party focused attention on the prisons, a tactic one scholar called "the most powerful political weapon that could be used by the North in securing Republican victories at the polls."[43] Although the Republican Party dominated the North, the sizable number of Democratic sympathizers there worried the Republican establishment. Since the white South remained anti-Republican, the possibility existed that a rejuvenated Democratic Party might challenge the Republican majority, threatening the hard-earned political power justified by the war. In the fall elections of 1867, *Harper's Weekly*, as usual, took the lead in reminding its readers of the stakes. Those "who love freedom, will vote for the Republican," the editor wrote, "while all who secretly wish . . . the Andersonville pen had succeeded, will vote for his Democratic opponent." On July 4, 1868, another *Harper's* article lamented that had the Democrat George McClellan defeated Lincoln in 1864, "the rebel army and the Andersonville jailers would have sung Te Deum." A week later, a *Harper's Weekly* editor referred to Andersonville as "the Palladium of Southern Democratic liberties."[44] Throughout 1868, Republican publications such as *Harper's Weekly* delighted in hammering Democrats by repeatedly charging them with behavior only slightly less traitorous than that of the Confederacy.

Over the last few months of the election, a torrent of similar sentiments flooded the northern press. On October 3, an anonymous letter to *Harper's Weekly* stated the obvious point of the agitation over Andersonville and the other southern prisons: "I should like to see a picture of that stockade, and on the left the United States Cemetery, with the Stars and Stripes flying over those poor boys' graves. I do believe," the author concluded, "it would clench the nail in the political coffin of Seymour and Blair." Three weeks later, with the election only days away, an illustration titled "The Political Andersonville" appeared in *Harper's*. The cartoon depicted the unfortunate Republican voters of the South as trapped in a giant stockade—symbolic of the white Democratic South's tactics of violence and fraud to ensure victory at the polls. A grim specter, the ghost of a dead Andersonville inmate, loomed over the scene. The caption quoted Wade Hampton, the ex-Confederate general and South Carolina gubernatorial candidate, as the main advocate of these abuses of democracy. "Agree among yourselves . . . that you will not employ any one who votes the Radical ticket," Hampton threatened, and "use all the means that are placed in your hands to control this element."[45] The denial of democratic liberties in the South and even the alliance between northern and southern Democrats, the engraving suggested, insulted the memory of the sacrifice that thousands of imprisoned soldiers made during the war. Over the course of the campaign, the Republican press succeeded in portraying the Democrats not only as corrupt, undemocratic, and unpatriotic, but as disrespectful of the dead Union prisoners.

In November, the war hero Ulysses S. Grant secured the presidency for the Republican Party. Given Grant's lack of political experience, the constant emphasis on playing to the patriotism of Republicans proved a sound strategy. That patriotism, of course, rested in part on attacks against anyone with even the slightest connection to the prison atrocities. The Republican victory further confirmed the versatility of memory as a political weapon. Along with blaming Henry Wirz and Jefferson Davis, in 1868, Republicans also held Democrats, North and South, responsible for the suffering at Andersonville and other southern prisons.

Even after Grant's election, Republicans continued to harp on the subject of Civil War prisons. In 1869, the House of Representatives published the results of one final investigation into the treatment of Union soldiers in Confederate prisons. "In a national and historical sense, the subject of rebel imprisonment," stated the committee, required "an enduring record, truthful and authentic, and stamped with the national authority." The report proceeded to endorse all the accusations of the Civil War and its aftermath, so that "these facts should live in history as the inevitable results of slavery, treason, and rebellion, and as an example to which the eyes of future generations may revert with shame and detestation." Nearly 270 pages of similar rhetoric seemed designed as much to justify the need for ongoing Republican control of the federal government as to warn posterity about the "unholy ambition" and the barbaric society of the rebel South. Besides officially endorsing the campaign propaganda of the late 1860s, the report served another purpose as well. Acknowledging the "heroism of the thousands of long suffering and martyred soldiers of the republic," the committee cited the sacrifice of these men "as an enduring example of that chivalric courage which elevates man above the common level of his race." The House also exonerated the Lincoln administration, as well as the Union military, "from any responsibility for these great sufferings and crimes."[46] With the Union absolved of any potential guilt and respect paid to the dead prisoners, the report accomplished its task of codifying the official Republican stance on the prison controversy. Rejecting even the possibility that the Republican government and military could have done more for the prisoners of both sides, the committee instead denounced the Confederacy as the barbaric product of a debased southern society and lauded the martyred figures of Lincoln and the Union prisoners. In part because of the constant repetition, few, at least in the North, disagreed. Memories of the Civil War remained too vivid to allow a more objective presentation of the events surrounding the prisons. Having won the war, the Republicans continued to press their rhetorical advantage in order to define the memory of the conflict and thus win the peace as well.

One of the reasons for the ongoing emphasis on remembering the wartime prisons by the Republican Party centered on the involvement of Union veterans through their main postwar organization, the Grand Army of the Republic (GAR), in mobilizing the Republican constituency. The GAR played several important roles during Reconstruction, with preserving the celebratory meaning of Union victory not least among them. The bitter memories of Civil War prisons influenced the GAR from its beginning, as initiation rites often included symbolic reminders of Union POWs and Andersonville. The need to honor properly the dead victims of Confederate prisons justified, indeed required, political involvement. In the late 1860s and early 1870s, according to historian Stuart McConnell, "the war's place in the popular estimation as a successful crusade allowed Union veterans to assume the role of savior, and they did not hesitate to do so." Between holding political offices at the national, state, and city levels and "marshaling the massive 'soldier vote' for Lincoln in 1864 and Grant in 1868," veterans affiliated with the GAR acted as a potent political base for the Republican Party.[47] The 1870 speech of General J. P. C. Shanks to the GAR post at Washington, D.C., indicated the continued centrality of the prison issue for the Union veterans and the Republican Party. "It is at the door of the confederate government I lay the charge of wanton and savage cruelty to helpless prisoners of war," Shanks thundered, before invoking the sympathies of the audience: "I would, if I could, call before your imaginations the gaunt, spectral forms of those thousands of robbed, frozen, starved, beaten, wounded, manacled, dogged, emaciated, neglected, crazed, and murdered men."[48] Shanks's oration testified to both the enduring power of the vitriol over the treatment of prisoners and the attractiveness of the easy political capital gained from recycling old allegations. The preeminence of Union veterans in the Republican Party, as evidenced by the subsequent elections of Grant, Rutherford Hayes, and James Garfield to the presidency, meant a natural focus on what best qualified them for public office—meritorious service to the Union cause. It also meant that the symbolic issue of Civil War prisons continued to be invoked by Republican politicians whenever convenient. Repetitious mention of the accusations of Confederate atrocity, the celebration of the sacrifice of the Union prisoners' bravery, and the innocence of the Union government all contributed to a political phenomenon known as "waving the bloody shirt."[49]

The 1872 reelection of Grant once again demonstrated the durable power of the memory of Civil War prisons to inspire righteousness in the North. On September 21, 1872, a Thomas Nast cartoon in *Harper's Weekly* conjured up the old animosity over the conditions at Andersonville. Presidential candidate Horace Greeley, a Democrat, stood, with hand outstretched to the South, while below him lay the vast stockade of Andersonville, filled with graves. Nast juxtaposed Greeley's quote "Let us clasp hands over the bloodiest chasm" with a sign featuring a skull and crossbones that stated "Andersonville Prison. Who Ever Entered Here Left Hope Behind."[50] Nast's setting proved telling. Instead of a battlefield such as Gettysburg or Antietam, two of the bloodiest battles of the war, Nast chose Andersonville to represent "the bloodiest chasm" of the Civil War. That choice mirrored the popular northern perception of Andersonville as a terrible anomaly, the result of demonic, deliberate cruelty. In a political culture still inflamed by the paradoxical need to both celebrate and hate, Nast expertly conveyed the message that a full reconciliation with the South was impossible and ultimately undesirable at this time, given the horrors experienced at Andersonville. To forestall that reconciliation, northerners needed to continue to vote Republican until the southern penance of Reconstruction was deemed complete. Undeniably effective as a practical political tactic, the persistent use of a one-sided memory of Civil War prisons, with its emphasis on the evils of the Confederacy and the purity of the Union, benefited Republican politicians in another, less tangible way—it enabled northerners to forget the similar experiences Confederate prisoners endured in the North.

Southerners, meanwhile, as the critics of the Wirz trial and survivors of Union prison camps indicated, remembered quite clearly, if more quietly, the sacrifices made in Union prison camps. Besides these few strident voices, however, in the immediate aftermath of the war many southerners suffered the accusations of the North in silence. The humiliation of defeat, augmented by the constant northern recitation of the memory of Confederate prison abuses, at first drowned out the southern voices who protested the North's selective recollection of Civil War prisons. Southern defenders of the Confederate prison record remained relatively quiet because the South, at least in the short term, wanted to move on. In the late 1860s and early 1870s, southerners faced the daunting task of putting their society back together, and the turmoil surrounding the process of first presidential Reconstruction and then congressional Reconstruction prevented debate with the North. "Reestablishing a normal life," according to scholar Gaines Foster, "left little time for dwelling excessively on the past and its pains" and "discouraged public lamentations." Despite Dixie's silence during Reconstruction, the South's "need to repeat their assertions of righteousness, honor, and manhood," and this "defensiveness toward northerners" foreshadowed an outpouring of southern frustration over the northern interpretation of Civil War prisons.[51] A few undaunted Southerners, however, began to frame the arguments that soon evolved into the standard defense of the Confederate prison record—a counter memory that defensively denied the validity of the northern accusations and deflected questions of responsibility for the prison suffering back toward the North.

Writing from a jail cell in 1865, former Confederate vice president Alexander Stephens echoed the Confederate congressional report on the problem of prisoner treatment, declaring that the harsh conditions in the Confederate camps resulted from "unavoidable necessity" rather than from "inhumanity of treatment." Since everyone in the Confederacy suffered from the lack of resources, Stephens opined, from the Confederate army to civilians, Yankee prisoners naturally endured the same hardships. Stephens suggested that in light of the quickly deteriorating state of affairs in the Confederacy by 1864, northerners prone to conspiracy theories about deliberate atrocities overlooked the obvious supply problems that plagued the entire Confederacy, not just Union prisoners. Despite the Confederacy's shortcomings, Stephens continued, "Confederates escaping from Camp Chase and other Northern prisons" found "their treatment in these places to be as bad as any now described in exaggerated statements going the rounds about barbarities at Andersonville, Salisbury, Belle Isle, and Libby." Stephens concluded that "there were barbarities . . . and atrocities on both sides," and that therefore, neither section should boast too much about their prison record.[52] Ex-Confederate president Jefferson Davis expressed sentiments similar to those of Stephens, according to the account published by the physician John Craven, who treated him during his imprisonment after the war. Craven summarized Davis's belief that Confederate officers cared for their prisoners "the best they could," but because "non-exchange" was "the policy adopted by the Federal Government," the Union abandoned its prisoners to their fate in the resource-starved South.[53]

In 1867, Louis Schade, one of Wirz's defense attorneys, stated that the question of responsibility for the dead prisoners "has not fully been settled." Like Stephens, Schade pointed out that given the collapse of Confederate infrastructure due to the Union naval blockade and the destruction of southern railroads and property, providing food and medicine for prisoners proved difficult, if not impossible. Schade insisted that "the Confederate authorities, aware of their inability to maintain their prisoners . . . urgently requested that prisoners should be exchanged," but to no avail. Not content merely to refute northern accusations, Schade asked, "Has the North treated her Southern prisoners so that she should lift up her hands and cry 'anathema' over the South?" Denouncing the North's "fearful record," which, according to the 1866 report of Secretary of War Edwin Stanton, consisted of an estimated 26,436 southern deaths in Union prisons, Schade pointed out how curious it seemed that "over 26,000 prisoners" perished "in the midst of plenty!" Using Stanton's figures, which claimed that 22,576 Union prisoners died in Confederate prison camps, approximately 4,000 fewer casualties than in the North, Schade wondered why northerners continued to adamantly attack southerners over the treatment of prisoners, especially when one considered the supplies available to prisoners in the Union but not to those in the Confederacy. After not so subtly suggesting that if either section deserved to be accused of atrocities committed against prisoners of war, perhaps it was the North rather than the South, Schade reminded readers that "puritanical hypocrisy, self-adulation and self-glorification will not save those enemies of liberty from their just punishment."[54] In the emotionally charged climate of the late 1860s, the arguments of Stephens and Schade reassured southerners of their brave and honorable conduct during the war. No one in the North took them seriously.

Despite the negligible impact of their ideas on northern public opinion, these southern defenders succeeded in creating their own deflective memory of Civil War prisons. Their version contained several components that not only excused the Confederacy's prison record but placed the burden of responsibility for the dead prisoners back on the Union. According to Stephens, Davis, Craven, and Schade, the Confederacy strove to fulfill its obligations to its prisoners even in the midst of total collapse. If the North had fought a more civilized war, refraining from destroying much of the Confederate heartland and preventing the import of medicine and other supplies, then tending to the needs of Union captives would have been far easier. Had the Union at any time acquiesced to the resumption of the exchange cartel the misery of the supposedly intentionally deprived Yankee soldiers would have ended. Finally, even with the concession that Confederate prisons took an incredible toll on Union prisoners, the fact remained that Union prisons killed Confederate captives at similar rates. While northerners scoffed at these arguments and dismissed them as selective, false, and conjectural, southerners clung to these rhetorical positions and began to repeat them, at first weakly, but eventually with growing confidence.

Like its northern counterpart, the southern memory represented a severe distortion of the truth about Civil War prisons. A clear preference for hypothetical alternatives defined the southern position. Such narratives are not surprising given the grim reality of the outcome of the conflict. As defenders of the Confederacy, through the power of hindsight, reflected on the war, the natural human tendency to revisit mistakes and to ask what if crept in and influenced their arguments. The more troubling aspect of the southern deflective memory lay in its defiant mirroring of the northern stance. The denial of all responsibility for the suffering in Confederate prisons combined with the insistence that the Union instead deserved sole blame not only was untrue but indicated just how deep the wounds inflicted by the Civil War, and constantly reopened, as with the Wirz trial, during Reconstruction, really were. And the telling refusal to accept the legitimacy of African American freedom as both cause and outcome of the conflict, or to own up to the racial brutality that so heavily influenced the prisoner exchange controversy, revealed a white South determined to persist in its traditional racism despite the forced changes of Reconstruction.

But even as the sectional fight over remembering Civil War prisons intensified, a third strand of memory emerged in the contest. Although white southerners used the debate over the wartime prisons to deflect attention from the lack of racial progress in the South, and northerners preferred to interpret Confederate brutality as confirmation of the virtue behind the Union cause, African Americans defined the memory of Civil War prisons for themselves. According to Blight, a black emancipationist vision of the conflict, focused on the abolition of slavery and consequent celebration of freedom, challenged the white supremacist trend, North and South, of resisting and ignoring the transformational issue of racial equality central to the Civil War.[55] For African Americans, the emancipationist war meant a redefinition of Civil War prisons as symbols not of atrocity, but of freedom. Although few black soldiers, no more than 1,200 total, experienced prison camps, the misery experienced within prison walls in the service of human rights, regardless of race, made these locations into places of honor, worthy of commemoration. Despite the small number of black prisoners—and the unpleasant similarity of imprisonment and slavery—the emancipationist memory clearly included Civil War prisons. As throughout the country, African Americans demonstrated a determination to pay respects to these sites of sacrifice as a way to both give thanks for and express their commitment to the cause of equality.[56]

Andersonville, in particular, showed the divergent—and controversial—power of the emancipationist tradition. Winslow Homer's well-known untitled 1866 painting, known variously as *At the Cabin Door* or *Near Andersonville*, depicted a female slave peering out from her cabin doorway while in the background Union prisoners of war are marched to Andersonville. The juxtaposition of black slavery with white captivity was intentional—the fight for emancipation and the plight of prisoners at Andersonville became one and the same. Homer's insightful recognition of the tangible connection between the prisons, abolition, and the uncertainty facing the newly freed slaves remains the most striking emancipationist image of Civil War prisons.[57] Such a painting also verified the reality that, alongside the one-sided sectional memories that enraged and frustrated white Americans, African Americans intended to embrace the location of Andersonville with a spirit of optimism about the future possibilities of freedom. No single human endeavor represents faith in progress more than the process of education, and in late October of 1866, a freedman's school, the American Missionary Normal School, opened in the old hospital buildings of the prison. Although soon displaced from the actual prison grounds, the school remained in existence for decades. During that time, generations of black students began their quest for a better life at the same spot that thousands died to create that opportunity. In its reincarnation as an educational institution supportive of the drive for equality, Andersonville became, fittingly, not just a symbol of emancipation but a tribute to the sacrifice, made willingly or not, by the dead Union soldiers. Although the Normal School's teachers, both white and black, were "generally shunned" by the white townspeople of Andersonville, a testament to the connection between memory and ongoing racial division, the positive emancipationist interpretation of Andersonville offered hope that the recollection of Civil War prisons might help heal instead of wound.[58] Before that could happen, of course, the recriminations would have to cease.

As the local white resentment of the Normal School indicated, the emerging importance of Andersonville as an icon of freedom implicitly criticized the southern deflective tradition. The power of the emancipationist legacy provided an unsettling reminder to white southerners that their memories of the past were challenged not only by northerners but by their African American neighbors as well. The intertwined political and racial hostility of Reconstruction manifested itself in the growing tradition of Memorial Day at Andersonville. Yearly commemorations, attended by mostly black audiences, openly revealed the seething racial tensions in the postwar South. A newspaper account, sensationally headlined "White Women with Nigger Beaus," of the 1870 "Andersonville frolic," which drew about seven hundred African Americans and "not over half a dozen respectable white persons," mocked the featured speaker, controversial Republican governor Rufus Bullock, as "His Expressellency." A bitter scene ensued, according to the writer, as "Mrs. Bullock and company were gallanted around by niggers!!!" Such open defiance of racial propriety unmasked "what Republicanism seeks to accomplish in Georgia." The black celebration at Andersonville testified to the importance of the emancipationist memory and offered a glimpse of not only an alternative past but perhaps the future for the South. The possibility of social change both profoundly frightened white southerners and encouraged them to cling ever tighter to their ideal-ized recollections of the Civil War and its prisons. Disturbingly, for local whites at least, the popularity of the "disgusting carnival" at Andersonville would continue to grow long after the era of Reconstruction.[59]

As the contested Memorial Day commemorations at Andersonville showed, throughout Reconstruction, and even by its end, the bitterness of divisive memory endured instead of fading. On January 10, 1876, Maine congressman James Blaine rose to criticize a pending bill that proposed amnesty to the last of the unforgiven Confederates on the grounds that it included Jefferson Davis. Davis, argued Blaine, deserved no amnesty, be-cause "he was the author, knowingly, deliberately, guiltily, and willfully, of the gigantic murders and crimes at Andersonville." Reaching back into his-tory for other brutalities, Blaine declared, grandstanding, that not even "the thumb-screws and engines of torture of the Spanish Inquisition begin to compare in atrocity with the hideous crime of Andersonville."[60] The debate over the amnesty bill offered yet another opportunity for northern manip-ulation of the memory of Civil War prisons in the name of politics as sup-port for Reconstruction faded and Democratic representation in the fed-eral government grew.[61] With Wirz and Winder dead, Davis provided the best remaining target for northern politicians determined to associate the Democratic Party with the Confederacy and its horrible prisons. Despite the applause, Blaine soon found himself in a storm of controversy. The first responses came from Representatives Samuel Cox, of New York, and Wil-liam Kelley, of Pennsylvania. Both regretted that, in the centennial anniver-sary of the United States, Blaine insisted on reviving the acrimony of the past. Just before adjourning, Benjamin Hill, of Georgia, obtained the floor.

The next day, Hill, speaking with the emotion of over ten years of pent-up frustration, delivered a rebuke not just to Blaine but to the entire North. Hill's speech ended the Reconstruction years of relative southern public si-lence over the prison controversy and demonstrated the rising influence of the southern defensive memory of Civil War prisons. Expressing sorrow that Blaine focused attention on the prison feud, Hill declared it his "im-perative duty to vindicate the truth of history" and protect the reputation of the Confederacy. "Whatever horrors existed at Andersonville," Hill contin-ued, "grew out of the necessities of the occasion, which necessities were cast upon the confederacy by the war policy of the other side." Hill proceeded to ridicule Blaine's claim "that no confederate prisoner was ever maltreated in the North" and insisted that "the time has passed when the country can accept the impudence of assertion for the force of argument or recklessness of statement for the truth of history." After rejecting Blaine's accusations, Hill questioned the constant use of the bloody shirt to attack southern honor. "Is the bosom of the country always to be torn with this miserable sectional debate whenever a presidential election is pending?" Hill asked, especially when "the victory of the North was absolute, and God knows the submission of the South was complete." But the reality of the political situation in 1876, Hill argued, showed a South "recovered from the humiliation of defeat," offering "no concession" to those in the North "who seek still to continue strife."[62] Hill's speech reflected a maturing, if still delicate, confidence in the white South that resulted from the preservation of much of the antebellum social order. By 1876, white southern males managed to regain political control in all but a few southern states, and northern interest in the South's affairs faded. Despite Reconstruction, the Thirteenth, Fourteenth, and Fifteenth Amendments, and a tumultuous period of economic and class turmoil within white society, continued southern white dominance over African Americans seemed increasingly possible. Although the amnesty bill went down to defeat, and Jefferson Davis remained unforgiven, the Hill-Blaine debate testified to the South's determination to protest the selective northern memory of Civil War prisons.

Two months after the controversy over the amnesty bill, a new periodical, the *Southern Historical Society Papers*, responded to Blaine's comments and devoted an entire issue, over two hundred pages, to the *"Prison Question."* Admitting that Union prisoners experienced some suffering in southern prisons, the editor nevertheless declared the conditions even worse for Confederates held in the North. In a manner reminiscent of the Confederate congressional report of 1865, the testimony of the southern defenders rehashed the South's counter memory of Civil War prisons. Although the inaccurate claims of higher mortality rates in Union prisons strained credibility, the strident, one-sided portrayal of the issue, intended to protect southern honor, helped cement a sense of solidarity in Dixie over the truth about the prisons. Despite a period of dejection, southerners, the *Southern Historical Society Papers* made clear, intended to fight the inaccurate northern charges and restore their reputation.[63]

In 1877, then, the hostility over Civil War prisons remained as strong as ever. The enduring passion behind the distorted memories of Civil War prisons must be understood in its context—Reconstruction was, at its core, an era defined by the search for new identities to replace those destroyed by the conflict. The ongoing anger over the prisons served as a verbal battlefield, a rhetorical framework, as African Americans, northerners, and white southerners fought to define their postwar goals and collective identities. Increasingly ignored by the North and consistently scorned by white southerners, African Americans remained steadfast in celebrating their unique memory of Civil War prisons as symbols of freedom during Reconstruction. But the forward-looking interpretation of African Americans prompted a dismissive response from whites of both sections, who not only clung to traditional attitudes of white supremacy but remained transfixed by the seeming impossibility of reconciling with the villainous enemy of the past.

The most vociferous recollections of Civil War prisons came from northerners, who justified the long, costly process of Reconstruction by "waving the bloody shirt," asserting their virtue, and reminding themselves of the South's barbarity toward prisoners during the war. The bitter rhetoric fostered a sense of obligation, based on appeals to the moral superiority of the North, which augmented support for the idea that the sacrifice made by the dead Union prisoners demanded that northerners complete the task of Reconstruction and support the patriotic party of Lincoln. Although these impulses were understandable, the irony of the northern memory of Civil War prisons was that it contributed to a series of contradictions that undermined much of the positive gain from the triumph. In celebrating the virtue of victory, northerners abandoned the cause of racial justice—emancipation as an accomplished fact was sufficient evidence of moral superiority—and ignored the injustices of Union prisons. The refusal to acknowledge the evils of the Union prison system was not a coincidence. As their memories hardened into gospel truth, righteous northerners, convinced by their own propaganda, refused to admit any wrongdoing. And the constant use of the prison controversy as a weapon against a series of convenient political targets had ramifications—it incited a sanctimonious indignation that precluded any meaningful sense of reconciliation in a nation that had suffered greatly in order to be preserved.

White southerners, initially relatively timid in mentioning their memories of the prison controversy and drowned out by the volume of northern intensity, over time rejoined the debate, albeit for different reasons. The frustration with the overbearing reminders of northern virtue encouraged southern apologists to mythologize the Confederate treatment of prison-ers. Forced onto the defensive by the relentless northern accusations, south-erners could not pretend—as did many in the North—that the atrocities committed in Confederate prisons did not occur. But they could, and did, attempt to deflect the barrage of criticism. The deflective memory con-structed by southerners blamed the Union government and war policies for the suffering and claimed that Confederate soldiers experienced far worse treatment in northern camps. With home rule all but established, and in a period of growing national support for the Democratic Party, southerners like Benjamin Hill enjoyed a renewed sense of confidence as they began to refute vigorously the northern charges. But for white southerners the war-time prisons raised even deeper emotions. The war, and the crushing nature of the defeat, shook southern faith in their society at the same time that the North attacked southern honor over prisons like Andersonville. While the North, in the revelry of victory, could overlook its flawed treatment of prisoners, the South, during the late 1860s and early 1870s, remained ex-ceedingly conscious of the aspersions cast on its honor. The rejuvenation of the southern defensive memory of Civil War prisons by 1876 thus served a multitude of needs for white southerners. As a component of the emerg-ing Lost Cause, defiance of the northern prison interpretation justified the honorable nature of the Confederate war effort, commemorated the sac-rifice made by Confederate victims of Union prisons, and demonstrated a sense of renewed optimism that the days of southern penance might soon end. The construction of this more comfortable past was not harmless. The deflective southern prison memory also encouraged resistance to racial equality by challenging, and ultimately rejecting, the legitimacy of the Af-rican American emancipationist remembrance of the prison tragedy.

Despite the divergent nature of the competing memories of Civil War prisons, these visions all shared a common durability rooted in and bound to the need for self-definition in postwar America. But beyond the need for identity, the intense emotions stirred up by Civil War prisons, still vivid more than a decade after the fighting, testified to the shocking human cost of the war and the desire to find meaning in the suffering. Begin-ning with the Wirz trial and continuing throughout the recriminations of Reconstruction, the prison controversy received so much attention in part because of the opportunity of political and financial gain, but mostly be-cause Americans remained unsettled by the scale of the tragedy. Even the war itself possessed identifiable, if controversial, origins. The 56,000 prison deaths, however, represented the apex of the Civil War's vicious nature and, at the time, made the most sense if understood as the brutality of a one-sided savagery. The existence of these Manichean, divisive memories created a deeply felt, if false, understanding of Civil War prisons that, throughout Reconstruction, obstructed the process of reconciliation and minimized the issue of African American equality. The possibility that the truth lay somewhere in between these divisive memories would have to wait for future generations even more bitterly schooled in the realities of modern war.

"This Nation Cannot Afford to Forget"

CONTESTING THE MEMORY OF SUFFERING, 1877–1898

In the period between the end of Reconstruction in 1877 and the onset of the Spanish-American War in 1898, despite the passage of time, the contested memories of Civil War prisons remained highly controversial. The dispute over the treatment of Civil War POWs continued—amid the larger national concern with the American future—as a transformative modernity redefined the United States as a country and society.[1] In the uncertain environment of the last decades of the nineteenth century, the legacy of the Civil War reassured Americans that the country had survived far worse. Americans took comfort and inspiration from the character and fortitude displayed by their forebears in the Civil War, including the sacrifice of those who suffered in enemy prisons. Honoring that sacrifice became paramount in these turbulent decades as Americans sought to make sense of their present. Testimonials to the dead Civil War prisoners represented the effort, made by northerners and southerners alike, to use their deaths to justify and garner support for the creation of an America worthy of these heroes.

During the late nineteenth century, northerners remained dominant in the battle to claim the moral high ground regarding the prisons of the Civil War. Sensing that the uneasiness caused by the memory of Union prisoners' suffering could still mobilize northern voters, Republican politicians throughout the late 1870s and 1880s continued to emphasize the unique brutality of the Confederate prison system. In 1879, James Garfield, future president of the United States, addressed a reunion of Andersonville survivors. "From Jeff Davis down," he declared, "it was a part of their policy to make you idiots and skeletons." That policy, thundered Garfield, "has never had its parallel for atrocity in the civilized world." As so often before,

Garfield connected the brutality of the Confederate prisons to the actions of depraved southern leaders. Garfield also renounced the possibility of reconciliation, suggesting that the individuals responsible for the prison suffering deserved the continued scorn of the North. "We can forgive and forget all other things," he stated, "before we can forgive and forget this."[2] Republicans recognized that emphasizing their role as the successful prosecutors of the Union war effort attracted the continued favor of voters. In order to maintain the public mandate supporting Republican officeholders, it helped candidates like Garfield to remind their northern constituents of the unspeakable horrors of the southern prison system. As a carryover from Reconstruction-era politics, this tactic made sense given the dominance of the Democratic Party in the South. The choice, as Garfield framed it, lay between the Republican Party of the civilized North and the Democratic Party of the immoral South.

Throughout the 1880s, national politics, and particularly presidential elections, often encouraged a revival of the old Republican bloody-shirt charge that the Democratic Party consisted of treasonous ex-Confederates who refused (as years of violence had shown) to accept the reality of Reconstruction. General William T. Sherman, a Republican political symbol if not an actual politician, as late as 1887, "divided the American people into Republicans and Confederates, and termed the Democratic Party the left flank of the Confederacy."[3] That same year James G. Blaine, the 1884 Republican candidate for president defeated by Democrat Grover Cleveland, published his *Political Discussions,* a compendium containing what he considered his most important speeches. Among them, Blaine included his 1876 address attacking the idea of extending amnesty to ex-Confederates, particularly Jefferson Davis. Once again northerners read Blaine's assessment that while "Wirz deserved his death," it was "weak policy on the part of our government to allow Jefferson Davis to go at large and to hang Wirz."[4] Despite his failed campaign, Blaine remained steadfast in his belief that the prison controversy offered incontrovertible proof of the need for Republican control of the American government. Only Republican administrations could act as a safeguard against the Democratic Party's allowing the return of ex-Confederates to power.

Although Cleveland's election to the White House in 1884 and again in 1892 demonstrated the diminishing effectiveness of bloody-shirt politics in general, Republicans nevertheless held fast to their accusations that the

Confederacy brutalized its prisoners. The calculated animosity with which Republicans denounced southerners such as Jefferson Davis and Henry Wirz continued to yield a tangible, if weakened, political dividend. It went over well with the northern public and army veterans, reminding them that the causes for which the war was fought were best served by keeping Republicans in office. By reinforcing the image of the Democratic Party as a sympathetic home to ex-Confederates, the ongoing utilization of prison memories stirred up the fading emotions of the northern voting public and obstructed sentiment for a reconciliation that fully absolved the South of its sins.

Throughout the late nineteenth century, the proliferation of published prisoner narratives by Union soldiers contributed to the politics of sectional bitterness. Capitalizing on the national appetite for reminiscences of the Civil War, numerous prison memoirs appeared in the North in which the animosity over the treatment of prisoners continued unabated. Many historians of Civil War prisons note that the motivation for publishing prison memoirs often derived from the desire to make a profit or to establish a right to a veterans' pension. These scholars offer persuasive evidence that authors of prison narratives, especially by the 1880s and 1890s, often exaggerated, fabricated, and plagiarized their accounts as they reinvented their experiences to help increase book sales.[5] But whatever the questionable motives or veracity of the ex-prisoners, the historical importance of the prison memoirs lies in the widespread acceptance of their stories by the northern public. Hundreds of thousands of readers bought these books because of their dominant narrative—the portrayal of the prison experience as an individual tale of courage appealed to a people still incredulous at the unimaginable scale of impersonal mortality in Civil War prison camps. The prison accounts not only reminded northerners of the Confederate prison atrocities, and in the process encouraged support for the Republican Party, but they also personalized the suffering of Union soldiers in a highly sympathetic manner. Despite their flaws, prison memoirs represented a legitimate search for meaning in the wartime suffering.

As with the Reconstruction-era prison accounts, the authors focused attention on their horrible treatment and struggle to survive, and they charged individual Confederate leaders such as Wirz, Winder, and Davis, among others, with committing deliberate atrocities against prisoners. Motivated by the desire to sell their stories of suffering, prison veterans eagerly camouflaged tales of drudgery with sensationalistic rhetoric. In 1880, Sergeant Oats recalled the misery he and his fellow "ragged, scurvied, filthy, vermin-eaten wretches" experienced at Andersonville. These pitiful specimens represented the lucky ones, as Oats made clear, because the "strongest struggled for life, and the weak died without pity."[6] Willard Glazier, self-styled "soldier-author," described the commandant of Libby Prison, Dick Turner, as "possessed of a vindictive, depraved, and fiendish nature ... there is nothing more terrible than a human soul grown powerful in sin, and left to the horrible machinations of the evil one."[7] Such brutal treatment, Glazier argued, could only have supernatural origins. The animosity toward individual Confederate leaders reached an apex in the account of John McElroy, another Andersonville captive. McElroy detested Wirz, but he saved most of his antipathy for Winder, whom he held most responsible for the atrocities at Andersonville. Although "neither Winder nor his direct superiors," and here McElroy singled out Jefferson Davis, "conceived in all its proportions the gigantic engine of torture and death they were organizing ... they were willing to do much wrong to gain their end." As their "appetite for slaughter grew with feeding," McElroy declared, "they ventured upon ever widening ranges of destructiveness." "Killing ten men a day" in places like Belle Isle, argued McElroy, "led very easily to killing one hundred men a day in Andersonville." The popularity of McElroy's well-written, if overwrought, account, due in part to his background as a newspaperman, was undeniable. Over 600,000 Americans purchased copies of McElroy's account after its publication in 1879, and its circulation, as well as the popularity of other prison narratives, helped cement the enduring power of the northern memory of Civil War prisons.[8]

Well into the 1880s and 1890s, these narratives showed, northern survivors of Civil War prisons blamed the unprecedented prison casualties on the "depraved" leaders of the Confederacy, the representatives of the old southern social order. The perception that "fiendish" southerners reveled in the committing of these atrocities appealed to the former prisoners for several reasons. Focusing their anger on men like Wirz, Winder, Davis, and Turner provided an outlet for the prisoners' bitterness, and the denunciation of the individual Confederate leaders offered a small measure of revenge for their suffering. With their infamous national reputations long established, Wirz and Davis served Union prisoners especially well in that northern audiences already perceived these men as villains, although the prisoners' attacks on other Confederate officials accomplished the same result. The explanation of the prison tragedy as the result of the actions of evil Confederate individuals also ensured acceptance in the North because it continued the long tradition of distracting attention from the shortcomings of the Union prison system. Finally, the bravery displayed by so many loyal imprisoned Union soldiers, even though confronted by unspeakable human cruelty, proved just how honorable and righteous their cause had been and reassured readers of the providence that a reunited America represented.

Thanks to its versatile appeal, the selective memory of Civil War prisons dominated northern survivors' memoirs as they discussed their captivity in the Confederacy. In the minds of a few prisoners, however, the explanation of so many deaths as the result of individual actions seemed insufficient. McElroy, although convinced of Winder's evil nature, found the escalating scale and efficiency of the brutality stunning and denounced the prisons in language that referred to "organization" and an "engine of torture and death."[9] Ex-Andersonville prisoner Herman Braun went even further than McElroy in searching for a different understanding of what went wrong in Civil War prisons. After describing Wirz as an individual of "efficiency and consideration," Braun assessed the organizational structure of Andersonville in a chapter titled "General Management of the Prison." "The management of the prison," according to Braun, showed "a persistent effort to prevent overcrowding," but the mortality from "the change in climate alone" doomed many prisoners despite the Confederate efforts. Focusing on Wirz or even Confederate organization, Braun felt, diverted attention from the most important lesson of the prison tragedy. The real responsibility for Civil War prisons should be attributed to the conduct of the Republican Party. Braun believed that the party of Lincoln deliberately discriminated "between the favored class and the rest of the people" by exempting wealthier citizens from military service and drafting the poor instead. "The seed beds of that policy were Andersonville and other Confederate prisons," as the Union government "assumed the right to expose citizens enlisted in its service to unparalleled suffering and sacrificed their lives for the sake of other citizens who were unwilling to aid in the country's defense."[10] For Braun, the evil of Civil War prisons resulted from the Republican government's callous abandonment of its soldiers, with their lower class origins, instead of the cruel actions of Confederate leaders.

The alternative explanations of the prison controversy offered by

McElroy and Braun revealed the growing importance of two interrelated concepts in American society. One involved what later historians referred to as the organizational synthesis, the idea that during the late nineteenth century organizational structure and behavior challenged the autonomy of individuals during the painful creation of modern America. McElroy's disdain for "organizations" and "engines," and his amazement at the efficient killing they were capable of in the case of Civil War prisons, directly reflected the suspicion and uncertainty many Americans felt with the role that organizations played in changing America. Braun shared McElroy's concerns with "efficiency" and "management" but made the even more ominous argument that the United States government itself represented a potential source of great evil in privileging the wealthier classes. By arguing that the Lincoln administration consciously sacrificed the poor in the prisons of the Civil War to benefit the rich, Braun implied that, in the America created by the Civil War, the growth of sinister government power made it impossible to accept that Wirz, Davis, or even the Confederacy itself could reasonably be credited with sole responsibility for the prison tragedy. Although the minority opinions of McElroy and especially Braun, whose class-based explanation of the prison controversy would never meet with acceptance, made little impact on public opinion at the time, in their refusal to accept the standard argument that depraved Confederate leaders intentionally slaughtered Union prisoners they not only anticipated concepts of modern, total war but asked thoughtful questions about the nature of an American society in transition.

Exceptions like McElroy and Braun notwithstanding, most of the post-Reconstruction era prison discussions aped the arguments of their predecessors in many ways. But along with the rehashing of familiar material and the escalating rhetoric, an emerging sense of purpose united these accounts. Three themes—rooted in the conviction of northern virtue—figured prominently in most of the newer presentations of prison memories. While continuing to vent hostility and attribute blame, the ex-prisoners also focused on the ideas of heroism, escape, and sacrifice. These themes, particularly sacrifice, were not new in the accounts of the late 1870s and early 1880s, but the emphasis given them was.

One of the primary reasons surviving veterans published accounts of their years in prison was to redefine what wartime heroism meant. Before the Civil War, according to public perception, heroism in combat almost exclusively manifested itself in battlefield charges, last stands, brilliant tactics, or personal fighting prowess. Young men entered the Civil War expecting a test of their manhood and character along these traditional lines.[11] Instead, over 400,000 imprisoned Union and Confederate soldiers experienced an entirely new test of individual fortitude. The patient courage they demonstrated, although less glorious, demanded no less of them than did fighting on the front lines. But as many prison memoirs indicated, the stigma of being captured combined with the unglamorous prison existence of waiting for exchange undermined the public acknowledgment of their heroism. Heroism required action in the nineteenth century, and so prison survivors set out to recast passive imprisonment as a harrowing tale of Yankee toughness overcoming southern brutality.

"The awful reality of the torments," wrote Asa Isham, Henry Davidson, and Henry Furness in 1890, "inflicted upon the unfortunate victims of this war in rebel hands can never be known, except by those who survived it."[12] Isham and his co-authors described in detail the horrible conditions they endured at Andersonville, including the lack of food, clothing, shelter, and medicine, but, despite the exhaustive depiction, warned their readers that mere words could not adequately convey the incomprehensible depth of their suffering. Through the exaltation of the misery they endured, Isham, his co-authors, and numerous other prison survivors hoped for public recognition that, although different from the carnage on the battlefield at places like Gettysburg or Antietam, being imprisoned by the enemy represented an equally traumatic experience. In his account of life in Salisbury Prison, Benjamin Booth asked "that the example of this noble heroism and loyalty to their country and their flag shall not be forgotten or treated as a mere trifle." Booth believed that the northern public needed these reminders of what happened in places like Salisbury because "this Nation cannot afford to forget."[13] The intensity of their trials, according to Alonzo Cooper, revealed the Union captives as "true-hearted patriots," who, in the words of Jesse Hawes, "never for a moment faltered in their devotion to their country."[14]

Unlike the more ambiguous diaries of the war itself, in which Union soldiers often pondered the role of their government in the failure to exchange prisoners, by the 1880s and 1890s few northern accounts even mentioned that the Lincoln administration played any part at all in the controversy. Proving their loyalty despite the hardships of Confederate prisons occupied the minds of most ex-prisoners, who seemed anxious to legitimize and explain their suffering as heroism on a par with any demonstrated on the battlefield. To that end James Compton dedicated his prison memoir "to the memory of that brave band of heroes," men "who were true to the flag and the cause of freedom when the monster death was looking them in the face."[15] The redefined heroism displayed in the southern prisons, these accounts suggested, deserved even more widespread recognition and respect.

Despite their inspiring tales of patient courage, the authors of the prison accounts also demonstrated their bravery by describing their heroic attempts to escape their Confederate captors. Almost every prison memoir published in the late nineteenth century contained a detailed report of an escape plot or exploit. Although escape stories figured prominently in the earlier prison texts, escape took on even more significance in the post-Reconstruction era. Instead of waiting for exchange, prisoners planned elaborate schemes of scaling prison walls or tunneling underneath them to freedom. According to H. Clay Trumbull, escape "was our duty," a sentiment shared by Madison Drake, who reminisced in 1880 that he "knew that a brave heart and unceasing vigilance would, sooner or later, offer me an opportunity of striking for liberty."[16] The idea of escape and its important role in the prison narratives restored the initiative to the captured soldier. Ex-prisoner John V. Hadley suggested that escape was a simple matter of "strength and will," a perception that empowered the prisoner.[17] Escape offered an active response to the inherently passive existence of imprisonment, and that desire for action resonated with the contemporary audience. Readers rooted for the underdog prisoner not only to escape the prison camp but to reach freedom despite the obstacles of guards, Confederate patrols, and hostile citizens. As Lessel Long, Andersonville prisoner, pointed out, the odds against successful escape seemed almost insurmountable when "every white man and woman in the South stood ready to assist in your re-capture."[18]

The authors of the prison narratives stressed that despite the apparent inevitability of recapture, they remained determined to try their luck at every possible opportunity. Andersonville survivors like McElroy wrote that as soon as they established their shelter, escape became "the burden of our thoughts, day and night."[19] William B. McCreery spoke about the hardships of Libby Prison and his attempt at freedom, emphasizing that he was no braver than the rest of his fellow inmates, of whom "nearly everyone was projecting some plan for escape."[20] And the public responded to the idea of escape, as the publishing of seven different editions of *Famous Adventures and Prison Escapes of the Civil War,* a popular collection of escape narratives, between 1885 and 1915 clearly indicated.[21] By emphasizing their escape attempts, the ex-prisoners focused public attention on their bravery and active determination to resist the Confederate villains holding them. Escape accounts, especially when successful, also appealed to the late nineteenth-century audience because they highlighted the ability of the individual to defy the power of the Confederate prison system. Although their audience appreciated the heroic sacrifices of the captives who died in the prison stockades and warehouses, they also appreciated a good story about the initiative of those resourceful individuals who actively fought to liberate themselves.

Whether they escaped or not, former captives of the Confederacy made their claims as Civil War heroes, according to historian Douglas Gardner, by basing their stories "on the metaphor of captivity leading to suffering and sacrifice and perhaps martyrdom, followed by some sort of redemption sanctifying and justifying the original suffering."[22] The dominance of Christianity in nineteenth-century America provided not only the archetype for the cultural understanding of sacrifice but the recognition that one of the most important proofs of faith involved the ability to sacrifice oneself for the greater glory of God and country. In a nation dedicated to belief in the martyrdom of Jesus Christ, the notion of wartime sacrifice particularly dominated the post-Reconstruction-era prison texts because it gave both the author and the reader a sense of meaning in the face of the unprecedented brutality that took place in Confederate prisons. The sacrifice of men like John Urban, who concluded his account by stating "a broken constitution and wrecked physical frame will ever be to me a horrible reminder of prison-life in the South," appealed to the author and audience because it lent a sense of purpose to and inspired appreciation for their prison experience.[23] Booth, who remained concerned that the public demonstrated too little appreciation for the misery endured in the Confederacy's prisons, asked "that the great sacrifices of my dead comrades shall not be suffered to pass into oblivion."[24] Sergeant Oats dedicated his memoir to "my comrades in suffering," an acknowledgment that the fraternal bond of sacrifice made the prison experience distinct in the Civil War.[25] The official Civil War history of Michigan reflected the destructive memory of Civil War prisons, accusing the Confederacy of "the most inhuman barbarities ever committed." But Michigan also acknowledged the "sacrifice" of "six hundred and twenty three braves," who "became victims of the horrid ordeal."[26] W. T. Zeigler, former Andersonville prisoner, recalled the suffering, but in an 1879 address, he spoke to his audience about the emotions he felt upon leaving Andersonville near the end of the war. "My heart grew sad," Zeigler stated, at the thought of those "who, in the defense of the cause they loved, had given their all, their life, and they lie there now in unknown graves." The sacrifice of "the martyred dead," he continued, would always remain in his thoughts.[27]

The recasting of the deaths of 30,000 Union soldiers in Confederate prisons as noble sacrifice revealed the desire of the former prisoners for public acknowledgment of their central role in the Civil War. Although during the war the misery of prisoners occurred far removed from the front lines of battle, prison narratives transformed suffering and death into a purposeful martyrdom that ultimately benefited the Union and reflected the moral certitude that God favored the northern cause. The prisoners' hardships were also retroactively justified as shortening the war by depriving the Confederacy of potential soldiers and resources. In endowing meaning to the prison suffering, these arguments proved attractive. In an 1889 speech to a Grand Army of the Republic post, William Chandler thanked the Union dead for their sacrifice, calling them the "saviors of our country."[28] According to northern memory, the sacrifice made by Union prisoners became an essential component of victory. But the concomitant reinvigoration of old animosities also tore at the scars of reconciliation.

As northern prison veterans reinvented their wartime experiences and stirred the embers of sectional bitterness, they also redefined the meaning of the Civil War. The prison memoirs of the late nineteenth century consistently minimized the racial implications of the conflict and stressed the paramount cause of Union. Although an occasional survivor such as Braun, who, when writing about the exchange controversy, argued that "the race question" was a "mere pretense" for the failure of the cartel, most ex-prisoners simply avoided the controversial subject.[29] Preferring to emphasize their warmly received tales of personal suffering, Union veterans of Confederate prisons risked alienating their audience with reminders that the Lincoln administration had not been above reproach during the sacred conflict. And the Union's wartime insistence on the connection between racial equality

and the collapse of the exchange cartel had long since lost relevance in a society where few whites regretted the regression of African American freedom. As white northerners, former Union prisoners wanted to remember
their sacrifice in the context of saving a reunited, if not yet reconciled, nation. Even the format of prison memoirs, according to scholar Ann Fabian,
"helped reconstruct racism for postwar white Americans." The removal of
African Americans from the story of Civil War prisons made white prisoners, who, in telling their tales of physical suffering and escape, "borrowed
descriptions of slavery," the central actors in the prison tragedy.[30] By sever-
ing the memory of Civil War prisons from the conjoined issues of emancipation, African American military service, and the Confederate "black flag"
prosecution of the war, white Union prisoners could define themselves as
active heroes instead of powerless victims. Although the rise of Jim Crow
during this time most strongly confirmed America's shameful retreat from
its commitment to racial equality, the racism inherent in the north's self-
congratulatory memory of Civil War prisons indicated the willingness of
the white northern public to abandon the cause of racial justice and its preference for a whitewashed recollection of the past.

The constant repetition of the themes of heroism, escape, and sacrifice
by Union veterans, as well as the exclusion of the racial dimension from the
prison controversy, was not accidental during the 1880s and 1890s—northern
prison survivors wrote and spoke about their terrible experiences in order
to better define their legacy. By emphasizing their heroism, the former prisoners hoped to bolster the national sense of respect for their suffering and
warn against premature reconciliation with the South. The spellbinding accounts of escape offered testimony to the individual courage and indomi-
table spirit that the prisoners displayed in the face of adversity and boosted
the entertainment value of their stories. Stressing their selfless sacrifices,
meanwhile, allowed the prisoners to make their most important appeal to
the American public—to remember the incredible human cost of the Civil
War and the need for loyal service to the nation. In a time when Republican
political dominance seemed increasingly fragile, these men felt a responsibility to revive flagging patriotism. They were gripped by a fear that, should
their deeds fade into obscurity, the purpose of the war as they wanted to
understand it, as a crusade to save the Union and not a revolution of racial
equality, might as well. The feverish intensity with which northern prison
survivors sought to ensure their interpretation of Civil War prisons reflected

the uncertain direction of the United States in the late nineteenth century. Prison survivors, through their discussion of deliberately chosen concepts, wanted to ensure that a reunified America would retain the proper northern memory of the Civil War as inspiration for its future.

The desire for a proper understanding of the Civil War and its prisons existed in the former Confederate states as well. During the late nineteenth century white southerners constructed the Lost Cause interpretation of the Civil War, defining the conflict as an honorably contested battle over constitutional principles. Embracing the Lost Cause not only restored a sense of purpose and glory to the South's defeat but offered "social stability" to a region deeply affected by sweeping changes in race, labor, and industrialization.[31] But northern accusations of Confederate atrocities against prisoners challenged the southern understanding of the war and represented a threat to the celebration of the Confederate legacy. Southerners, resenting what they thought was a northern attempt to further dishonor an already defeated opponent, angrily refuted these accusations and strove to legitimize their own defensive counter memory of Civil War prisons.

As in the aftermath of the Hill-Blaine debate in 1876, the *Southern Historical Society Papers* (*SHSP*) took the lead in both defending the Confederate prison record and attacking the hypocritical North. The continued intensity of the northern charges, the editors sought to show, represented an effort to obscure the true facts about Civil War prisons. Throughout the late nineteenth century, the *SHSP* stridently maintained that the suffering of Union prisoners in the Confederacy occurred because of the Union's own war policies. According to the *SHSP*, the prison casualties resulted from the combination of the blockade, which denied the Confederacy valuable materials and medicines; Sherman's campaign, which simultaneously destroyed resources and severed Confederate prisons from their supplying railroad lines; and the failure to exchange, a policy that the *SHSP* claimed proved both the hypocrisy and the brutality of the Union cause. But it was not enough to prove that the "*United States Government alone was responsible,*" as the *SHSP* stated in 1880. Since northern "authorities were responsible for the suffering of prisoners," the *SHSP* declared that "Elmira, Rock Island, Point Lookout, &c., are really more in need of 'defence' than Andersonville, with all of its admitted horrors." By vindicating the Confederacy and attacking the Union prison system, the *SHSP* offered an explanation of the prison atrocities that inverted the northern logic. Stanton and Grant replaced Davis and Wirz in the deliberate mistreatment of Confederate prisoners, while the suffering of prisoners in the South became the regrettable but inevitable consequence of the cruel Union policies. The deflective counter memory of Civil War prisons bolstered by the *SHSP* both reflected and contributed to the Lost Cause interpretation of the conflict—that the South had nothing to be ashamed of, prison record included, no matter what the Yankees might say.[32]

The zealous defense of the South undertaken by the *SHSP* during the late 1870s and 1880s also included publishing the experiences of ex-Confederate prisoners. In 1879 James T. Wells described the "gloom, privation, and starvation" of prison life at Point Lookout, Maryland. But Wells saved special contempt for Major Patterson, the provost-marshal of the prison, whose conscience, Wells stated, "must burn him." Patterson, claimed Wells, "was the impersonation of cruel malignity, hatred and revenge." Like his Yankee counterparts, however, Wells also detailed his efforts at escape. A scheme to tunnel out of the prison, a "bold" plan Wells and his fellow prisoners attempted, "required men of courage and determination and courage to undertake it." Unfortunately for Wells the escape plot failed, but he remained steadfast and loyal despite "the cruelty of the United States officials towards us." As in northern prison accounts, Wells and other southern prisoners emphasized the excitement of escape and testified that only heroic courage and a willingness to sacrifice their lives for the cause enabled men to survive the daily suffering of the prison experience.[33] In 1890, Charles Loehr addressed a meeting of the George E. Pickett Camp Confederate Veterans about his experiences at Point Lookout. Loehr recounted the Union attempts to starve the prisoners and the torture of being "bound and dipped head foremost in a urine barrel" for "trifling" offenses. "Expediency," claimed Loehr, motivated the Union, in sharp contrast to the Confederacy, which "did what it could for the prisoners that fell into our hands."[34] In an 1898 memoir, George Booth, who served briefly as a prison guard at Salisbury Prison, in North Carolina, testified that the Confederacy endeavored "to better the condition of the miserable men whom the fortunes of war had thrown on our hands." According to Booth, both the "poor confederates" and the "wretched federals" suffered tremendously because of the Union's "cruel, very cruel" refusal to exchange. In the end, Booth believed that "no phase of the war" seemed "more dishonoring to the federal arms than the policy they sanctioned . . . regarding prisoners."[35]

Booth's 1898 condemnation of the Union as singularly responsible for the failure to exchange echoed a southern vehemence on this particular point that had been building for years. Back in 1878, the *SHSP* declared that "*the sufferings on both sides were due to the failure to carry out the terms of the cartel for the exchange of prisoners, and that for this the Federal authorities (especially Stanton and Grant) were responsible.*" Emphasizing the failure of the exchange cartel as a deliberate Union policy choice remained a popular argument for proponents of the southern memory of Civil War prisons for several reasons. The focus on the Union's intentional manipulation of the status of wartime captives for political reasons deflected attention away from the actuality that the Confederacy's prison record revealed similar behavior. It also encouraged the southern fantasy that its chivalry during the war succumbed only to the cold reality of northern power—an argument that supported the myth that the Confederacy endeavored to prioritize humane care for its prisoners even during its collapse. Also of note in the southern attack was the omission of the Confederate "black flag" policy as a factor in the end of exchange. The refusal to admit any responsibility for racial atrocities indicated the southern determination to remember the Civil War as a failed revolution to protect white southern rights instead of a successful revolution to recognize African American citizenship. The removal of race as a central factor in the story of the Civil War, and its prisons in particular, fit the needs of a white southern society in the midst of reconstructing an idealized past through the rise of Jim Crow segregation. And finally, southern apologists, perhaps because they were already on the defensive in the battle for memory, seized on the exchange issue, despite the risk of reviving the subject of race, because it exposed an inherent contradiction in the northern memory of the prison controversy. During the war, the Lincoln administration justified refusal to exchange as an unfortunate but necessary measure to protect the rights of its African American soldiers. But with the end of Reconstruction, and certainly in the following decades, as northerners remembered the prison controversy, they deemphasized the connection between prison suffering and the establishment of African American rights. The northern abandonment of the racial explanation for the breakdown of exchange reflected the growing northern desire to define the Civil War as a war of nationalism instead of racial equality. The northern apathy toward racial concerns dovetailed with—and was encouraged by—an increasingly effective Lost Cause memory in the South that,

despite the historical evidence to the contrary, opportunistically manipulated recollections of the conflict. While southerners may not have consciously recognized this particular reason for the effectiveness of this challenge to northern memory, the realization that northerners could or would
not respond strongly on issues connected to the racial legacy of the Civil
War further encouraged their exploitation. Although cognizant that dispel-
ling the northern memory of prisons might take time, the *SHSP* publishers
felt "assured" that persistent repetition of these southern counterarguments
would lead to a memory of the war more favorable to the South than the reality of history had been. "If the present generation is not prepared to do us
justice," the *SHSP* declared, indicating the depth of its commitment to advocating the southern memory of Civil War prisons, "their children will."[36]

By the late 1880s and early 1890s, then, the *SHSP*'s elaborate defense of
the Confederacy's prison record helped reassure southerners that despite
the suffering at Andersonville and other prisons, the Lost Cause interpretation of the Civil War remained viable and southern honor intact. Another
major contributor to the southern defense of the Confederate prison system was the familiar figure of the ex-president of the Confederacy, Jefferson
Davis. In 1890 his article "Andersonville and other War-Prisons" appeared,
written expressly to "vindicate the conduct of the Confederacy" while en-
lightening those "who have generally seen but one side of the discussion."
Davis again revived the now standard southern argument that the "cold-
blooded insensibility" of the Union war policies and northern "inhumanity,"
not the actions of Confederate officers like Henry Wirz, whom Davis vigorously defended, caused the suffering that occurred in Confederate prisons.
Davis also wondered why, in the end, if the Confederacy was so brutal in its
treatment of prisoners, the Union prison record so closely mirrored that of
its beaten opponent. Davis suggested that the northern "authorities dared
not confess to the people of the North the cruelties, privations, and deaths
they were mercilessly inflicting on helpless prisoners." Although Davis expressed his desire to see the prison controversy fade away, he and his fellow
southerners did not really want the issue to disappear. The defensive southern counter memory of Civil War prisons served a lasting need in the Lost
Cause South. The coaxing and torturing of moral justifications out of memories of the wartime prisons helped inspire a rising southern confidence—
a sense that they need not accept a reconciliation dominated by northern
memories of the conflict. Until the North recognized and admitted its role

in the failure of the Civil War prison systems, or at least refrained from further attacks on southern honor, southerners remained eager and ready to argue the subject.[37]

And the debate continued. Appalled by Davis's argument, in 1891, General N. P. Chipman, a central figure in the government's prosecution and execution of Wirz, published his response, *The Horrors of Andersonville Rebel Prison*. In this work he promised to refute "fully" Jefferson Davis's "defiant challenge." Dismissing the cartel issue as "irrelevant," which effectively removed racial concerns from his argument, Chipman insisted that the end of exchange "furnishes no justification for unusual cruelty and starvation." After a lengthy recapitulation of the evidence presented at Wirz's trial, evidence that Chipman claimed conclusively proved both the brutality of Andersonville and the Confederate government's knowledge of the events, Chipman summarized why he found Davis's arguments so offensive. Davis hoped that the bitterness over the prison controversy should fade, but Chipman asserted that "so long as Southern leaders continue to distort history, so long will there rise up defenders of the truth of history." Instead of doing "a great service had he disproved the alleged complicity of his administration," Davis "chose to deny the horrors of rebel prisons rather than confess." Chipman spoke for many in the North who could not understand why southerners persisted in their perceived distortions and who resented the fact that the southern counter memory of Civil War prisons called into question the veracity of the Union government, Union veterans, and the Union cause. The dominant northern interpretation of the conflict, one that morally justified the cause of saving and reuniting America, depended in part on remembering Andersonville and other southern prisons as "unparalleled in the annals of crime."[38]

Undeterred by Chipman's vociferous reaction and the ongoing northern accusations, throughout the 1890s, led by the *SHSP*, the South continued to defend its honor in the fight to remember Civil War prisons. In response to the Davis-Chipman spat, the *SHSP* devoted many pages to further discussion of the conditions in Union prisons in articles such as "Horrors of Camp Morton," "Prison-Pens North," "Escape of Prisoners from Johnson's Island," and "Prison Life at Point Lookout."[39] These articles rehashed the cruelty that Confederate prisoners experienced in the North and extolled the bravery and sacrifices made by the loyal Confederate heroes. But more than anything else they sought, as Thomas Spotswood, author of the Camp

Morton piece, openly avowed, to refute the accusations of northern memory. "Since our friends on the other side have done so much to show how cruel the South was, and still continue to publish these sad and horrible facts," Spotswood declared, "it is but fair that we of the South should let the world know that the prison-pens of the North were no whit better than the worst in the South."[40] Although Spotswood and his fellow writers paid lip service to the idea of sectional healing, the persistent enmity provoked by the prison controversy indicated that the South would forget the past—and accept reconciliation—only when the North acknowledged the legitimacy of their claims. Since both sides understood history to be a product of memory, the competition to publicize the divisive memories of Civil War prisons continued to rage, motivated by the certainty that the correct version of history would exonerate either, and only, the North or the South.[41]

By the 1890s, southern confidence continued to rise as southerners actively sought ways to celebrate their memory of the prison dead while decrying the perceived northern hypocrisy over the prison controversy. While the *SHSP* led the fight to defend the reputation of the Confederacy's prisons, the *Confederate Veteran* spearheaded southern efforts to remember the dead Confederate prisoners, asserting that in regard to the wartime prisons, "history must affix on the United States government its lasting condemnation."[42] As the official voice of the United Confederate Veterans, the publication frequently included prisoner accounts and defenses of southern prisons couched in the same aggrieved terms as the *SHSP.*[43] But the reverent approach of the *Veteran* and its desire to praise the heroism of the Confederate soldier led naturally to a preoccupation with preserving the tangible evidence of that sacrifice, the graves of the dead prisoners in the North. The decades-old imbalance between the government-sanctioned, officially marked graves of those who died in Confederate prisons and the sporadically tended, shabby burial sites of those who died in Union prisons demanded redress if the South was to protect its memory of Civil War prisons.[44] In 1894, the *Veteran* announced plans to identify and order the graves of the Confederate dead in Indianapolis, which "lie leveled and unmarked."[45] The following year, in Chicago, "our monument" was unveiled on Memorial Day in commemoration of the Confederate dead buried in Oak Woods Cemetery, most of them casualties of the Union prison at Camp Douglas. At the dedication ceremony, Reverend Bolton, a former Union officer, honored "the brave men who died in our city, while prisoners of war," and celebrated those "men who were as true to their convictions, and as loyal to their leaders, as any class of men that ever put on the uniform, listened to the bugle-call, or marched to battle." Part of the reason for Bolton's magnanimity toward the Confederate dead, however, lay in his deeper understanding of the war's meaning: "To-day we stand with comrades at the graves that are not simply houses for the dead, but vaults in which the nation's power, fame and glory are stored."[46] While Union veterans such as Bolton demonstrated, according to the *Veteran,* a "soldier respect for soldier that you can not put into words," true ownership of the monument depended on sectional perspective.[47] Many southerners perceived the Chicago monument as evidence that, at long last, the momentum of their contest against northern memories of Civil War prisons was turning in their favor. The form of the striking memorial, well over forty feet tall and capped by a soldier standing aggressively, arms crossed in unrepentant defiance, certainly reflected the increased confidence southerners had in the authenticity of their prison memory. Most northerners, however, saw the monument as confirmation of a reunited Union in which a reconciled South, its heroism recognized and racism forgotten, participated wholeheartedly. The distorted understanding of both sections, provoked by their sectional memories, ensured that while commemorating the Confederate victims of Union prisons seemingly encouraged healing, it was only an illusion. In reality, such ceremonies perpetuated the one-sided nature of the memories of the wartime prisons.

The campaign to recognize the Confederate dead continued as a part of the larger southern desire to remember the war on its own terms. In 1896 and 1897, the *Veteran* publicized and requested support for the efforts, often supported by northerners for very different reasons, to care for "the graves of our known and unknown dead buried" at such places as Camp Morton, Camp Douglas, Camp Chase, Point Lookout, and Johnson's Island.[48] The *Veteran* declared that "it is our sacred duty," required by "the dictates of honor," to "keep fresh the memory and green the graves of those of our heroes whose arms are nerveless, many of whose families are helpless, and they sleeping so far away from homes and kindred."[49] Although the *Veteran* expressed the South's appreciation for northerners who assisted the process of decorating and memorializing the prison graves, the overall tone of the periodical in dealing with the prison controversy remained strident. According to Henry Howe Cook, in an article published in March 1898, "The

Federal Government was criminally negligent in her treatment of Confederate soldiers, and in many respects" committed "willful, intentional cruelty." Commemoration, even when both North and South participated together, still did not equate to a full reconciliation on the subject of Civil War prisons. Nor did it end feelings of southern defensiveness, evident in Cook's declarations that "we were a more civilized and Christianized people than were our Northern brethren."[50] The wartime animosities of the 1860s remained evident in the angry rhetoric of the 1890s. As the frustrating and painstaking process of officially marking the northern graves of captive Confederates unfolded, southerners, ever conscious of the constant insult that the lack of proper tribute represented, continued to resent the injustice of northern memory and to insist in the struggle to rewrite history.

And by the late 1890s, at least to the satisfaction of many white southerners, the southern defensive memory of Civil War prisons was firmly established as a part of the Lost Cause interpretation of the war. White southerners felt increasingly comfortable arguing that "there is no other feature connected with the great war in which the dominant power is so persistent as in keeping back the truth about treatment of prisoners" and expressing their disbelief that "good people North know of the 'horrors of Andersonville,' yet have hardly any knowledge that there were ever southerners in prison."[51] While they were not inaccurate, the nature of these selective criticisms showed just how carefully Lost Cause devotees were required to navigate in order to preserve an operational memory of the war. The singular focus on confronting northern failings ignored the Confederate government's deliberately cruel treatment of prisoners and completely removed the vital role of racist Confederate policies toward black prisoners from the prison controversy. But selectivity should not be confused with futility. In defining white southerners as the victims of the Civil War, the southern memory of prisons helped encourage and justify the growing consensus of white supremacy spreading across the South in the Jim Crow era.

Although whites, North and South, increasingly minimized and denied the racial implications of Civil War prisons, African Americans rejected those carefully edited memories in favor of their own. Throughout the 1870s, 1880s, and 1890s, African Americans steadfastly maintained a connection between Civil War prisons and the fight for racial equality as they remembered the prison controversy. The American Missionary Association continued its efforts to educate local African American children "near the spot made sacred by the sufferings of so many of the gallant Boys in Blue."[52] The gratitude felt by former slaves for what the Union soldiers had endured on their behalf manifested itself frequently at church gatherings in Andersonville. At an 1892 Thanksgiving service one elderly woman, remembering that the holiday used to be one of intense labor, remarked, "Thank the Lord I can come to the meeting myself to-day."[53] But the most telling evidence of the enduring power of the emancipationist memory remained the increasingly popular Memorial Day celebrations at Andersonville each May.

These yearly gatherings were held at the old stockade grounds, which, during the 1880s, were owned and farmed by former slave K. G. Kennedy. No single event revealed the contested nature of the competing prison memories as did the enthusiastic Memorial Day festivities at Andersonville. Although the Grand Army of the Republic played a prominent role in organizing the ceremonies, especially during the 1890s, most of the attendees were black, and the event took place surrounded by the watchful eyes of white southerners.[54] In 1888, a local newspaper report described how "the ground was literally covered with negroes," and estimated that 3,000 people attended the exercises. Along with a series of speeches, the day featured "strolling over the grounds and decorating the graves."[55] Two years later, 4,000 visitors descended upon Andersonville. The occasion was marked by a "considerably greater" white audience and "several slight affrays." These violent episodes occurred exclusively among the African American crowd, according to the local coverage, and testified to the atmosphere of rowdy revelry that attracted larger and larger crowds with each passing year.[56] By 1892, 10,000 people crammed into the national cemetery and prison grounds for "a great day at Andersonville." Although the GAR was "out in force," white attendees were "greatly in the minority," as the trains to Andersonville were reportedly "crowded to almost suffocation with negroes."[57] These commemorations helped preserve the unique emancipationist legacy of the Civil War, as blacks celebrated the sacrifices of the dead Union soldiers not just as the heroes of a reunited America, as did the GAR, but more precisely as martyrs to the cause of human freedom. Similar ceremonies occurred at other former prison sites. In 1895 approximately 1,500 African Americans decorated the graves of Union prisoners in Florence, South Carolina, as a sign of both appreciation for the changes wrought by the war and optimism that racial progress would continue.[58]

The inherent challenge of the emancipationist memory to the white supremacist interpretation of Civil War prisons did not go unnoticed. The proud and persistent displays by African Americans unnerved the white citizens of Andersonville—already frustrated by the presence of the GAR and the virtuous northern memory of Civil War prisons—and by the mid-1890s sparked a "lively discussion" of the "prospect of a riot."[59] The *Americus Times-Recorder* reported that "bloodshed" was "narrowly averted" at the 1894 Memorial Day event. The chain of violence began when Marshal Thad Aycock, a white officer, attempted to break up a fight between two African American men. One of the men shot Aycock, who was painfully but not fatally wounded, and the shooter was quickly seized by several of Aycock's companions. As the white mob began to depart the scene, they were in turn "overtaken by a mob of a hundred negroes," who forced "the release of the prisoner."[60] The social anger that nearly incited a race riot continued to infuse the subsequent Memorial Day gatherings. During preparations for the 1895 event, the white residents of Andersonville were "said to be arming for self-protection," since the promised arrival of 20,000 blacks ensured that "a drunken riot can very safely be counted upon." Although the ceremony thankfully occurred without "the event of emergency," the bitterness behind such real and imagined aggression indicated how tightly the conflicting prison memories were intertwined with racial identity by the 1890s.[61] Faced with the violence and oppression of the Jim Crow era, African Americans refused to accommodate the white desire to forget. As a result, each Memorial Day at Andersonville became a potentially explosive event at which African Americans ignored the social disapproval of whites and their sectional prison memories and instead celebrated the emotionally powerful memory of Civil War prisons as a symbol of their commitment to the legacy of emancipation.

Others recognized that the same controversy that fueled racial hatred also represented a financial opportunity. A new dimension to the recollection of Civil War prisons emerged in the late 1880s and 1890s as Americans found a different reason—one with highly capitalistic overtones—for preserving Civil War prison sites. The commercial potential inherent in the outrage provoked by the prison controversy had been apparent since the first sensationalized newspaper headlines and prison narratives, but during the last decade of the nineteenth century, two Confederate prison camps, Libby and Andersonville, evolved into national tourist attractions. In 1888, a group of Chicagoans, led by industrialist Charles Gunther, proposed the purchase and transfer of Libby Prison from Richmond to Chicago, where he planned to turn the former warehouse and prison into a for-profit museum of Civil War memorabilia. Gunther's project inspired sharp criticism from many Americans, particularly those in the North concerned about potential damage to the cause of reconciliation. Union veteran James Workman wrote a letter to the *Loudoun Times Mirror* in Virginia, declaring that the idea "horrified" him. Having lost his father and two brothers in the war, Workman wanted to let the past fade into "oblivion, which is impossible while a republican politician lives to wave the bloody shirt." The blatant commercialization of Libby Prison "would perpetuate in the North all the animosity of the war," he insisted, "and what can the people of Richmond be thinking about to permit it." Instead of allowing this travesty, Workman believed it would be better to "burn the building to ashes than for a few paltry dollars allow it to stand in a Northern city a standing shame on the fair fame of the South." But if some northerners, and veterans like Workman in particular, felt uncomfortable selling the memory of their sacrifices, southerners seemed content to let Libby go. Although the editor of the *Times Mirror* admitted that Workman's points met "with hearty approval," the lack of any organized attempt to preserve the Libby Prison site in Richmond not only indicated a southern willingness to distance themselves from one of the primary symbols of the prison controversy but also an acceptance of the memory of Civil War prisons as a viable commodity for commercial manipulation.[62]

Gunther's Libby Prison War Museum opened in 1889 and remained open for a decade. Ten years represented a successful run for a museum at that time, especially one that charged fifty cents per visit, far more than most workers in Chicago could afford.[63] Tied to the larger fortunes of Chicago, the museum's success rose and fell with the 1893 World's Fair and the economic troubles that followed it. During its career, however, the museum remarkably generated more profit than controversy. Inside the reconstructed prison, most of the collection contained nonprison related Civil War memorabilia such as manuscripts, letters, and weapons, while other items, such as shrunken Incan heads, indicated the museum's focus on entertainment rather than historical accuracy.[64] Although the very act of reconstructing Libby in Chicago confirmed the north's virtuous memory of the war—as the suffering in Union prisons such as the local Camp Douglas remained unrecognized—aside from the implicit reproach to the South the museum represented a new approach to the prison controversy. As a creatively presented commercial venture complete with its own gift shop, where one could purchase pieces of the old Libby Prison floor or small chunks of the Andersonville stockade, the new Libby Prison brazenly transferred northern resentment of the Confederacy's treatment of prisoners into profit.[65] By the 1890s, any misgivings about profiteering off the sacrifice of dead prisoners seemed prudish in light of the decades of hawking of prison narratives. History apparently possessed actual value beyond the intangibles of inspiring pride or the teaching of lessons learned in the past. In a culture increasingly driven by the siren song of consumption, history could be fabricated as needed to suit the needs of the masses. Many northerners enjoyed visiting the illusory Libby and purchasing prison souvenirs from Civil War prisons as a source of entertainment, even as they continued to commemorate the sacrifices of the heroic prisoners in a more solemn and sectional manner.

In contrast to the transformation of Libby Prison into a museum, the Andersonville site in Georgia remained quiet for many years, with the exception of the yearly memorial gatherings in May. But by the 1890s, the annual event attained such stature that the townspeople of Thomasville, Georgia, desired to take advantage of their relative proximity to the festivities. In 1893, the *Thomasville Review* dedicated its front page to advertising "must see Andersonville!" As the "Mecca for thousands of tourists each year," the paper asked, "can you afford to miss it?" After all, the prison inspired not only "patriotic pride" but also the "most wonderful forensic combat that ever occurred in our national legislative hall—that between the late lamented Senators Blaine and Hill." Special "elegant" train excursions shuttled interested parties between Thomasville and Andersonville and offered the opportunity to view the site in a more genteel serenity— which, not coincidently, would mean the absence of large crowds of African Americans.[66] Like their northern brethren, southerners embraced the opportunity to profit from the attention inspired by Civil War prisons like Andersonville and Libby. The mutual desire to use the controversial memories of Civil War prisons for financial gain marked a rare agreement between North and South on a prison-related matter.

As Thomasville embarked upon its tourism campaign, the surging curiosity about Andersonville prompted an interest from the Women's Relief

Corps (WRC). An organization affiliated with the Grand Army of the Republic, the WRC agreed in 1893 to purchase the prison site and care for the location. Although the government owned Andersonville National Cemetery, the prison stockade itself had been dormant under the ownership of the Georgia department of the GAR, which could not afford the expense of maintaining the location since purchasing it in the early 1890s. In 1896, the WRC started improving the site by building a cottage that also served as an informal visitor center and installing fences, bridges, roads, paths, and walkways.[67] By 1898, according to one newspaper headline, "The Old Prison Pen Is Now a Pleasant Park."[68] Since the WRC was a nonprofit organization, its efforts to preserve and beautify Andersonville focused on a more genteel and reverential commemoration in contrast to Gunther's overtly commercial Libby Prison War Museum. In practical terms, however, with nearby communities like Thomasville hoping to cash in on their proximity to a place of national interest, little difference separated the conversion of the old prisons into tourist attractions. The decades of animosity, and the ongoing bitterness of the debate over the horrors and responsibility for the treatment of prisoners during the Civil War, created a natural and abiding interest among all Americans, regardless of section, in these sites during the 1890s. The same desire to relive the halcyon days of the war that motivated Americans, and veterans in particular, to flock to the first national battlefield parks at places like Gettysburg, attracted visitors to the old prison grounds. Both the open commercialization of Libby and the "pattern of veneration and play" on display at Andersonville offered Americans an enjoyable opportunity to see for themselves firsthand the magnitude of what it meant to be a prisoner during the Civil War and simultaneously gain appreciation for the sacrifice of so many dead.[69] As northerners and southerners embraced the idea of using the prisons as a source of financial profit, the intermingling of patriotism with capitalism helped unify not only tourists but the sections themselves. The buying and selling of an idealized prison memory redefined a controversial past as part of a safe and comforting interpretation of American nationalism during a time of uncertainty and offered the first grounds on which reconciliation between North and South over Civil War prisons could finally begin. The seductive power of the illusion obscured reality, but the entranced public preferred the reconfigured version of the past. Although the bitterness of the divisive memories of the prison controversy still lingered, the transformation of Civil War prisons into commodities reflected the needs of an America determined to look forward as the turn of the century neared.

Although rancor still dominated the public perception of the wartime prisons, the exploitation of Libby and Andersonville indicated the beginning of a shift in the way Americans approached and conceived of the subject. Along with the increasing interest in memorializing and commercializing the prisons came the first opinions that, perhaps, it was time to let go of the old animosity over the prisons. In 1891, John Wyeth of New York wrote a letter to the editor of the *Springfield Republican*, a letter later published by the *SHSP*, in which he declared that any "reasonable and fair-minded being" knows that there was "as much culpability on one side as the other." The reason that passions remained heated after more than twenty-five years, Wyeth believed, was that "the Southern side of the prison question has never been made known to the Northern people. Though a good deal has been written, it appeared in Southern magazines" and as a result never found "its way to the masses of the North." In contrast, Wyeth argued, "the narratives of Union prisoners have been widely diffused through the daily papers, made the texts of passionate oratory by the statesmen of a day, elaborated by the illustrated journals, and emphasized by the immense circulation and influence of the Northern magazines." All this one-sided publicity, Wyeth asserted, prolonged the northern anger over the treatment of prisoners and prevented a true understanding of the "cold and unanswerable" facts.[70] Sir Henry Morton Stanley, imprisoned at Camp Douglas, instead of blaming either side, thought that "it was the age that was brutally senseless and heedlessly cruel." With this argument Stanley became one of the first observers of the prison controversy to find the real fault in the nature of modern war itself.[71] Although both Wyeth and Stanley based their desire for reconciliation on an incomplete conception of Civil War prisons, one that excluded both the deliberate nature of the inflicted suffering and the connected issue of racial equality, they at least demonstrated a willingness to assess more objectively the prison controversy. Their opinions, although certainly in the minority, offered evidence that at some point the sectional hostility over the memory of Civil War prisons might cease.

The work of one author, Herbert Collingwood, also showed a deep commitment to sectional reconciliation. In 1889 Collingwood published *Andersonville Violets: A Story of Northern and Southern Life*. Born in New England, Collingwood moved to the South in the 1880s and spent a few years farming in Mississippi before returning North and writing his novel, which he hoped would remind readers that it was "the duty of all patriotic citizens to lend their best efforts to the task of looking at the causes of the war, and its results, fairly and intelligently." The plot of the novel centered on the mutual respect between a Union prisoner who daringly escapes from Andersonville and a Confederate guard at the prison discharged for refusing to shoot a prisoner who crossed the deadline. When, years later, the two men find themselves living in the same Mississippi town, they recognize each other and become fast friends. Throughout the novel, in which Collingwood reveals his concerns about a South torn by racial questions and commercial exploitation, the horrors experienced at Andersonville represent the burden of the southern past. Despite the obstacles, however, Collingwood's characters find peace and strength in the bonds they formed at the prison, and "so much happiness" replaces "so much misery." Collingwood's optimism showed in his sincere belief that even the brutality of Civil War prisons should not discourage a spirit of forgiveness between the North and South. In reconciliation, he argued, America would discover new strength.[72]

Although the open-mindedness of Collingwood, Wyeth, and Stanley revealed the first signs of a desire to end the long hostility over the divisive memories of Civil War prisons, those signs remained overshadowed by the ongoing animosity that most Americans still held regarding the prison controversy. Bitter rhetoric continued to dominate the memory of prisoner suffering as it had since the 1860s. The intensity with which Americans disputed the meaning of Civil War prisons in the late nineteenth century reflected the uncertainty of a country in transition. The myriad, often conflicting interpretations of the wartime prisons by different groups existed as part of the larger process of shaping how an emerging modern America understood its past. Northerners continued to define the memory of the prison tragedy as they attempted to bolster support for the Republican Party, to instill reverence for the heroism and sacrifice displayed by Union prisoners, and to inspire a reunited country to honor the cause of American nationalism. White southerners, still on the defensive, refused to accept their assigned role as "depraved" villains and, as part of the emerging Lost Cause reinvention of the memory of the war, mounted a spirited rhetorical campaign to honor their dead prisoners and exonerate themselves—if not in the eyes of the North—at least in the verdict of history. Although white Americans, preoccupied with their selective memories, increasingly distanced themselves from, or, as in the case of many white southerners, defiantly rejected the cause of racial justice, African Americans continued to remember Civil War prisons, most notably with vibrant Memorial Day celebrations, as symbols of freedom. Along with the sectional arguments, however, new trends emerged adding further complexity to the recollection of Civil War prisons. For a few, the prison controversy reminded Americans of the powerlessness of the individual, no matter how heroic, against the increasing capability of governments and organizations for evil. The capitalistic recreations of Libby and Andersonville, meanwhile, offered Americans a chance to experience the history of Civil War prisons for themselves, testified to the potent influence the Civil War still had on American public memory, and even encouraged the tentative possibility of eventual reconciliation. Regardless of whether Americans restated old arguments or constructed new interpretations, the urgency with which they contested and invented their memories of Civil War prisons resulted from the shared sense that, in a rapidly changing world, the ability to define the meaning of the past offered the only real source of stability in the present.

╬═ 4 ═╬

"We Are the Living Witnesses"

THE LIMITATIONS OF RECONCILIATION, 1898–1914

I n 1898, the outbreak of the Spanish-American War confirmed the restoration of the bonds between the North and South. The sweeping success of the United States military in Cuba and the Philippines contributed to the growing feeling that perhaps the terrible divisions of the Civil War could be considered fully healed. As the war ended and the United States joined the ranks of imperial powers, America's destiny, once imperiled by the devastation of the Civil War, now appeared bright. On December 14, 1898, President McKinley basked in the afterglow of the convincing victory over Spain and remarked to an Atlanta crowd that "sectional feeling no longer holds back the love we bear each other." The proof, he argued, "is found in the gallant loyalty to the Union and the flag so conspicuously shown in the year just passed."[1] The popularity of the Spanish-American War, especially in the South, testified to the true patriotism of the maligned ex-Confederate states and heightened the spirit of reconciliation across America.[2] The resulting sense of optimism created by the Spanish-American War and the demonstration of American military prowess also fueled an increased national appreciation for the fading Civil War generation, the rapidly disappearing war heroes of the 1860s. With America secure in the knowledge that her fortunes were once again on the rise, the imminent deaths of the remaining Civil War veterans between 1898 and 1914 provided Americans with a final chance to acknowledge the shared sacrifices of the soldiers of the Union and Confederacy.

Between 1865 and 1898, celebrations held by and for Civil War veterans focused primarily on parades, monument dedications, and battlefield gatherings and were attended with increasing frequency by both Union and Confederate soldiers. Such reunions remained popular after the turn of the century. Year after year, famous battlefields hosted ceremonies where the dwindling numbers of blue and gray mingled, swapped stories, and relived the excitement of the war. Naturally the battlefields attracted the largest crowds, because the grounds consecrated by the tragic end of the thousands sacrificed to the cause of a reunified nation had become "sacred" sites for all Americans.[3] Northern acceptance of much of the southern combination of Lost Cause mythology and Jim Crow segregation contributed to the shared spirit of self-congratulation surrounding the Civil War. At these memorial events, speakers acknowledged the equal bravery and martial spirit of both sides, and with the important outcome—the preservation of the Union— achieved, the question of race faded from the American mind.[4] With the smashing success of the Spanish-American War, the growing sentiment of mutual forgiveness and shared celebration even seemed to encompass the still painful and controversial subject of Civil War prisons, as the rituals of reunions and monuments extended past the battlefield to old prison sites.

By the turn of the century, many northerners, inspired by the national sense of reconciliation, finally demonstrated a desire to forgive the Confederate transgressions against Union prisoners. In the immediate aftermath of the Spanish-American War, northerners embarked on numerous pilgrimages to the old Confederate prison locales at Andersonville and Salisbury. During the first two decades of the twentieth century almost all the northern states commissioned and unveiled monuments at one or both of these Confederate prisons in commemoration of the thousands of Union dead. As scholars Thomas Brown and Kirk Savage have shown, the establishment of Civil War monuments held great significance and represented an ongoing process of "negotiation" about the "cumulative" meaning of the war.[5] The construction of prison memorials offered a way to acknowledge specifically the sacrifice and heroism displayed by Union prisoners of war. These tributes recognized the dead, confirmed the cause of reunification, and testified to the example of courage displayed by those fortunate enough to have survived the ordeal. The process of dedicating these monuments also reflected and encouraged the national atmosphere of growing reconciliation. Instead of continuing to harp on the old divisive memories, many participants in the ceremonies at last seemed willing to part with their anger.

In 1898, New Jersey commissioned the building of a monument at Andersonville in the national cemetery, adjacent to the old stockade grounds, where the 13,000 dead prisoners rested in their graves. The $2,000 monument, constructed primarily of granite, honored the 235 New Jersey soldiers who died at the Georgia prison as "heroes" who, as the inscription on the monument stated, chose "death before dishonor." Dishonor would have been to swear loyalty to the Confederacy and gain freedom from the suffering inside the Andersonville stockade, an option taken by few Union captives. Capped by a statue of a standing soldier, the impressive tribute confidently radiated the virtuous northern memory of Civil War prisons. The active recasting of the dead prisoners as powerful, conscious saviors of the Union reflected the exultant mood of a nation savoring the victory of the Spanish-American War. In such a patriotic environment, the particular misery of Andersonville no longer mattered as much. The magnanimous atmosphere of the monument's dedication further confirmed that past sufferings had been repaid with current glory. The New Jersey contingent that attended the unveiling of the display on February 3, 1899, took pride in the "creditable distinction of having first erected a monument to the memory of its dead, buried in this cemetery." The northern rancor normally directed at Wirz, Davis, Winder, and the Confederacy in general was markedly absent from the proceedings. "The prison," the report of the dedication concluded, instead of being noted as a place of unprecedented brutality and inhumanity, "was a place where true character developed itself." New Jersey's attempt to recognize permanently the laudable aspects of Andersonville—northern prisoners caring as best they could for one another while suffering loyally, in a spirit of sacrifice, for the cause of Union—represented an important step forward in the process of sectional reconciliation. At last some northerners seemed willing to extend an olive branch despite the hard memories of Civil War prisons.[6]

Following New Jersey's lead, over the next decade more Union states commissioned and dedicated monuments of their own, and as the years passed, both the monuments and the ceremonies grew increasingly elaborate.[7] On December 7, 1905, Pennsylvania dedicated its $10,000 monument, a thirty-five-foot-tall archway topped with a bronze statue of a "dejected and sad" prisoner of war who stood overlooking the national cemetery. One dedication panel read, simply, "In Memoriam." Although not as strident as New Jersey's state monument, the Pennsylvania display similarly omitted specific reference to the horrors of prisoner suffering, as even the "dejected and sad" prisoner of war appeared to be in far better condition than most of the real Andersonville survivors. The dominant message remained one of gratitude for the sacrifice of the Andersonville dead.[8]

In addition to the funds lavished on the monument's construction, Pennsylvania spent an additional $16,000 on transportation so that the state's Andersonville survivors could attend en masse. Three hundred eighty-one of the former prisoners, nearly 80 percent of the 482 still living, made the trip to Georgia, an indication of their undimmed desire to remember their suffering. From the opening prayer, given by the Reverend J. R. Greene, a Grand Army of the Republic chaplain, the spirit of reverence for the sacrifice of the dead and the new atmosphere of sectional reconciliation dominated the ceremonies. Although the dead prisoners "fell not in the front of battle," Greene stated, "they were heroes every one," demonstrating "patient bravery" and suffering "untold agonies" out of an unwavering sense of "loyalty and honor." Descriptions of the martyrdom and heroism displayed by the Andersonville prisoners had been heard before. But as Greene continued, the importance of the Spanish-American War in finally starting to heal the wounds kept raw by the power of memory became clear. "Out of the carnage of war has come these days of peace," Greene declared, and "the animosities of the past have been obliterated, that the blue and the gray now mingle in fraternal sympathy, and that our sons and theirs go forth together to fight the battles of our common country, following the old flag, the one flag, in its victories on the land and on the sea."[9] Greene's prayer, reminiscent of President McKinley's belief that Americans had finally come to terms with the past, offered confirmation of the rising tide of reconciliation. Delivered at the actual grounds of Andersonville, the center of the postwar prison controversy, it showed the growing optimism felt by many Americans that perhaps the competing divisive memories of Civil War prisons might fade completely, to be replaced by a reunified patriotism.

As officials and dignitaries from northern states came to Andersonville to dedicate their monuments to the dead, the spirit of forgiveness they demonstrated corresponded to the warm welcome they received from their Georgia hosts. The guests from Pennsylvania, according to a December 8, 1905, article in the *Americus Times-Recorder*, received a "cordial welcome," and "fraternal good feeling was in evidence upon every hand." The event stirred such positive feelings of reconciliation that both hosts and guests would remember it "with much pleasure."[10] And with more northern states continuing to add to the rapidly expanding collection of monuments at Andersonville, residents of Americus, rather than displaying defensiveness and frustration, instead focused on providing southern hospitality. When Wisconsin scheduled its commemoration exercises for October 17, 1907, and Connecticut its monument unveiling for one week later, the *Times-Recorder* announced on September 13 that it welcomed the "distinguished party" to at least "stop in Americus" and extended an invitation "to make Americus headquarters during their stay in the South." After all, the editor continued, during the previous visit of the Pennsylvania delegation, the governor of Pennsylvania and the "entire party were handsomely entertained" just ten miles from Andersonville, and "with ample hotel accommodations" available, Wisconsin and Connecticut deserved the same courtesy.[11] Though the potential financial windfall of northern dollars no doubt contributed to the eager invitations, the cathartic, patriotic ceremonies at the prison indicated the maturing process of reconciliation between North and South. In 1911, when New York and Illinois added their monuments, an editor at the *Times-Recorder* declared the two new monuments "superb" and stated that "each state monument that is erected at Andersonville seems to display better taste and a more gracious spirit than its predecessors."[12] That spirit was the product of years of profitable interaction between the Union veterans and their once Confederate hosts as they met repeatedly at Andersonville to remember the horrors of the past. Although intended as a permanent tribute to the thousands of dead prisoners, the process of dedicating the northern monuments created a secondary effect—for many it defused the sectional memories of Civil War prisons as northern visitors and southern hosts cooperated to make each celebration successful.

While Andersonville remained the focal point of attention for northern memorials and visitors, Salisbury also served as host to northern delegations and monuments during the early twentieth century.[13] On June 8, 1908, the Maine contingent arrived to dedicate its tribute to the victims of the North Carolina prison. As at Americus and Andersonville, the people of Salisbury gave the northern veterans a warm reception. The mayor of Salisbury, ex-Confederate soldier A. H. Boyden, offered an "earnest, hearty welcome" and declared his excitement that "the season of heated blood has passed." Boyden's wife helped unveil the monument as the "Star-Spangled Banner" played. In response to such generosity of spirit, one of the Maine dignitaries, Adjutant General Augustus B. Farnham acknowledged that, happily, today "only the kindliest feelings existed" between North Carolina and Maine. After another Maine speaker, Charles Newell, reminded the audience of the patriotic example of the ex-Confederate turned Spanish-American War heroes Generals Fitzhugh Lee and Joe Wheeler, the crowd "repaired to the handsome home" of the Salisbury mayor, where the "visitors received their first real impressions of true Southern hospitality."[14] The report of the festivities omitted whether any of those who attended the harmonious ceremony noted that just two decades before, such an event would have been unthinkable.

As each northern delegation returned home, word spread of both the gracious generosity encountered in the South and, in particular, thanks to the dedicated efforts of the Women's Relief Corps in caring for the Andersonville site, the idealized beauty of the prison grounds. The pristine appearance of the cemetery—with its tree-lined boulevards and state monuments rising among the immaculate gravestones—created a scene of idyllic patriotism that imparted a comforting meaning to the particular horrors of Andersonville's past. Interest in Andersonville rose accordingly. Visitors no longer waited for Memorial Day celebrations or monument dedications to plan excursions to see the old stockade and national cemetery. By 1908, Sarah Winans, acting chairman of the WRC, remarked that maintaining Andersonville had become "arduous," primarily due to the constant job of "welcoming the increasing number of visitors, comrades especially" who traveled individually or in small groups to the prison to pay their own respects. With more state monuments planned for the future, the effort required of the WRC seemed likely to rise. Many members of the WRC realized that their organization had reached the limit of what it could accomplish at Andersonville and decided to offer the eighty-eight-acre site as a "free gift, unencumbered," to the national government, "because of a belief that these grounds should be under the control and protection of the United States." On March 2, 1910, President Taft accepted the gift, and later that year, at the official deed transfer ceremony, Lewis Call, one of the government's representatives, promised the WRC "that the grounds will ever be held as a memorial of the heroism of the men who there proved themselves the highest type of patriots."[15] The Taft administration's possession of Andersonville testified to the powerful immediacy and ambiguity of the conflicting emotions connected to memories of Civil War prisons. As the first and only former Confederate prison site preserved by the federal government, Andersonville became enshrined partly as a symbol of the un-speakable atrocities committed by the Confederacy. But the countering in-fluence of reconciliation was apparent as well, as the site also represented a permanent reminder of the brave sacrifice made by 13,000 Union soldiers and a celebration of the increasingly powerful country they died to save.

The persistent interest in Andersonville, and the tangible harmony dis-played at the memorial ceremonies at former Confederate prison sites, re-flected the pattern of sectional reconciliation that existed in early 1900s America. It was a trend made possible by several factors. The Spanish-American War and the patriotic fervor it generated healed some of the old wounds of the Civil War. For many Americans, attachment to the divisive memories of the conflict began to fade in an era of optimism. This develop-ment explained the celebratory imagery that dominated the northern state monuments erected at Andersonville, many of them topped by statues of soldiers, or, as in the case of Wisconsin, an eagle. National pride overshad-owed the need for continued sectional discord. The mutual racism dem-onstrated by both white northerners and white southerners further con-firmed feelings of unity. At the memorial gatherings at Andersonville and Salisbury the racial dimension of the Civil War went unmentioned. Re-moving race from the memory of Civil War prisons transformed the dead prisoners into martyrs to American nationalism, rather than to racial jus-tice. The redefinition of the conflict as a war fought solely for the cause of nation allowed both North and South to celebrate their heroic participa-tion and affirmed ongoing discrimination toward African Americans. And reconciliation was profitable. The income generated by northerners' visits to Andersonville and Salisbury convinced otherwise reluctant southerners to bury their lingering resentment out of self-interest. The combination of these impulses inherently challenged the former dominance of the divisive memories of Civil War prisons. For the first time, Andersonville began to take on a unifying role in American culture as a national shrine to an ideal-ized, if undefined, patriotic sacrifice.

But Andersonville's transformation to a symbol of national unity re-mained incomplete and contested during the early 1900s. Despite the seduc-tive attraction of reconciliation, the hardened recollections of the wartime prisons endured. While the ascendant themes of forgiveness and racial sol-idarity existed at each prison commemoration, an underlying bitterness remained noticeable as well. This pattern resulted from the paradoxical problem that Civil War prisons presented, as did all reminders of the war's destruction, in the narrative of reconciliation.[16] To recall the prisons was to recall not just suffering but deliberately inflicted cruelty. At least in the case of Civil War prisons, the horrific memories, reinforced over decades, would not allow many Americans to forget or forgive the crimes of the past. At the November 17, 1906, dedication of his state's Andersonville monument, Iowa governor Albert Cummins, even while remarking on the "harmony" of "emotions" of the moment, nevertheless implored the crowd to remember "the unparalled inhumanity" and "cruelty" of Andersonville.[17] Another Iowan, Ernest Sherman, who in 1907 published an account summarizing the experience of the Iowa delegation, included a sensationalized history of Andersonville reminiscent of those of the Reconstruction era. During the war, the Confederate authorities, Sherman claimed, openly "boasted" about the brutality of the Georgia stockade.[18] Even during the Pennsylvania unveiling, General Harry White, one of the official members of the monument commission, betrayed lingering anger concerning the prisons. White blasted the South for what he termed the "perversion of the actual facts of history" regarding the Civil War and its prisons and warned that the ongoing "disturbances" created by the southern counter memory threatened the "harmonies of the sections." Although Andersonville survivor Captain William Bricker followed White and declared himself "highly pleased" with the respect paid to the dead prisoners, the atmosphere of sectional reconciliation had been diminished by the defiant persistence of the northern memory of singular virtue.[19]

While the ambiguities caused by the clash of competing memories were on display at the memorial gatherings at Confederate prisons, there was less uncertainty in the prison memoirs of Union veterans during and after the turn of the twentieth century.[20] Many northern prison survivors, such as Private William Allen of the 17th Iowa Volunteer Infantry, showed little desire to abandon their hardened views of Civil War prisons. Allen repeatedly referred to Henry Wirz as a "demon" throughout his 1899 account of life in Andersonville prison.[21] In 1904 John Worrell Northrop, veteran of the 76th New York Infantry, recalled the "horrors of prison life" and the "barbarity of the treatment" experienced in Confederate prisons, which he described as "dark and loathsome spots."[22] Others were slightly more sensitive. At times northern prison survivors expressed, as in a 1910 address by John Read, member of the Loyal Legion, a "hesitation" about discussing the prison subject, which he referred to as "that dark episode." Despite his concerns, however, Read continued, hoping that the "desire in the hearts of all for reconciliation" would overcome the "harsh feeling of criticism." As he concluded, Read declared that "the lack of shelter" in Confederate prisons "cannot be understood or explained," a statement reminiscent of the old accusations of deliberate Confederate cruelty toward the Union prisoners. These potentially inflammatory statements, he attested, were necessary to "preserve the memory of the brave men who died for the honor of their country." By faithfully recounting the old tragedies, in this case to an audience of fellow veterans, Read and other prison survivors attempted to fulfill an obligation to celebrate the history of the Civil War and the successful quest for Union and also to recognize the memory of their fallen comrades whose sacrifices enabled victory. Although aware that this duty would jeopardize the process of reconciliation by freshly recounting the sins of the South, Read, along with many in the North, could not let the "memory be unspoken."[23]

By the twentieth century, then, in the minds of the remaining prison survivors in the North, there was a feeling that, before they died, they owed it to the memory of the thousands of dead Union prisoners to continue to pay homage to the heroism, bravery, and sacrifice of those who survived the ordeal as well as those who did not. In 1902, Ezra Ripple, Andersonville survivor, best summarized this sentiment as he began the tale of his prison experiences. He reminded his readers of the "suffering," the "great mortality," and the "horrors of the Southern prisons" and apologized, because "the subject is not a pleasant or attractive one." "We would all sooner listen," he acknowledged, "to a description of a grand battle where all the bravery and dash of trained soldiers in assault and defense is portrayed in the most vivid and glowing colors than to a tale which has little in it but that which is revolting, sickening and sorrowful." The reason Ripple subjected his audience to this depressing account, he claimed, was that it was "necessary to the preservation of the true history of those times."[24] Victory in the war itself, while satisfying, would not suffice. Before they disappeared completely, the northern prison survivors intended to win not only the war but the battle for posterity and the historical record. They naturally and understandably feared that if the orthodox memory of their suffering faded, it threatened to diminish the value of their experiences, their service, and their lives. Too many soldiers lay in the cemeteries of Andersonville and other southern prisons to allow Americans to forget. And so, as the remaining northern prison survivors entered the twilight of their lives they realized that while the Civil War officially ended in 1865, in the 1900s the fight to remember the conflict, prisons included, continued and would still persist long after they died.

If the growing obsession with history and memory by Union survivors of Confederate prisons motivated men like Ripple to share their perspective, it also revealed an irony about the nature of "true history." By 1902, when Ripple wrote, or 1912, when the account of George Putnam was published, decades had passed since the actual events described took place. Putnam openly avowed that, since "forty-eight years have elapsed," he could not "undertake to say that my memory can be trusted for all of the details or incidents." Putnam did pledge that his account had been composed in "good faith."[25] Ripple, meanwhile, boasted that he wrote his account from "a retentive memory on which the events had been indelibly impressed," though he confessed to reading "many other accounts of prison life." Although he insisted on the veracity of his memoir, in the end he argued that what was really important about his book was its message. "If you appreciate the sacrifice," he implored, "teach your boys and girls their duty in preserving to posterity this Union for which their lives were so freely given."[26] In appealing to his readers' patriotism, Ripple revealed the concerns of the aging prison survivors as to how Civil War prisons would continue to be remembered. Ripple and his comrades intended to remain heroes in the history of the Civil War, and that status demanded constant vigilance against southern heresy. By the early 1900s, prison chronicles no longer focused solely on the selective memories of the past, although the authors rarely missed an opportunity to rehash the old belief that southerners deliberately imposed cruel treatment on Yankee prisoners. Instead writers of the accounts, like Ripple, revised their presentations and cloaked their arguments in the guise of reconciliation and patriotism in the hope that the accumulation of subjective memories would eventually gain acceptance as objective history and cement the permanent recognition of the heroic sacrifice made by Union prisoners.

As the battle for history continued, on February 1, 1911, Lieutenant Thomas Sturgis, from Massachusetts, delivered a lecture on Civil War prisons to a New York branch of the Loyal Legion. Sturgis possessed a unique set of qualifications on the subject. During 1864, his regiment served as the guard at Camp Morton, a Union prison outside Indianapolis, and later that year, he was captured and imprisoned at Libby Prison in Richmond during the final grueling winter of the war. In his speech, reprinted in augmented form the following year, Sturgis offered insight into the northern perspective on the prison controversy and a sense of how, for many, little had changed after nearly fifty years. Concerning the treatment of the Confederate prisoners at Camp Morton, he insisted that "everything was done to minimize any unsanitary conditions" and that there "was no desire on the part of our men anywhere or at any time wantonly to take a prisoner's life." Sturgis concluded that "certainly our Government dealt with its prisoners with conscientious regard for life." Rebel prisons, such as Libby and Andersonville, however, existed as manifestations of a "spirit of malice or as a vindictive display of power." A sense of justification and righteousness infused Sturgis's words as he openly attacked the morality of the South. "We are the living witnesses," Sturgis declared, "rapidly passing away from this scene." "Before we go," he argued, "in the interest of history, in justice to the way our people conducted the war," in contrast to "the actions of our antagonists," we must "leave our testimony."[27] This need to testify confirmed the need of the aging survivors to preserve the legacy of the Civil War as they understood it.

For northern veterans like Sturgis the war always remained the ultimate experience of their lives, the years that defined them and gave meaning to their postwar careers. As they participated in saving the Union, reconstructing the nation, and the decades of growth that saw the United States emerge as a world power, America's success confirmed the worthiness of their sacrifices at prisons like Libby and Andersonville and reassured them that there was a purpose to the horror, a greater good to emerge from the suffering. That comforting understanding depended, however, on maintaining the traditional memory of Civil War prisons. Union prisons represented good, while Confederate prisons represented evil. The half-century of American progress, in the eyes of Sturgis, Ripple, and other survivors, owed its origins to their heroism in overcoming that evil, and they intended to continue reminding America of their sacrifice.

Another reason for the strident language of Sturgis and other Union veterans centered on the appearance of a new phenomenon—the first substantial histories of the various Civil War prison camps. The appearance of Clay Holmes's *The Elmira Prison Camp* in 1912 raised few eyebrows in the North, as Holmes, an Elmira native and devotee of the northern memory of moral superiority, described one of the worst Union prisons as being a place of "Christian humanity."[28] Likewise, William Knauss's 1906 *The Story of Camp Chase* focused not on describing the hardships experienced by Confederate prisoners at Camp Chase, the Ohio prison located near Columbus, but instead on the spirit of reconciliation. Knauss spent many years trying to restore and decorate the graves of the more than 2,000 Confederates who died at the sizeable prison during the war. Despite some resistance that included threats of violence, Knauss persisted in his efforts "with no thought but that of pride and admiration for the great American people, regarding no North or no South, but a land rich in memories of its brave deed."[29] Both volumes were written by locals who defended the conditions of the Union prisons and rejoiced in the national climate of reconciliation after 1898.

In 1911, however, the first ostensibly national history of Civil War prisons appeared as part of Francis Trevelyan Miller's *The Photographic History of the Civil War in Ten Volumes*. The bulk of volume 7, covering prisons and hospitals in the war, came from the pen of Holland Thompson, who originally hailed from North Carolina but at the time held an assistant professorship in history at the College of the City of New York. Over the course of several brief chapters, interspersed with dozens of photographs, Thompson discussed various aspects of the prison controversy, such as the experiences of prisoners on both sides and the question of why the policy of exchange ended, necessitating the creation of prisons like Andersonville. For the first time, pictures of both Union and Confederate prisons and prisoners appeared side by side, and Thompson intentionally juxtaposed the images to support his argument. Thompson suggested that the mortality in "the prisons of the Civil War, North and South," resulted from the use of "temporary makeshifts, hastily constructed," that were unfit "for human beings in confinement." "If judged by standards now generally accepted," he continued, they "would have been condemned for the lack of the most elementary sanitary requirements." Thompson concluded that the suffering resulted from an unintentional lack of preparation, and he never discussed the possibility of deliberate cruelty. But his willingness to scrutinize the Union prison system caused consternation to northern readers. Such a position shocked veterans like Sturgis, because Thompson lumped the prisons on both sides together and labeled them as equal examples of inhumanity, so that Elmira and Camp Chase became kin to Andersonville and

Salisbury. Sturgis felt betrayed because Thompson had relied on him, along with Read and Putnam, for "courtesies" during the preparation of the manuscript. Thompson even thanked Sturgis in the preface to volume 7.[30]

Outraged by the public connection of his name to this distortion of history, Sturgis attacked Thompson in the 1912 printed edition of his 1911 New York speech. While crediting Thompson with an "earnest effort" at impartiality, Sturgis considered it his duty to remind readers of flaws in Thompson's work. Not only had Thompson been born after the Civil War, and so relied entirely on "second-hand" information, but he was also "a native of North Carolina." These "insurmountable difficulties," according to Sturgis, proved that Thompson suffered from "unconscious bias."[31] Only a southerner, Sturgis insinuated, could possibly conclude that the prison systems of the Union and Confederacy shared more similarities than differences. With heretics like Thompson challenging the dominant memory of Civil War prisons, Sturgis and his fellow veterans felt compelled to protest, urgently and vociferously, these perceived injustices and perversions of history. If their message sounded shrill and strident, it was because they knew that they were running out of time "before we go."

The defense of "true history" explains in large measure why the familiar tone of animosity persisted among Union veterans, even in the midst of monument dedications devoted to spreading the message of forgiveness about Civil War prisons, and after the healing impact of the Spanish-American War. The paradoxical feelings of the survivors of Confederate prisons testified to the still uncomfortable juxtaposition of the positive story of reconciliation with the ongoing power of divisive memory. Former Union prisoners shared the national excitement over the achievements of the United States since 1865 and were proud of their role in winning the war that put America on that path to glory. In that sense men like Read and Ripple recognized that the rancor of the past seemed less important in a more optimistic and forward-looking present. Yet a fear remained that during that rapid march of progress, public remembrance of their part in the Civil War, or even the war itself, might fade into oblivion. As they revisited the hatred inspired by and encountered in the prisons, survivors apologized for disturbing the process of reconciliation. Compelled by the need to preserve their place in history, however, they refused to stop. Even for men accustomed to sacrifice, to allow a sanitization of their past proved more than they could bear.

The enduring bitterness of former Union prisoners of war also testified to the distinct conflict between the purpose of public and personal memory. From a national perspective, as evidenced by the statements of President McKinley, the Spanish-American War represented confirmation that the United States had fully recovered from the trauma of the Civil War. The monuments built at Andersonville and Salisbury showed that many northerners agreed with McKinley. Thus these monuments provided a final opportunity to acknowledge the sacrifice of the Civil War generation before Americans permanently turned their attention forward to the national future. As individuals, however, former prisoners felt that no statue, ceremony, or statement could suffice to repay their suffering. Only death would end many of the personal grudges of the prison survivors. No matter how much time passed, for many northerners, especially ex-prisoners, the old accusations and sense of outrage at the actions of the Confederacy, particularly regarding the treatment of prisoners, defined the meaning of the war and permeated any attempt at discussion or objective analysis of the issue. Much of the tenacity with which those northerners clung to their antipathy reflected a natural frustration as the construction of public memory, with its positive interpretation of reconciliation, inevitably overpowered the personal memories of those individuals who could never forget the bitter past.

If some northerners feared and resented the disappearance of sectional hostility, during the Spanish-American War and its immediate aftermath, southerners eagerly participated and welcomed the conflict as well as McKinley's declaration that reconciliation was complete. Perhaps naively, southerners assumed that that reconciliation extended to the subject of Civil War prisons and that northerners might finally acknowledge the suffering that occurred in Union prisons during the Civil War. At the 1898 United Confederate Veterans (UCV) convention, Surgeon General C. H. Tebault tested the waters by delivering a defense of the Confederate prisons. He stated that the "responsibility of all this sacrifice of human life . . . rests entirely upon the authorities at Washington."[32] Southerners received an additional morale boost from the publication of Union veteran James Madison Page's *The True Story of Andersonville Prison*, portions of which appeared in the *Confederate Veteran* and southern newspapers. Page's popularity in the South resulted from his conviction that "prejudice" and "warped" memory fed the northern perception of Wirz as a demon. Page, a prisoner for seven months in Andersonville, explained his motivation for writing his account. "After forty years we can at least afford to tell the truth," he argued, that "we of the North have been acting unfairly." "We profess unstinted friendship towards the South," Page continued, but "we charge the South with all the blame for all the horrors of the Civil War." Page believed that the time for recrimination was past and that the North, with its hypocritical treatment of the South concerning the memory of Civil War prisons, was only prolonging the bitterness. Southerners delighted in the fact that at least one Yankee finally understood.[33]

With their confidence on the rise once again, many southerners focused their energy on the ongoing campaign to care for and mark the graves, particularly those of former prisoners, of Confederates in the North. By 1901, however, their efforts yielded little progress. The report that year of Samuel Lewis, commander of the Charles Broadway Rouss Camp of the UCV, located in Washington, D.C., discussed the painstaking process of disinterring and reburying the remains of 264 Confederates in Arlington cemetery, as well as marking their new graves with marble headstones. Although the process met with McKinley's approval in 1899, not until 1901 were the necessary funds allocated and the process completed. Even more sobering, from Lewis's perspective, was the intimidating prospect of dealing with the "28,000 Confederate dead remaining uncared for in the North." "Attention to the care of these dead," Lewis argued, "would be productive of much good" and help "remove from discussion a still fruitful source of irritation."[34]

Decorating and restoring the often overlooked graves became a priority for southern memorial organizations like the Confederate Southern Memorial Association and the United Daughters of the Confederacy (UDC). These two groups expressed a desire to honor properly these 28,000 southern heroes in a manner reminiscent of the northern monuments built at Andersonville and Salisbury. One small success came in 1899, when the Ladies Memorial Association dedicated a monument in Americus to the 115 Confederate prison guards who died at Andersonville. Their graves had been "neglected" at Andersonville, and in 1880 their bodies had been reinterred in Americus, just a few miles away. The "suitable" monument and the new marble headstones offered a much more fitting tribute.[35] But the refurbished Georgia graves offered little solace to southerners still concerned about the thousands of Confederate dead in the North. During the early 1900s, although memorial efforts persisted to decorate graves in Chicago, site of Camp Douglas, and New York, the location of Elmira, the UDC focused much of its attention on Camp Chase, Ohio, where Union veteran and prison historian William Knauss continued to labor for the cause of sectional reconciliation. In the mid-1890s, Knauss undertook the cause of caring for the more than 2,000 Confederate graves because of the "unutterable loneliness and shameful disorder of Camp Chase Cemetery." Over time his efforts helped lead to the creation of a Columbus chapter of the UDC, and by 1902, the chapter members stood ready to take over the care of the cemetery grounds from Knauss. All that remained were the ceremonies of June 7, 1902, the day that the UDC helped unveil a memorial arch near the entrance of the cemetery. Tellingly, the monument was topped by a statue of a soldier standing at rest, leaning on his rifle—an assertive posture that, like the Andersonville monuments, testified to the southern determination to venerate its own version of prison memory. Financed by Knauss and his friends, the first monument dedicated entirely to Confederate victims of Union prisons bore the simple inscription, "Americans," a sentiment that seemed appropriate in the new climate of sectional reconciliation. Unlike the unveiling of the Andersonville monuments, however, where the northern delegations enjoyed a warm reception, locals, many of whom resented this challenge to their understanding of the Civil War and its meaning, anonymously threatened to vandalize and even dynamite the monument. Although the ceremonies proceeded without interference, and as Ohio governor Nash declared in his comments, the commemoration confirmed a joyous "epoch of fraternal love and peace," the promised, though unrealized, violence tarnished the proceedings.[36]

On the surface, the 1902 dedication of the Camp Chase monument represented the positive post-1898 culmination of reconciliation and provided an example of cooperation between North and South. But it also reinforced the growing suspicions of many southerners that perhaps the process of reconciliation, particularly in reference to the memory of Civil War prisons, remained tantalizingly close but impossible. Although the 1906 Foraker Act required the War Department to shoulder the burden of caring for the graves of dead Confederate prisoners in the North—and by 1914 a handful of government-sponsored monuments at Union prison sites such as Alton, Point Lookout, Elmira, and Fort Delaware had been erected—the national government demonstrated only a cursory interest in memorializing these locations. The plaques at the base of the monument shafts honoring the dead Confederate captives at Alton and Fort Delaware were identical—

only the numbers of the dead prisoners of war, "whose graves cannot now be individually identified," were changed.[37] These halfhearted efforts in honor of their dead only inflamed the passions of southern memorial groups like the UDC. Reconciliation promised forgiveness to the South, but as southerners examined the enduring northern attitude of superiority on the subject of prisons after 1898, they increasingly remembered that, according to their memory of Civil War prisons, they had done nothing to be forgiven for, or at least nothing that the North had not also done to them. From the perspective of southern defenders, if either section owed an apology over Civil War prisons, it was the North to the South for the decades of unfair accusations. At the very least, to confirm the sincerity of northern claims of reconciliation, northerners needed to stop denigrating the Confederate prison record and protesting Union innocence in the treatment of Civil War prisoners. Southerners, after all, peacefully and openly welcomed Union veterans to Andersonville and Salisbury year after year and listened to magnanimous Yankees forgive them for their sins. When an occasional southern-sponsored monument to Confederate prisoners was built, however, as at Camp Chase, northerners threatened violence. As a result of this clear disparity in the competing memories of Civil War prisons, where the North erected monument after monument, emphasizing the singular brutality of the Confederate prison system, while only a few generic memorials and thousands of dilapidated graves testified to the South's inability to convince northerners of their part in the tragedy, southerners realized that the offer of sectional reconciliation came with an increasingly apparent catch. To further the process of reconciliation, the South needed to accept the northern interpretation of Civil War prisons. For many southerners, the northern acceptance of much of the Lost Cause mythology and Jim Crow segregation by the early 1900s made it easier to accept blame for the prison controversy, especially when, as in the case of Thomasville and Americus, their communities benefited financially from the attention. Other southerners, meanwhile, remained dedicated to the fight for "true history."

Ever since the late 1860s and 1870s, when Jefferson Davis, Alexander Stephens, and Benjamin Hill defended the Confederacy's prison system, many southerners steadfastly refused to accept the northern memory of Civil War prisons. Even at the turn of the century, the campaign to clear the record about the wartime prisons continued as an important part of a larger effort to resist what southerners thought was no less than the rewriting of history by the North in an effort to permanently humiliate the South. In November 1899, a *Confederate Veteran* article, "School Histories in the South," republished the report of Hunter McGuire of the Grand Camp Confederate Veterans. In his statement, McGuire avowed that the South faced an insidious threat from "false teachings" of history. Southerners were either being "misled" or else were "foolishly" ignoring "the principles and convictions of the past." "We are enlisted," McGuire implored his fellow southerners, "against an invasion organized and vigorously prosecuted."[38] For McGuire, reconciliation on northern terms threatened to obliterate the true meaning of the war. Winning the war alone would never satisfy the Yankees, who persisted in denigrating southerners and reminding them of their treachery.

In response, southerners continued to construct their own alternative version of history based on the deflective counter memory of Civil War prisons. In 1899, the Southern History Association republished an article from the mid-1890s by Adolphus Mangum describing Salisbury Prison, which, after Andersonville, represented one of the worst Confederate prisons. A resident of Salisbury for part of the war, Mangum felt inspired to write about the prison, and the efforts made there to care for the Union prisoners, primarily because of two questions: "Why, then, all this unrelenting bitterness—this bloodthirsty, inexorable vengefulness towards the South," and "where is the apology for the barbarities and murders of Northern prisons?" "Impartial history," Mangum concluded, "will show that in the article of prisons," the South "'was more sinned against than sinning.'"[39] The challenge raised by McGuire and Mangum of exonerating the South through history did not go unheeded. Throughout the early 1900s, the *Confederate Veteran* and *Southern Historical Society Papers* continued their long-running campaign of opposition to the northern perspective on the wartime prisons.[40]

Southern survivors of northern prisons also produced more accounts of their suffering throughout this period as well—memoirs that still displayed a deep-rooted anger at the northern public's insistence of the superiority of Union prisons.[41] In his 1904 book, John King, motivated by the northern "spirit of enmity," confessed that he lacked the ability to properly depict his experiences at Camp Chase. "I have no words at my command," he stated, "with which to describe the horrors of the Yankee prison at Camp Chase. One would have to follow 'Dante' in his descent to Hell, and in his wanderings among its inmates, to find an approach to it."[42] Like Sturgis, King and his fellow chroniclers of prison life in the North felt compelled to write even after all these years because they shared the same goals, if opposing viewpoints, and similar tales of suffering. As death approached, the need to clarify the "true history" of their prison experience, their sacrifice to the failed cause of nation, became paramount. Leaving behind a published record that contradicted northern memory allowed former prisoners to preserve their identity as heroes of the Confederacy and remind their fellow southerners to take pride in their defensive memory of Civil War prisons.

During the early 1900s, southern prison survivors like John King were well reinforced in the battle for history. A combination of southern voices, male and female, sons and daughters, joined in protest against the northern memory. The reclamation of history, from the southern perspective, continued to drive memorial organizations. The 1904 *History of the Confederated Memorial Associations of the South* declared that the chief purpose of these Southern women centered on the "sacred duty," the "determined effort to perpetuate in history the testimony of the broken hearted women and maimed heroes of'61–'65." And, like Sturgis, a sense of urgency infused the organization and the discharge of its duty "before the march of time decimates our rapidly thinning ranks."[43] In 1905, the solidarity of the UCV, UDC, Sons of Confederate Veterans, and the Ladies' Memorial Associations as "guardians" of "vital Confederate historical interests" was "gratefully" acknowledged at the annual report of the historical committee at the UCV convention. The "extreme vigilance in guarding our posterity against error," stated committee chairman Clement Evans, protected southern "intelligence, patriotism, courage, and honor."[44] With their very identity at stake these southern organizations promised to hold firm against the Yankee appropriation of their history.

By 1905, the United Daughters of the Confederacy possessed a reputation as one of the most "zealous" of the memorial organizations in the South and as vigorous defenders of the historical memory of the Confederacy.[45] At the annual UDC convention in San Francisco that year, the president of the Georgia Division, Sarah Hull, unable to personally attend the "far-off" proceedings, instead sent a report updating the progress of the ninety-one Georgia chapters to the gathering. After some discussion of fund raising, scholarships, and memorial events, all part of "fulfilling" the "sacred duty we owe to our great dead," Hull concluded her statement:

There is one memorial work to which we wish it were in our power to direct the attention of the United Daughters of the Confederacy. This is the erection of a monument at Andersonville. We have nothing there to refute the lies and slanders proclaimed in marble on all sides, nothing to bear witness to the Truth, and to the brave testimony of Wirtz and the men who died with him. What greater work is there for us, when the monument to our President is completed, than to turn our attention to this, and so proclaim to the world in the simple, straightforward language of Truth, which needs no adornment, the facts of that prison at Andersonville. Awful they were, we know, but no more so than the prisons in which our own men were held; and we had this palliation: Our government did the best it could, and the prisoners fared as well as our soldiers in the field. Truly the work will never end, Daughters of the South, and the more we do the more we find to do, as is always the case in life.

Following Hull's announcement, the convention listened to the report of Mary Young, historian of the Savannah chapter. Since the northern monuments at Andersonville "inscribed a false presentation of Wirtz," duty called the UDC to right the injustice committed against southern honor and proper history. She suggested that a national fund-raising campaign commence, with the goal "to erect a suitable memorial to his memory," including "a lasting record of his murder under false charges."[46] So began the most heated battle over the memory of Civil War prisons since the Hill-Blaine debate of the 1870s.

During the fund-raising and planning stages for the Wirz monument, southern memorial organizations lined up in support of the UDC's proposal. The April 1906 *Confederate Veteran* publicized the initial campaign, announced the formation of three UDC subcommittees—"Selection of Site," "Inscriptions," and "Design"—and solicited "liberal" donations from loyal southerners willing to support the project.[47] That same year, R. A. Brock, editor of the *Southern Historical Society Papers,* expressed his excitement about the monument, stating that "it is gratifying to be informed that the cruel stigma may be removed from the memory of Henry Wirz."[48] By November 1907 the UDC commissioned C. J. Clark of the Americus-based Clark Monumental Works to build "the handsome marble shaft."[49] No doubt the fine craftsmanship Clark exhibited in building several of the Andersonville and Salisbury monuments contributed to his obtaining the

Wirz monument contract. The nearly thirty-foot-tall obelisk, when completed, seemed destined for either Americus or, as originally conceived, the Andersonville prison grounds as a "rebuttal to the State monuments" located at the prison and cemetery."[50] As news of the Wirz monument reached the North, however, controversy flared.

On January 28, 1908, the editor of the *Americus Times-Recorder* announced that the UDC's proposed tribute to Wirz had "kicked up" a "storm of indignation" in the ranks of that "fanatical element of south haters," the Grand Army of the Republic. Instead of placing the monument in the town of Andersonville—itself a compromise location since the Women's Relief Corps and the national government had no intention of allowing the Wirz monument anywhere on the Andersonville prison grounds or national cemetery—the editor suggested that in order to calm the "tempest," the town of Americus would accept the monument, further preventing any estrangement between "the two sections."[51] Many southerners recognized that perhaps the monument would cause less controversy if located away from Andersonville. A former member of the Georgia UDC, E. F. Andrews, wrote her friend, a Mr. Oglesby, in April 1907 and acknowledged that even though she was no longer part of the organization, she hoped "that the kind-hearted women of Georgia will place their monument either on Wirz's grave, or in some Georgia town where it will stand a chance of being treated with respect."[52] The debate over where to build the memorial grew throughout 1908, and members of the UDC, motivated by what the *Times-Recorder* called "strenuous objection in all parts of the state towards putting the monument at Andersonville," considered placing the monument at several locations, including Richmond, Virginia, as well as Macon, Americus, and Andersonville.[53] By December 8, 1908, the monument appeared headed to Richmond to stand "in close proximity to the graves of the Davis family," and the *Times-Recorder* declared in exhaustion that the "vexed question has been settled at last."[54]

One week later, the *Times-Recorder* reported that some "dissatisfied" Georgia members of the UDC requested a "reconsideration" of the "decision to remove the monument from Georgia soil" and announced a new convention, scheduled for March 1909, at which a final decision on the location of the Wirz monument would be reached.[55] On March 18, 1909, after a vote of 125 for Andersonville, 65 for Macon, and 5 for Americus, the *Times-Recorder* announced, with resigned relief, that "Andersonville was selected as the site for the famous Wirz monument." The resolution of the controversy ended "the discussion that has been raging for four years," although the construction and unveiling of the monument still remained.[56]

Although many residents of Andersonville approved of the town's designation as the permanent home of the Wirz memorial, they also harbored concerns about the impact of the monument on local race relations. The simmering tension and violent outbreaks that had marked past Memorial Day gatherings persisted into the early 1900s. Sensational descriptions of the controversial gatherings overshadowed the local newspaper's coverage of the speeches and decorative rituals. Four African American deaths were reported at the annual ceremonies between 1898 and 1900 despite the attendance of the Americus Light Infantry. This military presence was deemed necessary by local whites, since for "the unbleached brother," "Andersonville Day" represented "Christmas, Thanksgiving and the Fourth of July boiled down into one. For weeks past he has whetted his razor and hoarded his pennies for this occasion of superlative and inexpressible ecstasy when he can fill his tank with red coffin paint and shoot craps and dance all day." Whites celebrated the effectiveness of the military crackdown, which in 1900 led to eleven black arrests and "had the effect of making the unruly ones walk a chalk mark all day."[57]

The repetitive scenes of black violence certainly offended white residents of Andersonville, who complained that the "riot, bloodshed, murder and gambling" were "a disgrace for the state and those participating." So frustrated were white Georgians by the uncontrollable nature of the African American celebration that they openly wished that blacks would cease such improper behavior and instead placidly conform to the northern memory of Andersonville as a shrine to patriotic sacrifice. The 1901 newspaper report of the festivities lamented that many African Americans ignored the "impressive occasion" of the official proceedings, which in the early 1900s included musical performances, prayers, speeches, and annual readings of the Gettysburg Address as highlights of the day's activities. "He never goes there," the article scolded, "but in the thick woods nearby they dance, gamble and fight to their heart's content." Although white southerners remained defiant in their challenge to the northern prison memory, they clearly preferred the decorum of the Grand Army of the Republic to the disorder of African American crowds. African Americans, meanwhile, continued to dispute the dominant white sectional memories and instead transformed "Andersonville Day" into a vibrant reminder of the emancipationist tradition.[58]

As the campaign to build the Wirz monument accelerated, Andersonville residents recognized the need to impose stricter controls on the black celebration of Memorial Day. According to town historian Peggy Sheppard, "many letters" warned the UDC that "thousands of Northerners and Southern Negroes assembled in Andersonville every May" for Memorial Day exercises.[59] Thus it was no coincidence that by 1906 several years of military presence began to disperse the formerly unruly African American throngs. Attendance began to drop with the "muzzling" of the "negro excursion," and in 1906 the *Americus Times-Recorder*'s description of the commemoration announced what was, from the white southern perspective, good news. One headline celebrated that "No Murder is done by Zulus on Trip," while another noted that the gathering featured the "Smallest Crowd in a Decade." By 1914, crowds that had once numbered in the tens of thousands dwindled to no more than a few thousand. Although blacks still outnumbered whites, "very good order was maintained and there was not rioting or murderous assaults among the negro excursionists as disgraced the occasion in other years." This "muzzling" clearly reflected the desire of white southerners to reclaim Andersonville as an integral piece of their identity.[60] The persistent interpretation of Andersonville as a symbol of nation and/or freedom by northern whites and African Americans caused resentment among white southerners who disdained the inherent challenge to their understanding of the war's meaning. The palpable contempt for these geographical and racial outsiders dominated these letters to the UDC and influenced the newspaper coverage of the proceedings. Sensationalized descriptions of the ceremonies as chaotic, violent scenes of "rampant" intoxication led to fears that these people were capable of "desecrating the monument."[61] These worried admissions represented the recognition among white southerners of the enduring presence of the emancipationist memory of the Civil War. Controlling the Memorial Day events and establishing a monument to Wirz was more than just a rebuttal to the North—it marked another episode in the ongoing contest to preserve white supremacy in the postwar South.

Throughout the process of turning the proposed Wirz monument into reality, progress, particularly in terms of the selection of the site and the final decision on the inscription, moved slowly. Fears of racial unrest contributed to the delays, but so did the dogged resistance of Union veterans to the very idea of such an affront to the northern memory of Civil War prisons. The Iowa delegation that visited Andersonville in November 1906 demonstrated a keen awareness of and indignation about the growing southern support for the Wirz monument. In his speech at the Iowa dedication, General E. A. Carman praised the women of Georgia, who demonstrated a "womanly tenderness" toward the Union prisoners. The "sympathies" of those women, Carman announced, in a direct attack on the UDC, "will be remembered long after the names of those who seek to erect monuments to the memory of one whose cruelty was a shock to humanity shall have been forgotten."[62] In his summary of the Iowa proceedings, Ernest Sherman expressed his disgust at the actions of Wirz's defenders. "God grant that the proposition of certain misguided women," Sherman stated, "to erect a monument to the memory of Captain Wirz, may never be realized. There are some things in this world that are best forgotten. This arch fiend of Andersonville is one of them."[63] By early February 1908, an encampment of the Grand Army of the Republic issued its official response to the Wirz monument. "This insult to the honored dead of the Union should be stopped," the veterans declared, "if by no higher authority then by the conscience of the Southern women, who would as violently denounce any similar desecration of the memory of their own justly honored heroes." Any "consummation of this contemplated slur upon the martyred dead," the outraged northerners resolved, would "disregard" the "truth of history."[64]

Although the salvos of northern vitriol toward the Wirz monument divided the UDC members and delayed the selection of the final site for the shaft, the verbal attacks on southern women only further galvanized the support of the Southern Historical Society and other memorial organizations for the Wirz cause. In 1908, J. R. Gibbons, a soldier in J. E. B. Stuart's cavalry, wrote in the *SHSP* that "we will stand many things" in the South, but when northerners say "anything about our women," it "gets all of the fuz turned the wrong way." Gibbons declared that, furthermore, "it is a little peculiar that the people of the North can put up their fine monuments in the South, right under our noses, falsifying history, and think it is all right, but the Southern people must say nothing." Even if the Union veterans abhorred the idea of the Wirz monument, Gibbons pointedly commented, "the ladies of the South are going to erect one, and it will be built just as tall as it will be possible for them to get the money to build it, and they will inscribe upon it the truth, the whole truth, and nothing but the truth."[65] Throughout 1908, the *Confederate Veteran* also staunchly supported the Wirz monument, although one editor confessed that "the inscription is anticipated with anxiety."[66] What the final monument would say remained a secret. While awaiting its appearance, southerners, men and women alike, continued to defend their historical perspective against the northern memory of Civil War prisons and to reject what they perceived to be the insincere promises of reconciliation.[67]

On May 12, 1909, the Wirz monument, after surviving the arduous debate about its merits and location, made its public debut in the "historic little town" of Andersonville, a short walk from the prison grounds and cemetery. The *Times-Recorder* estimated that some 3,000 to 4,000 cheering spectators turned out and without incident enjoyed the "magnificent" occasion. The UDC deserved congratulations, the Americus paper admitted, for "this splendid consummation of their work of love and devotion to the cause which they represent."[68] Unlike the dedication of the northern monuments at Andersonville, however, no mention of forgiveness escaped the lips of the southern presenters. The towering obelisk, placed in the middle of Andersonville's town square, stood as a symbol of the isolated but unrepentant defiance of the defensive southern memory of Civil War prisons. Continuing the Lost Cause tradition of inverting northern arguments, the monument recast Wirz not as villain but instead as "the victim of a misdirected popular clamor." According to the southern defenders of history, Wirz, as a Confederate "martyr" and symbol of "humanity," offered a true contrast to "the North's terrible policy" and Edwin Stanton's "cold blooded cruelty." Another inscription on the finished shaft quoted Jefferson Davis, a constant defender of the Confederate prison system and one of the few Confederate figures vilified even more than Wirz. "When time shall have softened passion and prejudice," Davis once, either optimistically or naively, stated, "when reason shall have stripped the mask of misrepresentation, then justice, holding even her scales, will require much of past censure and praise to change places."[69] Those scales seemed a little more balanced, at least on that day, for the southerners who witnessed the ceremonies.

After the unveiling of the Wirz monument, northerners continued to express disgust at the audacity of the UDC and the "misguided" southerners who supported their efforts. Just over a month after the mid-May Andersonville ceremony, the Women's Relief Corps held its annual convention in

Salt Lake City. The Andersonville Prison Board reported that "the beauty" of the park "is grand," with only "one object to mar" the "view, and that is the monument erected to the infamous, inhuman keeper of this prison." The members of the WRC openly wished for a "thunderbolt" to "lower the statue with the name 'Wirz' chiseled upon it."[70] In 1910, General John Stibbs, the last surviving member of the military commission that tried Wirz, shared his thoughts regarding the Wirz memorial at a speech in Iowa City, Iowa. "After a monument was erected to perpetuate the memory of Wirz and he was proclaimed a martyr who had been unfairly tried and condemned," Stibbs explained, "I wanted" to "tell, as I alone could tell," the "unanimous action of the Court in its findings." Stibbs swore to the impartiality of the Wirz commission and reminded his audience that "there were no dissenting opinions" among its members. As "for myself," he insisted that "there has been no time during the forty-five years that have intervened since this trial was held when I have felt that I owed an apology to anyone, not even the Almighty, for having voted to hang Henry Wirz by the neck until he was dead."[71] Thomas Sturgis, unsurprisingly, also entered the fray in his 1911 speech, condemning the "personal brutality" of Wirz. "I am led to speak" about Wirz, Sturgis said, "because many of our younger generation are ignorant of the facts, and because the women of Georgia recently erected a statue to him as a martyr."[72] The ongoing northern outrage, inspired by the contradiction between the Wirz monument and their cherished memory of Civil War prisons, reflected the larger concern, particularly among veterans like Stibbs and Sturgis, that if the South won more historical victories by establishing more monuments like that to Wirz, the cause of "true history" faced grave peril.[73] Although the immediate urgency of the political uncertainty of the postwar decades now appeared resolved, it remained important to preserve the fading memory of southern evil. Future generations, without the actual presence of the "living witnesses" to remind them, might unknowingly begin to accept the heresies symbolized by the Wirz monument as truth.

The bitter controversy over the Wirz monument dispelled any illusion of authentic reconciliation between North and South, at least as it pertained to the memory of Civil War prisons. Northerners, incredulous at the perverse dedication of southerners to a wrongheaded understanding of history, revived their old selective memories of the conflict and quickly distanced themselves from the language of reconciliation. Until and unless southerners came to their senses and accepted the terms of northern memory on the subject of Civil War prisons, a full reconciliation would remain impossible. White southerners showed no less determination, however, to uphold their own defensive memory. The pressure created by the combined and competing influences of the black memory of emancipation and northern memory of the righteous cause of Union—demonstrated annually each Memorial Day—only hardened the white southern refusal to compromise an identity long rooted in defiance. Although African Americans vigorously continued their celebration of emancipation, their unique recollection was increasingly driven out of the public realm by open white hostility. Despite the singularity of their divisive memories, however, Americans of both sections shared one commonality. As they continued to search for meaning in the prison tragedy they still required an external explanation of the evils done in Civil War prisons.

That so many voices on all sides of the controversy concerning the memory of Civil War prisons continued to extol their own virtues and the faults of their former enemies between 1898 and 1914 was ironic, given that from a national perspective, it was truly an era of sectional reconciliation. But the same factors that encouraged national reconciliation continued to promote discord in the specific instance of Civil War prisons. The first trend involved the impending deaths of the Civil War generation in the years immediately following the Spanish-American War. As they passed from the scene, veterans on both sides rejoiced that they lived long enough to witness the incredible emerging power of the United States on the world stage. And as both sides met at battlefield reunions, no one could dispute the intensity and devotion displayed by the North and South. Regardless of side, all congratulated themselves that the martial spirit of their mutual brotherhood remained strong in the current generation of soldiers. But that shared recognition of what it meant to be a soldier only extended to the battlefield. In the prison camps of the Civil War, however, the vast majority of soldiers who endured capture saw only the one terrible half of the equation, the experiences that many could never forgive or forget. Before they died, prison survivors, and those dedicated to their memory, felt a duty to remind future Americans of the horrors of the prison camps, and thus, over and over, they reopened the wounds anew. Their personal resentments inhibited the process of reconciliation. But the once inflammatory memories of Civil War prisons, stripped of their political relevance by the Spanish-American War, no longer excited strong emotions in most Americans. The bitterness that surrounded the divisive memories of the prison controversy limited—but could not prevent—the prevalent trend of celebrating reunion while ignoring the legacy of emancipation.

The other reason for the lingering hostility over the memory of Civil War prisons during this period comes from the very nature of reconciliation itself. The idea of reconciliation implies a mutual sacrifice, to be made by both aggrieved parties, who admit to their sins and agree to attempt to put the past behind them. But for the prison survivors and those, North and South, who remained emotionally invested in the controversy, reconciliation could become possible only with a complete annihilation of their distinctive memories of the previous forty years. In the North, Union veterans, their health destroyed by their prison experiences, devoted their energies throughout the rest of their lives to denouncing the brutalities of the Confederate prison system, and in the South, Confederate veterans did likewise against the Union prisons. Having ravaged them physically and mentally, the prison camps of both sides committed a final injustice against these men—defining their identities and hardening the prejudices of memory throughout their final decades. That was why, by 1914, at least for the actual prisoners and those convinced by their arguments, reconciliation on this particular subject remained impossible. Northern overtures of forgiveness came with the condition that the South accept the northern version of memory on the subject of Civil War prisons. When the South, by then accustomed to northern receptiveness to Lost Cause memories of the conflict, rejected these terms, the rhetorical war over memory continued to rage. Not until the unreconciled Civil War prison survivors finally died and Americans discovered anew the horrors of war—and the provocative circumstance that evil was a human affliction, rather than a uniquely Union or Confederate condition—would a sincere reconciliation, and not just a facade, be truly possible.

"The Prisons at Richmond—Union Troops Prisoners at Belle Isle,"
from *Harper's Weekly*, December 5, 1863.

"Camp of Rebel Prisoners at Elmira, New York,"
from *Harper's Weekly*, April 15, 1865.

"Prison in Casemate No. 2, Fort Lafayette, New York Harbor,"
from *Harper's Weekly,* April 15, 1865.

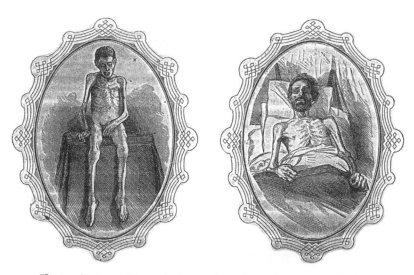

"Living Skeletons," from the House Joint Committee on the Conduct
of the War's 1864 report, *Returned Prisoners.*

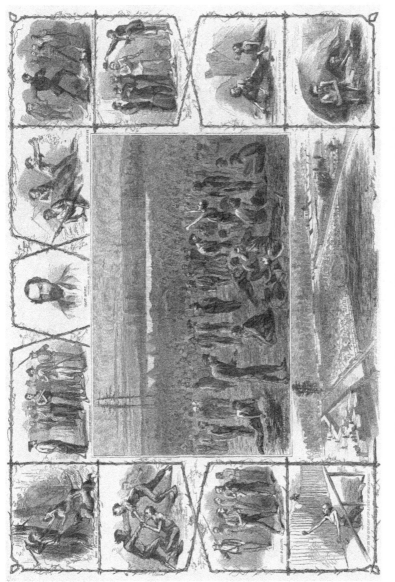

"Andersonville Prison Scenes, Illustrating Captain Wirz,"
from *Harper's Weekly*, September 16, 1865.

The Execution of Henry Wirz, November 10, 1865.
Courtesy of the Library of Congress.

"The Political Andersonville," from *Harper's Weekly*, October 24, 1868.

"Let Us Clasp Hands Over the Bloody Chasm," by Thomas Nast,
from *Harper's Weekly*, September 21, 1872.

Memorial Day at Andersonville, 1897.
Courtesy of Georgia Archives, Vanishing Georgia Collection, sum152.

The New Jersey monument to its Andersonville dead, dedicated 1898.
Photograph by author.

Andersonville National Cemetery, circa 1910.
Courtesy of Georgia Archives, Vanishing Georgia Collection, sum101.

The entrance to "Andersonville Prison Park," circa 1905.
Courtesy of Georgia Archives, Vanishing Georgia Collection, sum102.

The monument to the Confederate prison dead at Camp Chase, Ohio, dedicated 1902.
Courtesy of the Ohio Historical Society.

The Wirz monument, located in the town square of Andersonville, dedicated 1909.
Courtesy of Charles W. Plant.

The Georgia monument at Andersonville, sculpted by William Thompson, dedicated 1973.
Photograph courtesy of the National Park Service.

African American Girl Scouts decorate graves at Andersonville National Cemetery
in preparation for Memorial Day, 1976.
Courtesy of Georgia Archives, Vanishing Georgia Collection, sum119.

The National POW Museum, opened 1998.
Photograph courtesy of the National Park Service.

The current interpretive landscape of Andersonville National Historic Site, which
includes state monuments, the reconstructed prison stockade,
and the National POW Museum.
Photograph courtesy of the National Park Service.

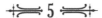

"A More Proper Perspective"

OBJECTIVITY IN THE SHADOW OF TWENTIETH-CENTURY WAR, 1914–1960

By 1914, fifty years separated the Civil War generation, most of them long since gone to their graves, from the terrible suffering experienced in the war's prisons. Despite the passage of time and veterans alike, the memories of those horrors still evoked powerful emotions, as the controversy over the Wirz monument made apparent. But with the onset of the shocking carnage of World War I, the even greater devastation of World War II, and the uneasy brinkmanship of the early Cold War, many Americans gained new perspective as they remembered Civil War prisons. Instead of overt sectional bias determining where the blame or guilt should fall for the 56,000 dead Civil War prisoners, the generations in the midst of learning anew man's destructive capabilities increasingly began to look beyond the passions stirred up as they reminisced about the Civil War. The flood of prison accounts rehashing the old sectional memories slowed to a trickle and then all but stopped, replaced by the appearance of objective attempts to reassess the treatment of Civil War captives. The diminishing intensity of the divisive memories of Civil War prisons was a positive sign that heralded a potential end to the lingering animosity between North and South over the persistent controversy. But the news was not all good. It also testified to the critical but depressing realization that, when interpreted in the harsh new light of the wars of the early and mid-twentieth century, the prison experience of the Civil War did not represent a break from the past but perhaps instead the origins of a grim pattern. An understanding emerged that suggested places like Andersonville or Elmira were not isolated examples of unparalleled human cruelty but were, when compared to the Nazi concentration camps or Japanese internment camps of the 1940s, similar symptoms of the cost of modern war.

In 1914, however, thanks to Woodrow Wilson's official policy of neutrality, the growing horrors of war still seemed far away. Both North and South continued the honoring, and in the process defending, their treatment of what had become, in the words of New York's Andersonville Monument Dedication Commission, the "handful of survivors of the many thousands of their comrades with whom they had shared unutterable privations in the war that saved the Union."[1] Two years later, Minnesota added its monument, a granite pedestal topped with a bronze statue of a Union soldier "of moderate heroic size," dedicated to the state's ninety-five Andersonville victims who sacrificed their lives, according to the tribute's inscription, "in the service of the United States in the war for the preservation of the Union." Minnesota's contribution to the collection at Andersonville further cemented the power of the northern memory of Civil War prisons.[2] By 1916, the northern transformation of Andersonville's landscape into a shrine to the virtuous cause of Union included displays from Connecticut, Indiana, Iowa, Maine, Massachusetts, Michigan, Minnesota, New Jersey, New York, Ohio, Pennsylvania, Rhode Island, Wisconsin, and, curiously, Tennessee. Confirming Tennessee's status as one of the states most divided by the Civil War, in 1915 Grand Army of the Republic veterans from the state dedicated a monument at Andersonville to the 712 Tennesseans who died there. Made of Tennessee marble, the relatively short memorial lacked a statue atop the monument, unlike the more elaborate northern state displays, although a patriotic eagle was carved above the inscription. The monument committee admitted that while the final, "somewhat inartistic" sculpture could not match the beauty of the other more lavishly funded northern monuments, some of which cost $10,000 or $20,000 each to build, it accurately reflected the "rugged loyalty" of the Union men from Tennessee. Despite some embarrassment at raising only $866 for the project, $750 of which went to the construction of the monument, the finished product took its rightful place in Andersonville as a testimonial to the "patriotism of the men."[3] The lack of financial support from many Tennesseans revealed the ongoing division between Union veterans who wanted to preserve their memory of what they felt was unparalleled sacrifice and southerners who remained frustrated with what they felt was unparalleled hypocrisy at the one-sided remembrance of Civil War prisons.

Although state monuments dominated the Andersonville prison and cemetery grounds, the Women's Relief Corps continued to play an important role in memorializing the prison site. During the first few decades of the 1900s, the organization dedicated several small monuments at Andersonville, including one in 1915 honoring Clara Barton—with a granite tribute highlighted, appropriately, by a red cross—for her role in organizing the national cemetery and identifying the names of more than 12,000 of the 13,000 dead prisoners.[4] Four years earlier, the WRC proudly constructed the "Sun Dial" monument, a bronze sun dial placed atop a polished granite base. The "Sun Dial" display, built to honor the transfer of the Andersonville grounds from the WRC to the national government, commemorated, according to the monument's inscription, "the patriotic work" done by the WRC "in the preservation and improvement of this historic site."[5] Although the monument was far from modest, such self-congratulation was all but indiscernible amid the larger northern displays that confidently dotted the Andersonville landscape. In 1936, the WRC brought this period of monument construction to a fitting end with the unveiling of the "8 State Monument," a $500 tribute to the dead from states that had yet to build their own shrines. The monument recognized the nearly 1,500 victims of Andersonville from Delaware, Kansas, Kentucky, Maryland, Missouri, New Hampshire, Vermont, and West Virginia.[6] With all the Union states officially represented at Andersonville, the process of honoring the patriotic sacrifice of the prison dead in confirmation of the northern virtuous memory of Civil War prisons finally reached completion. Several decades would pass before new monuments appeared at the Georgia prison site.

As the final state monuments went up at Andersonville, the few living Union survivors of Confederate prisons offered their testimony about what they endured in captivity. In 1922, Captain H. M. M. Richards compiled a tribute to one of the last prison survivors, Samuel B. Trafford. One more time the old memory of moral superiority surfaced, as Richards described the "deliberate attempt to starve the prisoners to death" and lamented how Union captives "were driven insane" by the Confederacy's treatment of them.[7] When Peterson Cherry published his 1931 memoir, *Prisoner in Blue: Memories of the Civil War after 70 Years,* along with his discussion of the "awful confinement," he included inflammatory drawings of prisoners being attacked by hounds. Cherry's rehashing of the traditional insults toward the South negated his attempt at magnanimity when he concluded, despite "my being chased by bloodhounds, my capture and terrible mistreatment," the "Civil War is so far past that, no matter what was done by either side in the heat of conflict, such spiteful letters and acts should stop."[8] Appropriately then, Cherry's account was one of the last Union prison memoirs that had, since the 1860s, recycled the same arguments of exceptional southern cruelty.[9] By the 1930s, with the deaths of all the Union veterans of Confederate prisons, the accusations finally started to diminish. Only a very few edited prisoner accounts appeared in the next few decades as the animosity of northern memory finally began to fade.[10]

In response to the rhetorical broadsides from the last living Union prisoners, southerners, particularly former prisoners and those affiliated with memorial organizations like the United Daughters of the Confederacy, continued their defense of the southern counter memory of Civil War prisons. The last survivors of Union prisons released accounts such as *The Life Record of H. W. Graber*, which discussed Graber's imprisonment at Camp Chase and Fort Delaware in a chapter titled "The Inhumanity of the Federal Government."[11] Graber's still vibrant anger was not isolated, as the chronic bitterness of the southern deflective memory permeated the 1914 memoir of David E Johnston. Discussing his captivity at Point Lookout, Johnston recounted his amazement at losing nearly forty pounds in just over two months as a prisoner. "Carrying out the ratio," he stated, "if I had stayed there six months I would have weighed nothing."[12] Like their Union counterparts, Confederate survivors displayed an unswerving commitment to their version of the truth about the wartime prisons until the end.[13] And even as they disappeared they left behind fervent devotees to continue the contest.

After 1914, the loudest defenders of southern innocence in the prison controversy came from the organizations that had spent the previous decades venerating the Lost Cause. Although after 1913 the *Southern Historical Society Papers* focused on reprinting the proceedings of the Confederate Congress, the *Confederate Veteran*, until its final issues in the early 1930s, remained steadfastly devoted to the southern memory of Civil War prisons. Within its pages, month after month, articles appeared discussing the prison controversy. Some pieces, like "Seventeen Months in Camp Douglas," described the "barbarity" of the Chicago prison.[14] Periodic discussions of "Treatment of Prisoners of War," and "Prison Horrors Compared" also indicated an ongoing desire to vindicate the South's reputation and triumph in the fight to properly remember Civil War prisons.[15]

Other defenders of southern honor included stalwart groups such as the Sons of Confederate Veterans (SCV) and the United Confederate

Veterans, who joined the UDC in protecting the South's good name. During the aftermath of World War I, the SCV published *The Gray Book,* a "purely defensive" publication designed to fend off the "attacks and untruthful presentations of so-called history."[16] Although *The Gray Book* reflected the traditional general defensiveness of the South, its publication was also intended as a specific response to the parallel drawn between Wirz and the German atrocities of World War I. As a January 1919 *William and Mary College Quarterly Historical Magazine* editorial declared, "it is certainly lamentable" that "the case of Major Henry Wirz" and "the execution of this unfortunate officer" were, during World War I, "instanced as a just precedent for the execution of Von Tirpitz and the other detested leaders of Germany."[17] To answer this grievous affront, the third (and longest) chapter of *The Gray Book* was titled "Treatment of Prisoners in the Confederacy." Motivated by the comparison of "Confederate treatment of prisoners with Prussian outrages in Belgium and France," the author of the chapter, Matthew Page Andrews, declared his regret that even now, after a reunited America had fought and won two major wars since the Civil War, the "sweeping condemnation of James G. Blaine," delivered back in 1876, "is still, in a general way, believed by Americans."[18] That belief remained deeply rooted among many Americans, stated UCV General A. T. Goodwyn in a 1926 speech, because the execution of Captain Wirz "was a smoke screen to divert the attention of the good people of the North from the prisoners-of-war question, as well as to misrepresent the South in its treatment of prisoners." The northern government used this tactic, Goodwyn argued, because they were "conscious that they themselves were morally responsible for the painful conditions prevailing in prisons."[19] What the North called history Andrews and Goodwyn called conspiracy. Overcoming the distortions of the past and restoring the South's reputation depended on challenging northern memories of Civil War prisons at every opportunity.

Of all the defenders of the South after 1914, no one else demonstrated quite the vehemence of Mildred Lewis Rutherford, historian general of the United Daughters of the Confederacy. Throughout her career Rutherford used her position to redress supposed historical injustices that she and her supporters felt were damaging to the South. In 1914, Rutherford gave a speech titled "Wrongs of History Righted," in which she identified glaring historical inaccuracies, ranging from the causes of the Civil War, to the character of the institution of slavery, to Andersonville Prison, Henry

Wirz, and the "Cruelties in Northern Prisons," which "we of the South have borne too long and too patiently." Against the ongoing condemnation of the North and "the falsehoods that have crept in and are still creeping in, "the only chance to combat this "anti-Southern atmosphere," Rutherford declared, lay in restoring the "truths of history." This process, she believed, would help preserve a sense of pride and honor in southern memories of the Confederate past.[20]

A few years later, in 1921, in her capacity as state historian for the Georgia chapter of the UDC, Rutherford set out specifically on a crusade against the northern memory of Wirz as an inhuman devil. Like Matthew Andrews, Rutherford resented the connection of the Swiss-born Wirz, and therefore the Confederacy, to the German atrocities of World War I. Another factor motivating Rutherford was an incident of vandalism in the town of Andersonville. In May 1919, three American (and presumably Yankee) soldiers painted part of the Wirz monument red, black, and gold—the colors of the German flag.[21] Instead of causing people to forget Wirz and his (mis)deeds, World War I created anti-German sentiment and re-ignited the hatred toward the German-speaking Wirz. In an attempt to show the misguided nature of the continued anti-Wirz prejudice, Rutherford wrote a book defending Wirz, *Facts and Figures vs. Myths and Misrepresentations: Henry Wirz and Andersonville Prison.* Primarily a compendium of excerpts from the trial of Wirz, a discussion of his execution, and a review of the tumultuous process of creating and dedicating the Wirz monument, Rutherford's book broke little new ground. But Rutherford was more interested in argument, as her concluding question revealed: "Is it any wonder that those boys of the North reading in France such vilification of the South should attempt to desecrate that Wirz monument when they returned to America?" By making the truth "known," Rutherford hoped to dispel what seemed to her and many southerners an irrational, and at this point in time, unnecessary, prejudice in the North against Wirz.[22] Given her obvious pro-southern viewpoint, however, she convinced few not already in the fold.

Rutherford's fanatical approach infused the UDC with the most endurance of all the southern memorial organizations on the subject of Civil War prisons. Throughout the late 1920s and into the decades to come, the UDC continued to maintain the southern counter memory of Civil War prisons. And occasionally, as in Margaret Mitchell's 1936 novel, *Gone with the Wind,* these arguments still surfaced in mainstream popular culture. Mitchell was not the first famous American author to imbed the sectional memories of Civil War prisons into their fiction. In 1919, Sherwood Anderson began the opening chapter of the powerful *Winesburg, Ohio,* "The Book of the Grotesque," by describing an elderly Andersonville survivor still brokenhearted over his brother's starvation in the prison.[23] The power of the image of Andersonville as a symbol of the grotesque resonated with northerners long accustomed to belief in the singular cruelty of the infamous prison. But if "Andersonville was a name that stank in the North," Mitchell wrote in rebuttal to the memories of northerners like Sherwood Anderson, "so was Rock Island one to bring terror to the heart of any southerner who had relatives imprisoned there."[24] Rutherford herself could not have stated the UDC's position more succinctly—if Confederate prisons were bad, so too were those of the Union.

While the prison controversy obviously received only peripheral attention in Mitchell's sprawling depiction of the destruction wreaked upon the old South, these types of minor successes encouraged the UDC in its devotion to the cause. In 1937, the UDC unveiled a monument to the approximately 3,000 dead Confederate prisoners at Elmira, New York. The Elmira statue was not as openly defiant as previous Confederate prison monuments. The figure of a solemn soldier, hat removed in tribute to his dead prison comrades, was embedded into the front of the monument, rather than the more confident and customary placing of the form atop the memorial. But even the muted nature of the Elmira display still represented the enduring power of the old southern prison memory, and it joined the ranks of existing Confederate monuments at Camp Chase, Johnson's Island, and Camp Douglas, among others, as the UDC strove to balance history by equaling the amount of bronze, marble, and granite deposited at Andersonville.[25] Aside from this symbolic effort, throughout the 1940s and 1950s, as the strongest remaining voice of the pro-Confederate South, the UDC continued to publish articles in its monthly periodical such as "Henry Wirz, the Martyr."[26] But at this late date, with the original and most dedicated generations of Confederates and those devoted to their memory long since dead, the tenacity of the UDC made little impact on the battle for the historical record. Only southerners hypersensitive to the negative perception of the South maintained interest in continuing a listless debate with northerners increasingly oblivious to the fact that a controversy over Civil War prisons even existed.

The fading intensity of the old sectional memories and, tellingly, the public visibility of the black emancipationist legacy were also evident in the nature of the Memorial Day exercises held at Andersonville between 1914 and the 1930s. Although the annual event still consistently attracted crowds of several hundred to a little over a thousand, including a strong African American presence, much of the formerly spontaneous celebration gave way to formalized ritual. By 1924, reports of the event declared that the racial "disorders" that previously turned Memorial Day at Andersonville into a rowdy affair had "entirely disappeared and a public aid of solemnity now surrounds the annual observance." The "quiet" occasions, stripped of their violence and marked only by the decorum of music, speeches, and monument dedications, showed the remarkable outcome of the turn-of-the-century contest between white northerners, white southerners, and African Americans to remember Civil War prisons. Although the divisive memories of northerners and southerners still grated against each other, at Andersonville a compromise between the two visions existed, born out of a shared resistance to the emancipationist tradition. The northern memory dominated the landscape of Andersonville and each Memorial Day gathering in the name of nationalism, but this unwelcome reality was ameliorated for white southerners by their success in using years of military force to restrain the African American celebration.[27] The constant presence of African Americans at Andersonville represented a still firm commitment to the emancipationist memory, but the carefully restricted nature of black participation showed how completely whites, North and South, embraced the reassuring social order of Jim Crow–era racism. The vital questions of race, freedom, and equality raised by the Civil War and its prisons were increasingly—and comfortably—ignored.

The bonds forged by northern and southern whites as they mutually negotiated the remembrance of Andersonville testified to the reality that, by the 1920s and 1930s, the traditionally controversial prison memories, although still framed in terms of argument, no longer threatened entrenched sectional identities. The divisive memories served not to convince Americans that either the Union or Confederacy deserved all the blame for the prison tragedy, but instead catered to older generations who remembered the Civil War as the central event of their childhood or as the source of compelling stories told them by their Confederate or Union grandfathers. Recalling Civil War prisons was a part of reaffirming, for Peterson Cherry and his northern contemporaries, their identity as the saviors of the Union and offered consoling evidence of their important contribution to history as death approached. For Rutherford and her southern supporters, railing against the northern memory of moral confirmation likewise played a part in preserving their identity. Unlike the days of the Blaine-Hill debate, however, or the printed exchange between Davis and Chipman, no one in the North bothered to respond to Rutherford. Even so, the UDC-led campaign to remember retained importance, as it contributed to the white southern Lost Cause orthodoxy and reinforced attitudes of white supremacy. The divisive memories succeeded in muting the African American emancipationist legacy and became entrenched as history, albeit in dualistic form. But that very success came with a hidden cost. With the monuments built, memoirs written, and stories told, the urgency behind the sectional memories began to fade. The combined impact of two important changes ultimately brought an end to the dominance of the old bitter memories of Civil War prisons. As the Civil War, and its prisons, retreated into history, the war became less controversial, ironically because the existence of a defensive southern memory of the prisons had become an accepted tradition in the culture of American reconciliation and at this late date posed no real threat to the entrenched northern interpretation. Many Americans saw little point in contesting the peculiarities of the Civil War—the final outcome of the Union preserved was all that mattered. And when the gruesome brutality of World War I shocked Americans into the modern world, the context of prison suffering changed rapidly, defying the attempts of the old defenders of true history to define the memory of Civil War prisons in shades of black and white at the very moment that those defenders finally exited the stage.

The changing nature of public interest in the prison controversy did not mean the disappearance of the subject of Civil War prisons—instead it represented a transition that often occurs in the construction of historical memory as events lose the context of their immediate relevance and become the property of those who interpret and adapt them to fit contemporary needs. Although most Americans forgot about or were oblivious to the once emotional prison tragedy, the fading intensity of the selective sectional memories also presented the opportunity for a more critical appraisal. As a result, a new strand of Civil War prison memory emerged in the 1920s and 1930s. American scholars started to revisit the prisons, not to assign blame to the Union or Confederacy, but instead to seek objective understanding of, and perhaps solutions to, the universal problem of how to treat more appropriately future prisoners of war.

In 1924, Major Herbert Fooks, a retired U.S. Army officer turned civilian lawyer, wrote *Prisoners of War,* a comparative examination of how prisoners of war fared in captivity from as far back as Philip of Macedon and the Punic Wars of Rome (not well) through the end of World War I (somewhat better). But while Fooks briefly touched on the treatment of prisoners of war throughout history, he devoted most of his attention to the Civil War and World War I. He found that Civil War prisons "were poorly organized" compared to World War I prison camps and that "an extreme scarcity of food" plagued Civil War prisoners, in contrast to the more "fortunate" World War I captives. Fooks also noted an unfortunate similarity between the two conflicts; some prisoners in both wars suffered from maltreatment. Fooks admitted that because of the "civil strife" between 1861 and 1865, "the exact truth" of what happened at places like Andersonville remained somewhat clouded by "unpleasant memories, passions, and prejudices." Nevertheless, he believed that what was now paramount was "determining the basic cause of these inhumanities." Both sides, according to Fooks, simply fell victim to "the harsh customs of previous wars." After exonerating the "humane" behavior of the United States toward German prisoners during World War I, however, Fooks overlooked his prior statements about the obscuring potential of emotion and denounced the German treatment of captives as "frightful." While Fooks's objectivity in making that statement may be questioned, ascertaining the degree of German guilt for various atrocities matters less than the fact that he refrained from rehashing the old accusations as he discussed the prison camps of the Civil War. For Fooks, distinguishing between the Civil War prison systems of the North and South was less important than learning from the mistakes made by both sides. His argument emphasized that the traditional sectional perception of either the Union or the Confederacy as representative of aberrant brutality toward prisoners no longer made as much sense when one considered the actions of the Germans during World War I.[28]

Another benefit of examining the prisons of past wars in a comparative manner appeared as Fooks assessed each conflict on its own merits, stripping each event (World War I excepted) of the bitterness endemic to the discussions of the past. When viewing the overall pattern of treatment of prisoners of war throughout history, Fooks concluded that there was reason for optimism. The days of killing or enslaving prisoners seemed safely in the past; "great progress has been made." Here Fooks revealed that despite that progress, the recent experiences of the Civil War and World War I showed that a "great task" remained—to ensure that future generations of prisoners fared better, so "that the lives of all those who have suffered and died to bring about these results shall not have been sacrificed in vain." Civil War prisoners, according to Fooks, did not sacrifice their lives to a sectional or racial cause, but instead for the greater good of their fellow POWs. In the end he declared, in a touching if somewhat naive statement, that only when all nations "bear in mind the golden rule," a paradoxical concept during times of war, will prisoners of war finally receive the fair treatment they deserve. No matter how unrealistic the use of the golden rule might be as a protective shield against atrocities toward captives, Fooks's book heralded a new era of Civil War prison memory. Instead of adding to the vilification provoked by Civil War prisons in the past, Fooks recognized that, in the aftermath of World War I and its own controversy over prisoners of war, perhaps the old story of Civil War prisons contained some lesson about how to solve the enduring challenge of how to improve ourselves as captors and captives. It was a lesson especially needed in a modern world.[29]

Like Major Fooks, William Hesseltine had World War I in his thoughts as he approached the issue of Civil War prisons. He realized that the reappearance of such horrors begged impartial investigation. As the first and, until recently, the only work by a professional historian to analyze thoroughly the topic of Civil War prisons, Hesseltine's landmark 1930 work, *Civil War Prisons: A Subject in War Psychology*, represented an inconsistent but significant challenge to the power of divisive memory. From the opening page, Hesseltine, born in Virginia but professionally trained at Ohio State University, assured readers of his objectivity. "The hatreds of those war times have been cooled," he stated, and the war finally "may be dealt with in a more proper perspective."[30] According to his peers, Hesseltine succeeded in his attempt to handle the volatile subject delicately; reviewers hailed the "judicial spirit" and "cool detachment" of the "critical study."[31] Drawing primarily on evidence from *The Official Records of the Union and Confederate Armies* as well as the scores of published prison accounts, Hesseltine reduced the overall controversy over Civil War prisons into individual pieces, including the issue of prisoner exchange, conditions in the prison systems on both sides, and the heated emotions generated by the suffering. He then, at least to his own satisfaction, systematically and dispassionately explained the reasons behind the tragedy of the Civil War prison camps.

Hesseltine began his dissection of the prison controversy by exploring the question of responsibility for the breakdown of the exchange cartel. Had the policy of exchange continued throughout the war, instead of halting in 1863, camps such as Andersonville and Elmira need never have existed, and so Hesseltine spent over a third of the book sorting out how exactly the exchange process came to an end. This required him to engage with the selective perspectives of both sections, and Hesseltine outlined the familiar arguments for his readers. Since the 1860s, northerners insisted that the Confederacy's refusal to recognize the rights of African American prisoners prompted the Union's principled stand of not exchanging prisoners with the Confederacy—unless black troops received the same treatment as white Union soldiers. Southerners fired back that the Union government always opposed the cartel because it returned Confederate soldiers to the front lines, obstructing Grant's strategy of attrition, and that defending the rights of African Americans existed purely as a political smokescreen to distract northern families from the fact that Lincoln and Stanton made conscious decisions to sacrifice their sons in Confederate prisons. On the cartel issue, Hesseltine clearly sided with the southern view, claiming that the Union government waited "until the country showed signs of restlessness" with the lack of exchange to declare the South's policy toward captured African American soldiers as "reason for the non-exchange of prisoners." Hesseltine's discounting of the impact of race on the prison controversy showed just how seductive the conjoined memories of reconciliation and white supremacy remained in 1930.[32]

But if Hesseltine favored the traditional southern position on the issue of exchange, he took a different stance on the conditions experienced in the camps of both combatants. Hesseltine believed that one of the major components of the story of Civil War prisons was the scrambling of "both belligerents" to create proper "organization for the care of prisoners of war." Union and Confederate prisons operated on an impromptu basis throughout the war, he argued, first in 1861 as prisoners began arriving behind the lines, and then all over again in late 1863 and 1864 as the war reached its destructive peak just as the exchange agreement collapsed. Despite the lack of foresight on both sides, Hesseltine credited the Union with executing "definite plans" to organize its "prison system" and acknowledged the structure of "military administration" in the North. Of the Confederate "prison system," Hesseltine described it as "less worthy" and as "the result of a series of accidents." Not until "the last months of the war," far too late to make a difference, did the Confederacy finally establish a proper administrative structure for its prisons. This clear discrepancy, Hesseltine argued, led directly to the terrible suffering in southern prisons, which he detailed in individual chapters on various Confederate camps.[33]

In his emphasis on "organization," "plans," and "administration," Hesseltine offered a novel theory about the reason behind the tragedy of Civil War prisons—bureaucratic inefficiency. This approach, once hinted at by former Andersonville prisoners John McElroy and Herman Braun, represented a major break from the divisive memories of the relative guilt or innocence of individuals like Wirz, Davis, and Stanton. Hesseltine suggested that those involved in the contest of vilifying or defending these polarizing figures were caught in a circular and ultimately unanswerable debate. Individuals certainly should and could have done more, Hesseltine believed, but the widespread scale of the suffering testified to the need for a deeper explanation of the "prison system." Andersonville, as the worst individual prison of the Civil War, provided Hesseltine with his most powerful evidence in support of the organizational explanation. Recounting Andersonville's origins, Hesseltine described how the "execution of the plan" to construct the Georgia prison suffered from "distance," "delay," and a lack of men and supplies. "In the midst of the preparations for equipping the prison," the Confederate government started shipping prisoners to the site "before the preparations for their reception had been completed." From Hesseltine's perspective, prisoners accumulated and died at Andersonville because of poor planning and bureaucratic mismanagement, not inhuman cruelty.[34]

Hesseltine's argument that the Confederate prison system lacked organization compared to the Union's camps brought him to the final piece of the prison controversy. Why, if the Confederacy was derelict in its duty to Union captives, were the death rates of Confederates in Union prisons comparable? "Polemical" northern writers, Hesseltine claimed, "were faced with a problem when they came to an enumeration of deaths to prove their thesis that the South deliberately murdered prisoners. The numbers given in the official reports were not sufficiently large for those who desired to prove deliberate murder." As Hesseltine reported, traditional Union estimates placed mortality rates in Union prisons at 12 percent and Confederate prisons at 17 percent. Confederate defenders insisted that the casualty rates stood at 12 percent in Union prisons and only 9 percent in Confederate prisons. Whatever the real figures, however, what struck Hesseltine was that the death rates were markedly similar. Although the similarity between Union and Confederate prison mortality simply confirmed the prevalence of fatal diseases in all Civil War prisons, Hesseltine remained unsatisfied. His finding undermined the validity of the organizational explanation given his demonstration of the superiority of the Northern "prison system." Hesseltine concluded that while organizational failings explained the Confederacy's mistreatment of prisoners, another rationale was needed to clarify the Union's almost identically poor prison record.[35]

Hesseltine found his answer in the fashionable contemporary theory of psychoanalysis, which, as historian Peter Novick states, scholars of Hesseltine's era believed to be "devoted to unearthing objective truth."[36] According to Hesseltine, the grim record of the more prepared, wealthier, and provisioned Union prisons could be explained only as the result of "war psychosis," a psychological condition that he described as inspiring "the fiercest antagonism toward that country's enemies." As the war continued and northerners heard more about the sufferings taking place in Confederate prisons, "the inevitable reaction of the prisoners and the people of the North was to demand that the prisoners in the Northern prisons should be given a similar treatment." In other words, the psychological desire for revenge caused the public to inspire Union officials to treat prisoners badly by reducing rations and withholding supplies when, unlike in the South, the food and supplies existed to care properly for the Confederate captives. So thorough was "war psychosis," Hesseltine observed, that even as conditions deteriorated in the Union prison system, northerners still believed that "prisoners in the Northern prisons were accorded excellent treatment." One of the most remarkable features of Hesseltine's "war psychosis" involved its durability. After Appomattox, "war psychosis" still contained such emotional power that it continued to fuel the prison controversy during Reconstruction with the execution of Wirz, the "waving of the bloody shirt," and the appearance of scores of prisoner memoirs. Hesseltine thus categorized the postwar years of northern indignation over the prisons as a sincere, if hypocritical, reflection of the passion stirred up by the prison controversy during the war. His "study in war psychology" again attacked the traditional belief that evil individuals bore responsibility for the tragedy and instead confirmed the modern, more scientifically nuanced perception of how the world worked. Hesseltine's revisionist combination of objective psychoanalytic theory and the impersonal dominance of large bureaucratic organizations, with their capacity for mismanagement, presented the history of Civil War prisons in a more compelling, usable form, especially compared to the outdated sectional memories of the prisons.[37]

If Hesseltine leaned toward the southern interpretation of the prison controversy, one of the main reasons could be found in an article he published in the *Journal of Southern History* in 1935, titled "The Propaganda Literature of Confederate Prisons." In it Hesseltine expressed the understandable frustration he felt during his years researching his groundbreaking book as he sorted through the hundreds of memoirs that prisoners published, almost all of whom, he argued, "took up a reminiscent pen" in order "to convince his readers of the essential brutality of his captors." Hesseltine briefly traced how the Union government publicized the suffering in Confederate prisons during the war as well as how the postwar government continued to publish reports and investigations rehashing the treatment of prisoners into the late 1860s. These actions, Hesseltine argued, inflamed northerners and "made the recounting of atrocity stories an act of high patriotism." From Reconstruction throughout the late nineteenth century, as Union prisoners leveled exaggerated charges of Confederate brutality in their memoirs, they therefore drew much of their inspiration from official sources and the desire to defend the government, just as they had on the battlefield between 1861 and 1865.[38]

Since northern voices dominated the debate over the wartime prisons, the focus of Hesseltine's research on the prison systems and the immediate aftermath of the war naturally led to his somewhat pro-southern interpretation of Civil War prisons. In his attempt at objectivity, Hesseltine overcompensated in an effort to compare more fairly what happened in Andersonville and the other Confederate prisons to Elmira and the Union camps. Although he correctly perceived that the casualties in Union prisons resulted in part from deliberate political choices, his emphasis on the North's psychological desire for revenge minimized the consistently calculated nature of the Lincoln administration's policy toward prisoners of war throughout the conflict. The theory of "war psychosis" removed responsibility for the Union's actions; defined the harsh treatment of prisoners as an unavoidable symptom of the disease of war; avoided the question of racial justice; and minimized the legitimacy of the understandable, if overzealous, northern desire to both celebrate and find meaning in victory. His reliance on the organizational and psychological explanations so common in mid-twentieth-century academia ultimately prevented analysis of the human evil at the core of the prison tragedy. And while Hesseltine did not exonerate the Confederacy, his descriptions of the inept bungling and flagrant negligence that characterized the disorganized Confederate prison system reflected his tendency to accept the southern counter memory of Civil War prisons. Hesseltine factored neither the Confederacy's brutal no-quarter racism toward African American soldiers nor the Davis administration's consciously callous treatment of Union captives into his argument. Despite these flaws, Hesseltine's work represented an important achievement. In sifting through and rejecting much of the old divisive memories, Hesseltine helped shift the terms of debate over Civil War prisons. Neither North nor South, despite all their attempts to do so, could still legitimately contend that their prison record truly improved on their opponent's.

Between 1930 and 1960, historians, when commenting on the topic of Civil War prisons, based their objective arguments primarily on Hesseltine's work. Ella Lonn agreed with Hesseltine when she defended Henry Wirz in *Foreigners in the Confederacy,* published in 1940. Lonn claimed that Wirz, in part because of his Swiss birth, made an easy but undeserved target for the "inflamed war feeling" of the North and that his execution, or "sacrifice," as she termed it, occurred solely to satisfy northern demands for retribution.[39] In a review of Lonn's book, R. Walter Coakley agreed with her that Wirz was "unjustly cited."[40] Although not exonerating Wirz of all blame, Lonn followed Hesseltine's lead in arguing that responsibility in the matter of Civil War prisons could not possibly in fairness rest on the shoulders of one particular individual. Another scholar, William Maxwell, pointed out in his 1956 study, *Lincoln's Fifth Wheel: The Political History of the United States Sanitary Commission,* that the Sanitary Commission bore some of the responsibility for stirring up northern passion over the prisons with the release of its 1864 report on the "privations and sufferings" taking place in the Confederacy. Maxwell called the report, which attacked southern prisons while absolving northern camps of any wrongdoing, a "diatribe" and a "false position." The intensity of the war, Maxwell explained, in a statement reminiscent of "war psychosis," caused the commission to lose "their sense of fairness and objectivity, forgetting the suffering of Confederates in Northern camps."[41] And one of Hesseltine's own graduate students at the University of Wisconsin, William Fletcher Thompson, declared in his 1959 book, *The Image of War,* that the "conditions within the prison camps of both belligerents were frightful."[42] The old convictions of singular brutality in the prisons of either the Union or the Confederacy had finally been completely discredited, at least among historians.

Other scholars relied even more closely on Hesseltine's arguments. One of the foremost chroniclers of the Reconstruction-era bloody-shirt phenomenon, Reinhard Luthin, adopted Hesseltine's psychological vocabulary when he declared in 1960 that the goal of northern Republicans after the Civil War was to keep "the war psychosis alive." Republicans succeeded at this, in part, Luthin believed, because of the efforts of such men as James G. Blaine, who in 1876 famously "delivered an incredibly foul verbal attack" on the subject of Jefferson Davis's responsibility for the horrors of Andersonville.[43] Public reminders of Andersonville and other Confederate prisons cemented northern popular support for the Republican Party, Luthin suggested, and helped preserve the unity of the wartime period. The work of another scholar, Frank Byrne, also revealed the debt that historians owed to Hesseltine. In his 1958 article, "Libby Prison: A Study in Emotions," Byrne explored the implications of Hesseltine's "war psychosis" theory. Byrne concluded that, during the war, the raw emotions stirred up by the Richmond prison resulted from the "interaction of the guards' fear and the prisoners' hate." Libby Prison became, at its core, "a cauldron of emotions," and the intensity of feeling, as Hesseltine and Luthin suggested, would continue to linger long after 1865 in the form of "war psychosis."[44] By 1960 then, among professional historians, Hesseltine's psychological theory of "war psychosis" had met with widespread acceptance, as had his objective insistence that the tragedy of Civil War prisons resulted from the actions of both the Union and Confederacy. Importantly, Hesseltine's example also started to inspire those outside the circle of professional historians.

One example of the increasing influence of more rigorous scholarship on the subject of Civil War prisons appeared in the work of Richard Hemmerlein, author of the 1934 book *Prisons and Prisoners of the Civil War.* Although poorly researched compared to Hesseltine's volume—he did not even acknowledge Hesseltine in his brief bibliography—Hemmerlein's book took both North and South to task for abandoning "all human consideration" in caring for their prisoners and, like Hesseltine, concluded that both sides deserved their share of blame.[45] Hattie Lou Winslow and Joseph R. H. Moore's 1940 history, *Camp Morton, 1861–1865: Indianapolis Prison Camp*, was of higher quality. They based their study of Camp Morton on solid documentation and traced the wartime history of the facility from its origins as a recruiting and training ground for Union soldiers to its eventual conversion to a prison camp for Confederate captives. In its conception, the idea of a history of an individual prison broke no new ground. But unlike authors of earlier camp histories, such as Clay Holmes in his 1912 work on Elmira, Winslow and Moore made no apologies about the difficult conditions at Camp Morton and openly discussed the prison's shortcomings, including the role that the Union government played in the suffering. Many of the deaths of the winter of 1865, they argued, resulted "from the haggling over hospitals and winter quarters" for the prisoners, as poor communications between the officers in charge of the camp and Washington prevented proper preparations.[46] Winslow and Moore's focus on the managerial and bureaucratic nature of the problems that led to prisoner misery at Camp Morton once again reflected the growing acceptance of Hesseltine's organizational explanation for the tragedy of Civil War prisons. The honesty of their assessment led to favorable reviews in both the *Journal of Southern History* and the *American Historical Review*. Anyone interested in the subject of "man's inhumanity to man," reviewer Edgar Stewart declared, would find Winslow and Moore's book "well worth the attention."[47]

Inspired by Hesseltine's example, professional and amateur historians alike rejected the old selective memories of Civil War prisons and instead approached this particular example of "man's inhumanity to man" with the objective goal of more faithfully chronicling and explaining the horrors of Civil War prison camps in terms of scientific theory. The efforts of these scholars, coinciding with the deaths of the fiercest sectional defenders, started the process of reinterpreting Civil War prisons in the context of modern war during the 1920s and 1930s. But the victory for a more objective memory of Civil War prisons soon proved of insufficient satisfaction. The need for a usable past required continued attention. As the 1930s ended with the outbreak of World War II, an even more appalling story of "man's inhumanity to man" emerged. The context provided by World War II lent a further gravitas to the subject of Civil War prisons. In an overt response to the numbing violence of the fight against fascism in the 1940s, historians began to address the parallels between such atrocities as the Holocaust, the

Bataan Death March, and the prisons of the Civil War as common symbols of the destructive capacity of modern war. The dramatic escalation of the scale of atrocity frightened scholars and alleviated any lingering sentiment that the treatment of Civil War prisoners remained an abstract historical problem. Many turned with a new sense of urgency to the story of Civil War prisons in a desperate search for understanding. If the process of atrocity could be explained, then it might be prevented in the future.

In response to this imperative, the most eloquent discussion of the commonalities between the suffering that took place in Civil War prisons and the brutality of Nazi Germany came from the pen of James Bonner, chair of the history department at the Georgia State College for Women. In 1947, Bonner published "War Crimes Trials, 1865–67," in which he discussed the postwar controversy over the treatment of Jefferson Davis and the trial and execution of Henry Wirz. From the outset, however, Bonner made no effort to disguise his real motivation—the troubling connection between 1865 America and 1940s Germany, and in particular the question of how to accomplish justice in the aftermath of war crimes, whether at Andersonville or Auschwitz. "Thoughtful Americans," Bonner wrote, "attempting to find a rational submission to the reality of the Nuremberg trial" would unfortunately find little "tranquility of mind" from "our previous experiences with war crimes and atrocities." Bonner referred to the concept of "war psychosis," described how it unjustly fueled Wirz's execution, and raised the fear that history was repeating itself in the Nuremberg trials. The "atrocity stories" of the Civil War, Bonner argued, "bore some of the flavor of Dachau and Belsen," and Wirz "received more venomous invectives" in 1865 than "Heinrich Himmler, the Nazi Gestapo chief" in the 1940s. Although Bonner agreed with the outcome of the Nuremberg trial, as it sealed the "well-deserved fate" of "a group of evil men," the self-congratulatory attitude of America and its allies throughout the process troubled him. In assuming that they were somehow incapable of such atrocities, Americans ignored the precedent of Civil War prisons at their peril. "Will history," Bonner asked, "accept and justify the legality of the war crimes commission, or will future generations associate its proceeding with ex post facto and fait accompli achievements," and can we ever feel assured "that retributory crimes of vengeance will not be repeated—that two wrongs do not make a right?" Americans needed to remember the painful lessons of Civil War prisons and redouble their efforts for humanity and justice in the future, Bonner suggested, because what happened in Nazi Germany was not so far removed from the barbarities of the Civil War. To Bonner, the Holocaust and Andersonville, although separated by time and space, confirmed the fundamental evil inherent in modern society. The only defense against the shockingly easy acceptance of atrocity, Bonner warned, lay in constant vigilance—repeatedly reminding ourselves to guard against the mistakes of the past.[48]

The influence of World War II also appeared in the work of one of the most prolific historians of the Civil War, Bruce Catton. Like Bonner, Catton based his interpretation of the story of Civil War prisons in part on Hesseltine's interpretation that both sides bore responsibility for the disaster. He also held the personal conviction that Andersonville and the other prisons remained relevant to the present as a cautionary tale about the nature of modern war. In a 1959 *American Heritage* article, Catton enthusiastically reminded his readers that "the passage of the years has at last brought a new perspective." Andersonville remained "the worst of a large number of war prisons," but all prisons, North and South, "were almost unbelievably bad." "The real culprit" for the suffering, Catton declared, was not "Wirz, the luckless scapegoat," but "war itself." Catton's focus on the inherent evil of modern war reflected a sense of weariness with the tragic development of world events. By 1959, the experience of the Civil War, World War I, World War II, and the Korean War convinced Catton and many Americans that, starting with the Civil War, in each and every instance war meant the infliction of unspeakable cruelty, no matter when or where it took place. "If the people of the North in the fall of 1865 had used the language of the late 1940s," Catton argued, "they would have said that Captain Wirz was a war criminal who had been properly convicted and then had been hanged for atrocious war crimes." The only difference between 1865 and 1945, then, was that in a nineteenth-century world unfamiliar with the atrocities to come in the twentieth century, Wirz had been demonized and executed as a symbol of everything peculiarly wrong with the South. Given the decades of ongoing bitterness represented in the divisive memories of the prison controversy, Wirz's death, Catton wrote, "did not help anybody very much." No one would feel better about the atrocities of 1865, and in turn the atrocities of the 1940s, unless they viewed these horrors with the "proper perspective" of war's inevitable cruelty.[49]

Historians, by the nature of their common pursuit to find patterns of meaning in the past, led the search for links between the atrocities of different generations in an effort to better understand the tragedy of Civil War prisons. But, as is often the case, historians did not engage in this quest by themselves, and their voices were overshadowed. By the late 1950s, popular authors, most famously MacKinlay Kantor and Saul Levitt, were already inspired—if such a word could be appropriate—to revisit the story of Civil War prisons. Through the lens of fiction, they sought to come to terms with the awful reality of the present and find some explanation as to why such horrors continued to haunt humanity. The pragmatism inherent in that mission also testified to how the memory of Civil War prisons had changed by the 1950s. For the Civil War generation and their immediate descendants, contesting the prison controversy provided ammunition for the ongoing rhetorical war about the justice of the Union or Confederate cause. Beginning with Fooks and Hesseltine, however, historians and writers, who benefited from emotional distance from the prison tragedy, remembered Civil War prisons not just as historical events, but as a chance to investigate and perhaps even comprehend the contemporary horror of modern war. The influence of this new purpose of memory clearly existed in the work of both Kantor and Levitt. Although they wrote about Andersonville, the constant shadow of the Holocaust throughout their work revealed their desire to make sense of their present.

In 1955, MacKinlay Kantor published his massive novel *Andersonville*. At the time, the native Iowan had already established a sterling reputation in the literary world based on the merits of his many books, most notably *Long Remember*, a 1934 retelling of the Battle of Gettysburg that, before Michael Shaara's *The Killer Angels*, was widely considered the best fictional description of the battle, and *Glory for Me*, a story of the reintegration of World War II veterans back into American society, which was adapted to the big screen in 1946's Academy Award-winning *The Best Years of Our Lives*. But for all his success on these and other projects, *Andersonville* represented Kantor's crowning achievement. The idea of a novel about the notorious prison camp first occurred to Kantor in 1930, which, perhaps not coincidently, was the same year Hesseltine published *Civil War Prisons*. Over the next twenty-five years, in fits and starts, Kantor researched and worked on the manuscript. He finally summoned the will to complete the book after a visit to the Andersonville prison grounds in late 1953. In an October 1955 article written for the *New York Times Book Review*, Kantor described how at five o'clock in the morning he stood at the site of the old stockade and listened to the ghosts of the thousands of dead Union prisoners. "They had come," he wrote, "to tell me that there must be no compromise. I had invoked their name and thought for nearly twenty-five years; they were thronging at last to force me to the task. I was crying. I had not cried in many years, but now I was crying."[50] That emotion permeated the 700-plus pages of the finished novel.

Although emotional, *Andersonville* was carefully calculated to resonate with a contemporary audience. Kantor, who visited the concentration camp at Buchenwald near the close of World War II, approached the topic of Andersonville and atrocity in general with the recent shock of the Holocaust at the forefront of his thoughts. The telling of the story of Andersonville represented an opportunity for Kantor to use the setting of the Civil War, according to scholar Jeff Smithpeters, "to sift mid-20th century discourses into a more digestible substance." The Holocaust made *Andersonville* more accessible to the public by providing a natural frame of reference. The power of Kantor's novel derived in part from the natural connections readers made between the images of German concentration camps and the descriptions of emaciated Union prisoners. Kantor counted on evoking the Holocaust, not to further denounce the Germans, but instead to facilitate American comprehension of the universal nature of atrocity. A pragmatic sense of, and support for, the contemporary politics of anti-Communist consensus motivated Kantor to encourage forgiveness for and understanding of the Germans, who by the 1950s had been transformed from enemy to Cold War ally. Andersonville thus became Kantor's subject because he wanted to establish "that a real concentration camp and a semblance of a Holocaust had happened in America."[51] Kantor intended for the emotions stirred by recalling Andersonville to serve the needs of present Americans for a narrative of Civil War prison suffering as a source of unity, rather than as a reopening of the scars of the bitter memories of the past.

Despite the strong influence of the Holocaust and Cold War politics on the novel, at the core of *Andersonville* lay Kantor's self-described mission of recreating "an accurate history of the Andersonville prison." Although the inhabitants of the town of Andersonville were fictitious, as were many of the prisoners, Kantor prided himself on creating "portraits" of the Confederate prison officials and some of the prisoners who actually suffered in the stockade.[52] But suffering belonged not solely to the thousands of Yankees prisoners—Kantor also presented a moving portrayal of how the war slowly

destroyed the town of Andersonville and degraded the Confederate officials and guards in charge of the madness taking place inside the stockade.
Kantor implied that, the long decades of divisive memories notwithstanding, neither the Confederacy nor the Union alone deserved excoriation on
the specific issues of exchange or treatment of prisoners, but instead both
sides together merited universal condemnation for allowing such a tragedy.
The horrors of modern war overwhelmed Union and Confederate characters alike, in keeping with the now orthodox objective understanding of
Civil War prisons, and the clear influence of the recent scholarship on the
wartime prisons on Kantor's work did not go unnoticed. The eminent historian Henry Steele Commager proclaimed the novel "the greatest of our
Civil War novels" and praised it for creating a sense of how the prison "sub-
merges" all involved, whether prisoner, guard, or observer "in a common
humanity or inhumanity."[53] Lawrence Thompson, another scholar, compli-
mented Kantor for achieving "Olympian objectivity" toward "human beings caught in the maelstrom of war." While "no student of Civil War history need be told that Buchenwald and Belsen would have had no special
horrors for anyone lucky enough to have survived the pest-ridden valley
at Anderson Station in central Georgia," Thompson declared, the sublime
nature of Kantor's achievement could be attributed to the author's desire
"to find out what made Wirz and millions of his contemporaries behave as
they did."[54] For readers like Commager and Thompson, the merit of Kantor's novel was not its entertainment value, but the sincerity with which it
recognized and meditated on the urgent need to better understand the nature of wartime atrocity.

From a purely literary standpoint, Kantor's novel qualified as a thorough
success. Not only was the book widely acclaimed and selected as the *New
York Times* November 1955 book-of-the-month; it won Kantor the Pulitzer
Prize, no doubt in part because of its timely and undeniable emotional appeal. Kantor's vision of Andersonville showed how barbaric supposedly civilized people become when officials and guards forget their shared humanity
with their prisoners, when captives prey upon each other, when bureaucracy
pushes paper instead of solves problems, and when the local townspeople
do nothing to ameliorate the suffering. The power of this insight derived
from the heightened awareness of the repetitious pattern of atrocity in the
modern era, of the persistence of apathy, blind obedience, and misguided
patriotism, and the role these human failings played in history from the

prisons of the Civil War to the concentration camps of the Holocaust. Although *Andersonville* pinned responsibility for the suffering on all involved, as did Hesseltine, because Kantor was a novelist and not a historian, he also took certain liberties in the interest of a good story. And every story involving good and evil needs a villain.

In the case of Andersonville, Kantor had two tailor-made historical figures for the role: John Winder and Henry Wirz. As could be expected, giving the sprawling nature of his achievement, inconsistencies crept into Kantor's work. Perhaps no aspect of the novel revealed this more than Kantor's struggle to reconcile the contradictions inherent in his depiction of Winder and Wirz. Both were central figures in the decades of emotional bitterness caused by the contesting memories of Civil War prisons and, even a century later, remained controversial. The problem for Kantor, bent on a message of unity, was how to employ these characters without reopening old wounds. Clearly intrigued by Hesseltine's concept of "war psychosis," Kantor chose to depict his villains as psychologically disturbed. Winder was insane with "hatred" for his father, whose failed generalship led to the British capture of Washington, D.C., during the War of 1812. He also seethed with rage against the national government as a "composite demon" because it refused to recognize his military accomplishments and held his father's failures against him, an injustice that turned Winder's "blood to black." "John Winder," Kantor wrote, "desired that children should be trained to scorn the National government as he scorned it, to loathe the Yankees as he loathed them, to crush all supporters of that Faith as one would snap the shell of a cockroach with his boot sole and feel the shell pop." This irrational hatred finally led Winder "to kill as many of the prisoners as he could. It was as simple as that." Wirz, meanwhile, driven crazy by constant pain from a wound at Seven Pines, thinks of the prisoners under his care as animals rather than people. Although, also in keeping with Hesseltine, Kantor infuses Wirz with the organizational desire to bring an "orderly" spirit to the administration of the prison, Wirz's psychological failings lead him to view the Union captives as "fast-bred rodents." While Kantor's novel warns us of the inherent predilection of man for evil, by portraying Winder and Wirz, the two men most directly responsible for the prison, as essentially insane, he dilutes the power of his message. By making the immorality of Winder and Wirz result from their personal demons and individual failings, Kantor undermines his criticism of the capacity of modern government and society for evil and thus mimics the excuse of the old divisive memories of Civil War prisons—that while modern society may allow such horrors it takes inherently depraved men to accomplish them. Kantor also exaggerates Wirz's tendency to lapse into his native German, punctuating Wirz's dialogue with "ja," "nein," and "ach." Through the constant German mutterings of the Swiss-born Wirz, Kantor overtly seeks to tie the atrocities of Andersonville with the Holocaust. Although consistent with Kantor's motivation, his primary concern with contemporary atrocity deflects attention from the fact that while what happened at Andersonville paralleled the descent of German society into brutality, the events of the Civil War resulted from the cracks in our own civilized veneer. The distorted depiction of these two key characters has the important effect of externalizing evil—linking it to the Nazis—thus lessening any specific criticism of American values or society. Given that Kantor wrote in an era of conformity, his avoidance of the issue of specific responsibility for the suffering that occurred in Civil War prisons was unsurprising. Part of the novel's appeal lay in its clever manipulation of contemporary fears—Kantor simultaneously decried modern society while subtly pardoning Americans from worrying that such horrors could ever occur here again.[55]

Not everyone appreciated Kantor's effort. Ironically, given how his work anticipated *Andersonville*, William Hesseltine despised the novel, and in his 1956 essay "Andersonville Revisited" seemed to revel in the opportunity to criticize Kantor. Calling Kantor "uninfluenced" by "critical scholarship," Hesseltine ridiculed Kantor's claims of historical accuracy, declaring the book a "perversity" whose "errors and inadequacies should not be allowed to hide behind the literary form in which it appears." But the most damning aspect of *Andersonville*, according to Hesseltine, lay in its perpetuation of the old northern memory, the "myth of Andersonville," instead of endorsing Hesseltine's objective argument that "it was the war system itself that produced the graves in the Georgia village."[56] Although part of the offense taken by Hesseltine in response to *Andersonville* contained legitimacy, particularly as it relates to Kantor's pompous attempt to present a novel as meeting the standards of analytic history, most of Hesseltine's outrage seemed a product of envy at the attention (and book sales) generated by Kantor's work. The accusation that Kantor inflamed the memory of northern virtue reflected the fact that Hesseltine always demonstrated a proclivity toward the southern counter memory and minimized the obvious point that Kantor, unlike Hesseltine, was writing about a Confederate prison infamous for its horrors, rather than comparing the prison systems of both Union and Confederacy. As for the charge of ignoring the rising dominance of the objective interpretation of Civil War prisons, Kantor cited Hesseltine's *Civil War Prisons* in *Andersonville*'s bibliography. Petty jealousies aside, the work of both men shared far more in common than Hesseltine cared to admit. Neither succeeded completely in shedding the divisive memories of Civil War prisons even as they claimed objectivity; both agreed that Andersonville, like all wartime prisons, reflected the unsettling, even inevitable, connection between atrocity and modern war.

Despite Hesseltine's objections, in its timing and complexity *Andersonville* revealed the degree to which the memory of Civil War prisons had changed by the late 1950s. Ostensibly a novel about the treatment of Civil War prisoners, Kantor's novel combined numerous perspectives on the prison controversy in that it included but refused to pander to the traditional animosity inherent in the material, nodded to the objective historical interpretations pioneered by Hesseltine, and recast the prison's history in the context of the Holocaust and the Cold War. The ambition of *Andersonville* may or may not have reflected Kantor's goal to become America's "spokesman," but it certainly showed the belief that remembering the tragedies of the past provided a means to understand the horrors of the present.[57] At its core, *Andersonville*—in the spirit of Hesseltine, Bonner, and Catton—offered a cautionary tale about the fragile nature of morality, the insidious capacity for evil inherent in humanity, and the need for vigilance against future atrocity. It was a powerful and optimistic message. Despite its eloquence, however, *Andersonville* also represented the limitations inherent in the objective memory of Civil War prisons. Kantor, like his contemporaries, admitted that evil had been done in the wartime prisons. But the categorizing of that evil as typical of modern war—an intellectual construct motivated by the desire to place Civil War atrocities in the context of the pattern of the recent world wars—created an inherent excuse for the horrors of the Civil War. A new myth about Civil War prisons took the place of the old. The suffering of Civil War prisons was not the result of deliberate cruelty but instead simply happened as a part of the process of war. The passivity of this new perspective had an important consequence. The removal of blame relieved Americans of the moral responsibility to confront the true nature of the evils committed against Civil War prisoners.

With the celebration of Kantor's novel in the form of awards, recognition, and publicity, *Andersonville* garnered prolonged attention across America in 1955. As an unintended consequence, perhaps one appreciated by Hesseltine, the popularity of the novel also generated a new wave of interest in Andersonville and the subject of Civil War prisons. Between 1955 and 1960, academic journals like *Civil War History, Nebraska History,* and the *Alabama Historical Quarterly* all published previously unpublished wartime journals or postwar reminiscences of Civil War prisoners.[58] In the December 1956 issue of *Civil War History,* Ovid Futch's article about the Andersonville raiders, six Union prisoners who terrorized their fellow captives, appeared, followed soon after by Virgil Carrington Jones's June 1958 piece "Libby Prison Break," an account of how hundreds of Union prisoners, fifty-nine of whom succeeded, plotted their escape from the notorious prison.[59] And as Richard Barksdale Harwell prepared his two volumes, *The Confederate Reader* and *The Union Reader,* published respectively in 1957 and 1958, he included the testimony of prisoners from both sections.[60] *Andersonville* seemed to spark a renewed public appetite for the topic of Civil War prisons, although Kantor's influence was not inevitably positive. In their 1960 textbook *The New Nation, 1865–1917,* Columbia University historians Dumas Malone and Basil Rauch, in describing how the Wirz trial reflected the bitterness of Reconstruction, utilized the popular psychological interpretation of Wirz and referred to him as "the crazed and cruel Swiss-American who was in charge at Andersonville."[61]

Of all these Andersonville-inspired publications, one of the most important was the 1957 reprinting of *This Was Andersonville,* by John McElroy, one of the Andersonville prisoners whose work, first printed in 1879, not only contributed to the enduring power of the northern memory of Civil War prisons but also influenced Kantor.[62] The new edition contained an introduction by Roy Meredith, who placed McElroy's incendiary works in the emotional context of Reconstruction and explained that "McElroy was extremely biased" and made "erroneous statements in the heat of anger at his captors." The real importance of McElroy's book, as interpreted through the eyes of Meredith seventy-eight years later, came from its relevance as an account of the most "appalling incident during the Civil War, which had no precedent until the Second World War, when the prison camps of Belsen and Dachau and the unforgettable Death March in the Philippines overshadowed anything that had gone on before in warfare." Meredith finished his introduction by stating the lesson so painfully learned not just at Andersonville, but in the much more recent past. "All that can be said for Andersonville, after almost a century, is that it stands as an indictment against war in all its forms," Meredith claimed, "and places the Civil War in the category where it belongs, as one of the most terrible wars the world has ever known."[63] Although depressing, the subject of Civil War prisons, if confronted, Meredith hoped, offered a way for Americans not just to reject what happened at Andersonville and in the Holocaust as unacceptable, but to caution future generations to guard against such horrors.

Besides the thought-provoking questions of morality and responsibility inspired by Kantor's novel, *Andersonville* also sparked a revival of interest in the prison site itself. Since the flurry of monument dedications in the early decades of the 1900s, Andersonville had slowly returned to quiet anonymity. On May 28, 1957, an editor for the *Atlanta Journal* stated that "until the publication of McKinley Kantor's best-selling novel, 'Andersonville,' this peaceful cemetery and prison park was seldom visited by tourists and usually ignored by nearby residents." With the "throngs" now jumping "by leaps and bounds," the editor reported, "park employees are bracing themselves for an increasing influx of visitors."[64] A few days later, W. S. Kirkpatrick wrote an article in the *Atlanta Constitution* declaring that "The Bitterness Is Gone at Andersonville." According to Kirkpatrick, Kantor deserved credit for providing "evidence to show that Southerners of the 60s were not the beasts the hysteria of the times caused them to be considered in the North."[65] As a result more and more tourists came to Andersonville each year, not to re-hash old arguments but simply out of a curiosity to see the grounds after reading Kantor's novel.[66]

With traffic through and around the town of Andersonville on the rise, it came to the attention of the Georgia UDC that the old monument to Wirz, which stood "in the midst of a cluttered commercial-garage district, oftimes surrounded by garbage," badly needed repair.[67] In January 1958, the UDC sponsored a resolution in the state House to appropriate Georgia public funds "to clean the stained and corroded statue." Even fifty years after its construction, controversy over Wirz's memorial flared quickly. Although the resolution passed, seventy-year-old Representative Ulysses S. Lancaster, a descendant of a Confederate guard at Andersonville and also "a former school-teacher with a knowledge of history," voted against the measure, stating that "according to what I've heard about it we did a lot of the things we've accused the Germans of doing."[68] Tellingly, the Georgia legislature never approved the funding. Popular *Atlanta Constitution* columnist Celestine Sibley, whose remarkable career spanned from World War II until her death in 1999, explained, with her trademark tone of moderation, the core of the controversy to her readers. Although proud of "ouah sacred heritage," Sibley wrote, given that "latter-day historians" referred to Wirz as the "the Himmler of the Confederacy," prudence was needed. Criticizing the UDC for having "slipped a sleeper" resolution into the Georgia House, Sibley referred to Kantor's "weighty" and "well-documented" novel, declaring that "the fact that Yankee prisons were bad too and Confederate soldiers suffered similarly doesn't excuse in many minds the wanton acts of cruelty attributed to Wirz." Those acts, she concluded, weren't "likely to be popular with Georgia legislators of today."[69] Sibley's reasoned stance—and the reluctance of most Georgians to support the Wirz resolution—would have been inconceivable in the early 1900s but was understandable in the context of the 1950s. Some white Georgians, unnerved by the rising tide of the Civil Rights Movement, preferred to reassure themselves by clamoring for renewed devotion to the heroes of Confederate mythology. But many locals started to realize the potential benefits of abandoning the shrill defense of Wirz and instead displaying a more positive and accommodating attitude toward those interested in remembering the prison controversy. The growing acceptance of the objective theory of Civil War prisons as a mutual rather than sectional failure not only helped restore the reputation of the Confederacy but also brought financial rewards through tourism. For moderate southerners like Sibley, choosing this moment to make a public stand in defense of Wirz, always one of the most controversial figures of the Civil War, made little sense—except to the UDC—because it threatened the profitable goodwill created by Kantor's novel.

As the attention surrounding Andersonville grew, writer Saul Levitt also found himself captivated during the 1950s by the historical events at the Georgia prison, and by the figure of Henry Wirz in particular. Around 1956, Levitt started the script for what eventually became *The Andersonville Trial*. Originally conceived as a television program (a one-hour version aired on the CBS show *Climax*), over time Levitt's idea grew into a full-length play about the Wirz trial. On December 29, 1959, *The Andersonville Trial* made its debut on Broadway, and it eventually made its way to London and Andersonville itself. From the outset, Levitt expressed frustration with the reviewers of the show, who inferred a connection between the Wirz trial and the Nuremberg trial. In an interview he tried to explain his motivation for the play. "I didn't write this play because of a dedication to Civil War events," Levitt declared, and "I also didn't write it because I wanted to make a preachment about war criminals linked to the experience of our own time with the trials of the Nazi leaders at Nuremberg."[70] Given the content of the play, critics could be forgiven for scratching their heads at Levitt's cantankerous response.

The Andersonville Trial commences with the beginning of the Wirz trial proceedings, and for the first three-fourths of the script, Levitt recreates the aura of the actual Wirz trial, even accurately keeping the historical identities of most of the important characters. To give the audience a feel for the atrocities committed at Andersonville, Levitt condenses the huge Wirz trial transcript into a few key witnesses who testify about the horrible conditions Andersonville prisoners endured and whether or not Wirz personally killed any of the prisoners. From the outset, Wirz has no illusions about the purpose of these proceedings, exclaiming in the first act that "all that is wanted of me is my life." Although the outcome of the trial is never in doubt, as the government's case against him accumulates, in the second act Wirz takes the stand to defend himself. The resulting battle of wits between Wirz and Chipman, the prosecutor, directly reveals the theme of Levitt's play. In his attempts to defend his actions, Wirz repeatedly states that his duty as an officer in the Confederate army requires him to obey his superiors, in this case John Winder. "One does," Wirz argues, "as he is ordered." Even though he watched the suffering of the thousands of Union prisoners, the "situation," Levitt has Wirz declare, "was General Winder's responsibility—not mine." From the perspective of Wirz, the terrible suffering "was to me a military situation." Chipman, however, refuses to accept Wirz's argument that following orders absolved him of personal responsibility. "Why did you obey," Chipman asked Wirz, when "we who are born into the human race are elected to an extraordinary role in the scheme of things. We are endowed with reason and therefore personal responsibility for our acts." By failing to follow a higher law than that of the chain of command and find some way to ameliorate the suffering of the captives he ruled over, Wirz deserves the death sentence that the play concludes with. As Wirz's lawyer, Baker, exits the courtroom following the verdict, he tells Chipman that the prosecutor's faith in human potential is naive given humanity's inherent weaknesses. "It was a worthy effort," Baker explains in frustration, "though it hasn't anything to do with the real world. Men will go on as they are, most of them, subject to fears—and so, subject to powers and authorities. And how are we to change that slavery? When it's of man's very nature?" Levitt's dark conclusion reflected his desire to convey the seductive ease with which personal responsibility could be avoided in the modern bureaucratic world and deny any validity to the idea that following orders constitutes a legitimate defense for atrocity.[71]

Levitt's main theme in *The Andersonville Trial*, the responsibility of each individual when torn between organizational duty and individual conscience, betrayed his statements to the press. By fictionalizing the proceedings and putting Wirz on the stand, which never happened in the 1865 trial, Levitt clearly wanted to make a statement about human nature and about how people often fail, as did Wirz, when forced to choose between their morals and the demands made on them by institutions. The reason so many critics immediately associated the play with Nuremberg instead of Andersonville involved not only the timing but Levitt's focus on the question of responsibility, an issue perceived much differently in 1865 than in the 1940s and 1950s. In the actual Wirz proceedings, responsibility applied to Wirz because northerners knew his job entailed dealing with the Union prisoners. The assumption in 1865 was that when Wirz failed, he did so as an aberrant individual motivated by demonic evil. Had he been a better man the atrocities of Andersonville would never have transpired. By the 1940s, when Nazi war criminals explained that they merely followed orders in committing their atrocities, that explanation, although dismissed as untenable, sent shivers down the spine of Levitt and other observers familiar with the same kind of shadowy existence, where, thanks to entrenched bureaucracy and organizational structures, responsibility often took a back seat to conformity and evil became a relative condition inherent in all of humanity. Levitt's suspicion that "man's very nature" encourages atrocity came directly from the fearful reality of the Holocaust. Even though his play ultimately focused on the themes of the present, it also revealed the essential connection between Wirz and the Nazis. The only difference between the two tragedies involved the scale of the slaughter, while both confirmed that the belief in man's innate capacity for good faced a constant challenge from the ability of institutional power to facilitate the darker side of human nature in the modern world. Even the destructive pattern inherent in modern war, however, refused to deter Levitt from exhorting his audience to resist organizational evil and trust their individual morality.

But there was a hidden danger in the morality tales woven by both Levitt and Kantor. For these authors, whether they admitted it or not, the compelling connection between the Holocaust and Civil War prisons gave their work its contemporary appeal. The conflation of World War II with the Civil War provided a dramatic canvas on which to explore important universal themes and question the nature of modern humanity. There is an important distinction, however, between atrocity and genocide. As horrible as Civil War prisons were, they were not Nazi concentration camps. The ahistorical repackaging of Andersonville as a World War II–style tragedy revealed the seductive mythmaking power of the new objective memory. Eloquently blurring the specifics of the past in a universalized lament about human failings generated profits and defused controversy. Americans, as always, preferred artfully constructed meaning to honest, more painful, reality.

Despite the pessimistic nature of the subject of Andersonville, or more probably, because of it, by 1960, the literary achievements of Levitt and Kantor showed that, almost one hundred years after their existence, the interest in remembering Civil War prisons persisted. Although the period following World War I brought the passing of the generations so consumed with the divisive memories of Civil War prisons as part of the identity politics of sectional and racial justification, a new generation of Americans, led most prominently by Hesseltine, Kantor, and Levitt, endeavored to redefine the perception of the prisons. They did so because, amazingly enough, the tragedy of Civil War prisons took on even greater relevance in the context of the destructive wars of the first half of the twentieth century. Traditionally the historical record of Civil War prisons divided Americans, but Hesseltine, Kantor, Levitt, and many others hoped that, in the modern world, avoiding future Andersonvilles or Dachaus could be possible if Americans were united through a usable interpretation of the prison camps. The excitement of placing the history of Civil War prisons in its proper context, and the resulting potential for human progress, was unmistakable. There was an urgency with which these intellectuals applied new scientific explanations, reminded readers of the need for vigilance against evil, and rejected the concept that just following orders excused atrocity in any form. The emergence of the new objective memory of Civil War prison was not without its flaws, however. In an environment dominated by the shadow of contemporary brutality, as Americans compared the atrocities of different wars the question of the important connection between racism and prison suffering during the Civil War remained sadly overlooked. And the fixation on the pattern of atrocity encouraged the widespread adoption of the belief that modern war inevitably brought a devastation for which no one was really to blame. Excusing both the Union and Confederacy as equally guilty allowed Americans to continue to avoid the daunting task of honestly and more accurately assessing the responsibility for the tragedy of Civil War prisons. Objective memory possessed increasing attraction for Americans by 1960—it was profitable and also helped validate America's claim to a position of moral leadership in the world. But even a successful illusion is still an illusion. Although the widespread destruction of the wars of the early twentieth century inspired the creation of a new remembrance of Civil War prisons, the emphasis of objective memory on shallow consensus, though understandable in its challenge to the divisive sectional memories, ensured that its promised goal of helping humanity start to learn from its past mistakes remained out of reach.

✦ 6 ✦

"Better to Take Advantage of Outsiders' Curiosity"

THE CONSUMPTION OF OBJECTIVE MEMORY,
1960–PRESENT

From 1960 through the early twenty-first century, the view that both the Union and the Confederacy shared a generalized measure of responsibility for prisoners' suffering and that both deserved criticism for their equalized failings became even more firmly entrenched. Instead of leading to the disappearance of the once heated prison controversy, however, the widespread acceptance of objective memory actually increased the attention that Americans paid to the subject of Civil War prisons. The diminished passions removed blame from the prison tragedy, and as the old stigma of deliberate atrocity faded, Andersonville in particular became the focal point of an accelerating trend during these decades—turning Civil War prison sites into tourist attractions. The success of the emerging tourist interest in southwest Georgia indicated that remembering Civil War prisons possessed commercial potential. And the enduring interest in the Civil War continued to thrive in American popular culture, as new prison histories, more prisoner accounts, and even movies about or featuring Civil War prison camps appeared. The proliferation of these products resulted from two paradoxical, yet inevitably intertwined, motives inherent to the American culture of capitalism. The commercialization of Civil War prisons transformed suffering, like any other raw material, into a profitable commodity stripped of its most controversial elements, but the avid consumption of objective memory also testified to an ongoing, unsatisfied curiosity in American society to understand more fully how such atrocities could ever have been possible.

The commercialization of Civil War prisons did not begin in the early 1960s, but the celebration of the Civil War Centennial represented a unique opportunity to turn memories of the conflict into profit. Initial enthusiasm for this commemoration ran high. Columnist Celestine Sibley feigned disbelief at the "great numbers of citizens who are as freshly, urgently, imperatively engrossed in some phase of That War as if it were day-after-tomorrow's nuclear threat."[1] A. B. Moore, executive director of the Alabama Civil War Centennial Commission, explained that naturally Americans anticipated their chance to relive the war, which, after all, remained "the great national adventure." Remembering "the sterling qualities" of the Civil War generation and cherishing "our great traditions" also provided an additional benefit, Moore believed—it protected the United States from "communist brain-washers."[2] Participation in the Civil War Centennial equated, at least for Moore, to a stand against the Communist Soviet Union. As a display of unity, the centennial offered North and South a chance to reconfirm the bonds of sectional reconciliation in the crucible of the Cold War.

That chance was not free from controversy, however. The necessity of avoiding the entanglement of objective Civil War memory with the rising tide of the Civil Rights Movement complicated the celebration for white southerners, at least some of whom, according to *Atlanta Constitution* journalist Harold Martin, "worried about the centennial" as a potentially "foolish thing." Stirring "the old bones of a lost war" might reopen the "old wounds" of racial controversy by upsetting the dynamics of a Jim Crow South in which white southerners had long since refused to acknowledge, let alone accept, the validity of the emancipationist memory of the Civil War.[3] Careful planning would be required. Despite the discomforting aspects of the centennial, a sense of excitement permeated the preparations. With so many Americans willing to express their patriotism by joining in the ceremonies, important Civil War locations prepared for a surge of visitors. Although tourism, especially at Andersonville, where the national government owned the prison site, predated the centennial activities, the longtime interest of Union veterans and the attention generated by MacKinlay Kantor's novel ensured that visitors inspired by the centennial would find the prison grounds of interest. By 1959, as plans commenced for the national festivities, it became clear that, especially in Georgia, the story of Civil War prisons deserved a place of prominence.

In part that recognition stemmed from the direction of the national Civil War Centennial Commission, which in January 1959 created the Committee on Historical Activities to make recommendations about how to effectively promote the centennial and encourage participation across the country. The committee reported that each individual state should set up its own Civil War Centennial Commission, which would help stimulate local interest and involvement and in the process allow for a more thorough recreation of Civil War events in each state. The committee also pushed for the publication of a national series of official guides to the war that would focus on "topics that need to be investigated," including "prisoners of war."[4] Instead of avoiding the subject, the Civil War Centennial Commission declared that the horrors of Civil War prisons, now objectively reinterpreted to fit the needs of American consensus, merited inclusion in the celebration. With these national guidelines in mind, Georgia rushed to prepare for its role in the centennial.

Led by its first chairman, Peter Zack Geer, the Georgia Civil War Centennial Commission emphasized a "grass roots" approach to commemorating the war in Georgia that between 1961 and 1965 encouraged the retelling of "the thousands of true stories of heroism." In the process, Geer, the future lieutenant governor of Georgia, hoped that "each story will endear itself in the hearts and minds of every Georgian."[5] From the outset, Andersonville featured prominently as one of the most important of Georgia's Civil War sites, as the prison appeared in almost every catalog of crucial war locations compiled by various centennial committees.[6] The Georgia Civil War Centennial Education Committee organized a list of ways, including field trips, to involve the children of Georgia in the events so that they might learn, in keeping with the climate of patriotism, "the need for adjustment from the Old South to the New." The Education Committee's register of approved "educational field trips" rated Andersonville as the fourth most important site to visit, behind only the battlegrounds of Sherman's 1864 campaign for Atlanta.[7] Radio advertisements frequently mentioned the chance for Americans to come to Georgia during the centennial to visit not only Atlanta but Andersonville too.[8] Instead of demonstrating embarrassment over Andersonville's infamous past, the citizens of Georgia responded to the centennial commission's lead and welcomed the prospect of featuring the controversial prison site as a part of the commemoration.

Although sentiments of patriotism and education certainly fueled the embrace of Andersonville by Georgians during the centennial, some pragmatic observers believed that the success of the occasion and the effectiveness of the centennial committee would be best measured in dollars and cents. In 1959, Bill Corley, the commission's director of promotion, declared that "if we don't sell a dollar's worth of souvenirs to each tourist who comes into the state, we're missing an opportunity."[9] On July 23, 1960, Milt Berk of Business Boosters, Inc., solicited Geer, informing him of Business Boosters' ability to manufacture some "80,000" promotional items. Selling these "gimmicks" emblazoned with the logos of the various flags of the Confederacy would generate interest among collectors as well as advertise the events of the centennial.[10] Although the products of Business Boosters never received official sanction from Georgia governor S. Ernest Vandiver and the Georgia Civil War Centennial Commission, a host of souvenir items, including tumblers, ashtrays, flags, cufflinks, cigarette lighters, key rings, bags, and cushions appeared during the centennial.[11] Walt Barber, head of Walt Barber Advertising Specialties and adviser to the centennial commission, explained why so many types of products were necessary. Georgia "expects to bring forty or fifty million visitors to our state," he stated, and "the tourists will spend money—forty to fifty million on souvenirs alone."[12] Although few, if any, state-sponsored products specifically bore the name or image of Andersonville, the idea that the celebration's purpose centered as much on tourism and souvenir consumption as on the proper remembrance of history dominated Georgia's centennial proceedings and eventually made an impact on the residents of Andersonville.

Despite the clear emphasis of Governor Vandiver and the state officials in charge of the centennial on the importance of tourism and souvenir sales, some Georgians feared that their efforts were not enough to take full advantage of the once-in-a-lifetime opportunity to cash in on the Civil War. In an April 1960 editorial in the *Atlanta Constitution*, Cooper Smith worried that Georgia trailed her fellow southern states, particularly Virginia, in the preparations for the upcoming centennial. "Georgia has on the national dunce cap again," Smith wrote, referring to the perceived slow development of the plans for the centennial celebration. "Will somebody tell me," he asked, "why this state always has to bring up the cow's tail?"[13] Although his concerns accurately reflected the bottom line mentality with which many Georgians approached the centennial, Smith's worries proved groundless. On February 23, 1964, John Pennington, born and raised five miles from the town of Andersonville, acknowledged that, even though Andersonville remained "a monument to an unhappy fragment of our national past," the Civil War Centennial "has called new attention to it." "Twenty years ago," Pennington argued, Andersonville "had faded almost from memory."

Thanks to the centennial, and Kantor's novel before it, even the prison's location "off the beaten path" could not stop the "thousands of tourists" who
"manage to find it yearly."[14] The successful incorporation of Andersonville
into the centennial celebration as both educational subject and tourist attraction indicated that, while its infamy persisted, the site also piqued a
profitable curiosity about the difficult memory of Civil War prisons.

Although Andersonville found itself the best situated to play a central role in the Civil War Centennial commemorations, other Civil War
prison sites also served as locations for anniversary celebrations. On Memorial Day, 1961, the town of Elmira, where the most notorious of the Union
prison camps once stood, hosted a New York Civil War Centennial Commission function with the dual purpose of "honoring the dead of all wars"
and uniting America against "the communist menace." Again the backdrop
of the Cold War and the need to maintain patriotic solidarity against the
Soviet threat provided strong incentive for Americans to celebrate the Civil
War as the story of how sectional division became national unity. In keeping with that message, one member of the New York commission, Wilbur
Glover, gave a speech in which he offered the standard objective consensus
memory of Civil War prisons. "In this year of 1961, we realize that savage as
the war became, later accounts have exaggerated the cruelties somewhat."
But today, "we recognize that Northern prisons—as well as Southern—left
much to be desired."[15] Tributes to prisoners also extended beyond the actual
prison sites of Andersonville and Elmira. In late 1963, the Centennial Center in Richmond, Virginia, opened an exhibit titled "The Civil War Prisoner," which featured some of the remains of the well-traveled Libby Prison
and artwork depicting "the capture and treatment of prisoners," "prison life,"
"prisoner exchange," and "retaliation and atrocity."[16] The theme of national-
istic unity dominated the Andersonville, Elmira, and Richmond centennial
activities and showed how thoroughly the objective memory of the once divisive subject of Civil War prisons had been reinforced by the environment
of Cold War patriotism.

Along with the increasing visits to the actual prison sites, the centennial also inspired a surge in the number of publications devoted to the subject of Civil War prisons. People who could not travel to Andersonville or
other prison locations could at least read about what took place there. Between 1961 and 1965, books about Civil War prisons generally took one of
two forms: official state centennial commission–sponsored histories of the

war, including prisons, or new editions of previously printed or unpublished prisoner accounts.[17] Both sources confirmed the dominance of the objective memory of the prisons, and the ready availability of these volumes testified to the centennial's ability to generate interest in Civil War prisons among the general public. And the success of the magazine *Civil War Times Illustrated* (*CWTI*), which made its debut in 1962 and remains in publication today, proved that stories about the Civil War, and prisoners of war in particular, still captivated and entertained audiences. From its inception, *CWTI* frequently ran excerpts of primary source material recorded by Union and Confederate soldiers. Previously unpublished prisoner accounts consistently appeared in the magazine over the years, beginning with the April 1962 debut issue's inclusion of "The Amazing Story of Pvt. Joe Shewmon," an article that recounted the horrors of Andersonville.[18] With an incredible variety of unpublished prison sources to choose from, the current editors of the magazine continue to print prison materials to satisfy the continued fascination of contemporary readers, a practice supplemented by occasional articles about the various prison camps.[19]

By including Civil War prisons in the national story of the larger war, the Civil War Centennial Commissions, on both the national and the state level, encouraged Americans to revisit the controversial issue of the treatment of prisoners as part of a positive celebration rather than as a reason for discord. Although the centennial presentations of Civil War prisons broke no new scholarly ground, the festivities exposed many Americans to the arguments of Hesseltine, Kantor, and Levitt for the first time. In the context of American patriotism and heritage, at the moment when the Cold War threat of communism peaked, the early 1960s, the national commemoration helped the objective memory of Civil War prisons gain further acceptance. Of course, the atmosphere of consensus among white Americans depended, as always before when remembering the prison controversy, on the avoidance of the connection between the fight for racial justice and Civil War prisons. Only when stripped of their accusative power to remind Americans of both their destructive nature and the subsequent failure to honor the full meaning of freedom central to the conflict could Civil War prisons be successfully transformed into profitable symbols of nationalism. Meanwhile, the aggressive marketing tactics of the various centennial commissions in fusing historical interpretation, tourism, souvenirs, and education set a precedent. After 1965, in order to take advantage of the ongoing public

interest in the subject of the Civil War and its prisons, efforts to commemorate the sacrifices of the dead prisoners increasingly combined with the
industry of tourism. Residents of Andersonville provided the foremost example of the business of remembering Civil War prisons, as the town embraced the commercial strategy of selling its past to a curious public.

Seeking to capitalize on the positive attention created during the Civil
War Centennial, the town of Andersonville, which sits directly across Highway 49 from the national park, started to openly embrace the stigma of its
past for the first time since the erection of the Wirz monument in 1909.
The appearance of scholar Ovid Futch's 1968 *History of Andersonville Prison,*
the first objective treatment focused solely on the prison and its infamous
past, confirmed that the animosity inspired by the prison was fading.[20] But
Andersonville's remarkable transformation really began when the Mullite
Company commenced mining operations just outside town that same year.
Taking advantage of the rich deposits of bauxite and kaolin, two crucial in-
gredients in the production of steel, many Andersonville residents took jobs
at the plant, and the town's economy boomed.[21] The infusion of mining dollars into Andersonville's coffers brought with it an important change. The
once predominantly agricultural town, despite its small population of approximately 300 inhabitants, started to accumulate disposable income—and
at this moment, local Georgians began to plan for an even brighter economic future.

In the early 1970s, Bobby L. Lowe, the executive director of the Middle
Flint Area Planning Commission and resident of nearby Ellaville, Georgia,
oversaw a scheme to capitalize on the historical notoriety of Andersonville
and in the process boost the economies of the surrounding towns as well.
The challenge lay in properly using the potential benefits of Interstate 75,
which ushered traffic just to the east of Andersonville and the surrounding region. Lowe believed that in order to lure tourists off the interstate
into the "real Georgia," the communities of southwest Georgia, the local
towns needed to unite their efforts.[22] Thus the idea of "The Andersonville
Trail" was born—a tourism campaign that cobbled together the historical
resources of Americus, Andersonville, and several other Georgia towns. By
linking these various historical sites, Lowe hoped to transform a once isolated area into what he in 1976 referred to as "a unique stop for interstate
travelers."[23] His decision to center the trail on Andersonville made sense
in light of the more positive objective memory of the prison so apparent

during the centennial commemorations and the lesson that the shame of the past could yield commercial benefits in the present.

Quickly embracing Lowe's ideas, the newly prosperous citizens of Andersonville, led by their mayor, Mullite Company executive Lewis Easterlin, developed an all-out marketing strategy in the early 1970s. In 1973, residents of the town formed the Andersonville Guild. The organization intended to turn "back the clock in Andersonville to make the town look much as it did in Civil War days."[24] If tourists traveled off the beaten path to revisit the controversy of the Civil War, Andersonville intended to give them what they expected to see. Flush with mining dollars, the guild put that money to work. Its early activities included moving an old log-cabin church from the outskirts of town into the downtown and installing an old railroad depot as the town's official information center.[25] By 1975, Easterlin and his guild supporters embarked on an even grander plan to increase Andersonville's tourist appeal with the proposal of the "Andersonville Mall." At an estimated cost of nearly $250,000, the initiative called for the sweeping redesign of downtown Andersonville. Containing shops, landscaping, and pedestrian walkways, along with ample parking, the mall, according to the town boosters, would entice tourists who visited the actual prison site on the other side of the highway to spend time and dollars in an authentic Civil War–era town.[26] The Wirz monument provided the main attraction as the literally central feature of the mall, given its location in the middle of the town square.

With the reconstruction of the town underway, and the Andersonville Trail drawing curious motorists off the interstate, the residents of Andersonville realized the need for an annual event to increase further the town's desirability as a tourist destination. In October 1976, the first annual Andersonville Historic Fair drew a crowd to the small village. The festivities included a parade led by Georgia lieutenant governor Zell Miller, who insisted on riding his own horse in the procession, and a performance of Saul Levitt's *The Andersonville Trial,* staged across Highway 49 at the national park.[27] Throughout the late 1970s and 1980s, to the delight of Easterlin and the guild, the fair brought thousands of participants to Andersonville each October. Over time, besides the traditional parade and play, the celebration expanded to include an outdoor flea market, bands, beauty queens, Civil War reenacting, magic shows, clogging, puppet shows, and, in 1985, "a circuit-riding preacher who arrived on horseback."[28] For all the entertainment the visitors enjoyed, however, the real magic trick involved the transformation of Andersonville's image. Although Easterlin and the Andersonville Guild used the infamy of the town to attract visitors, the general festivities that took place at the historic fair often had little or nothing to do with Andersonville's history. But as the word spread of the charming hospitality of the town, newspaper and magazine articles appeared praising the town's attempts "to shed its old image."[29] So thorough was the transformation that, according to one reporter, the "old Andersonville" and its "shackles of shame" had disappeared.[30]

The success of the Andersonville Historic Fair, followed by the creation of the Andersonville Antiques Fair each Memorial Day, testified to the profitability of Andersonville's public relations campaign. And the welcome publicity that accompanied Jimmy Carter's rise to the presidency of the United States from Plains, Georgia—located, like Andersonville, in Sumter County—only added to the growth of tourism along the Andersonville Trail. All the while, the marketing strategy devised by the Andersonville Guild of presenting their town not as the site of atrocity but instead as simply a Civil War village remained effective. Today, shops, museums, a bed and breakfast, and a restaurant still cater to the tens of thousands of tourists who descend on the community each year. Pens, postcards, pamphlets, and pins are just a few of the various Civil War memorabilia available for purchase at the town's gift shops. At the entrance to the town, a billboard welcomes visitors to "Andersonville, Civil War Village," while over in the town square, a short distance from the Wirz monument, sits a covered wagon with an identical message. By camouflaging Andersonville's specifically notorious past with a general presentation of Civil War period history, the opportune calculations of residents like Peggy Sheppard, Andersonville Guild member, town historian, and author of *Andersonville, USA*, continue to pay off. "I figured it was better to take advantage of outsiders' curiosity," Sheppard explained to one reporter, "than to resent it."[31]

The efforts made by Sheppard and the Andersonville Guild to employ pragmatically Andersonville's history as heritage were undeniably effective and, based on the financial results, intelligent. But as historian David Lowenthal eloquently argues, heritage can be both "good and evil."[32] The "good" behind Andersonville's choice to celebrate the entertaining aspects of its past is obvious. "We had to do something or disappear," Mayor Easterlin explained in 1983; "you've got to take what you got and use it. We had history. And if somebody doesn't preserve history, it's gone."[33] Any shame connected with the town's infamous past has nothing to do with the current residents, who do not—and should not be expected to—continuously apologize for the sins committed there during the Civil War. And the use of heritage to inspire new traditions, such as the Andersonville Historic Fair, ensures that the bonds of community remain intact from generation to generation. The ability of heritage to provide a comforting sense of both personal and communal identity explains much of its attraction.

But the "evil" must be recognized as well. The selective manipulation of the past, especially in the name of tradition, is, by its nature, exclusionary. The choice to revive the history of the Civil War, even in a generalized form, also indicated that race motivated Andersonville's transformation—Andersonville's makeover was in part a response to the social turmoil of the South during the era of the Civil Rights Movement. Despite Andersonville's small population, its racial diversity—approximately two-thirds white and one-third African American—meant that the reinvention of Andersonville served not only a financial but social purpose. The words and phrases Easterlin used to explain Andersonville's preservation ("we," "disappear," "it's gone") also applied to the common human need to protect preferred constructs of identity. Easterlin, Sheppard, and the Andersonville Guild members were white, and by taking active roles as town boosters, white Andersonville residents maintained political power and the accustomed social order. Thus, the seductive veneer of Civil War nostalgia not only generated profits but reaffirmed, in subtle but unmistakable terms, the intentional embrace of Confederate heritage as an important Andersonville tradition.

As a result, Andersonville, the home of the Wirz monument, also served as a central attraction for diehard pro-Confederate supporters of Wirz. The successful rehabilitation of Andersonville's reputation by the 1970s ironically also helped revive, on a limited scale, the flagging interest of white southerners who clung to the old southern defensive memory of Civil War prisons. Once again Wirz became heralded as a martyr to the Confederate cause. In the late 1970s, the Sons of Confederate Veterans and the United Daughters of the Confederacy began co-sponsoring annual November memorial services to commemorate Wirz's execution in 1865. This phase of devotion to the tattered shreds of Lost Cause mythology, at least pertaining to Wirz and Andersonville, peaked in the mid-1980s. In 1981, the SCV awarded Wirz the Confederate Medal of Honor. And in 1984, a speech praising Wirz—who chose "death over betrayal," making him a worthy symbol of Confederate heritage—given by Georgia's former governor Lester Maddox, himself a symbol of segregation, highlighted the event. The opportunity to confirm southernness by celebrating Wirz attracted white southerners who sought to assert the legitimacy of their heritage in a difficult era of turbulent race relations and political transition. The ritual celebration of Confederate mythology offered a reconfirmation of the traditional racial identities of the past. It was not coincidence that in the same speech in which Maddox, never one to shy away from controversy, portrayed Wirz as a symbol of southern virtue, he also took a thinly veiled shot at African Americans, criticizing welfare recipients as "bums and parasites."[34] Such sentiments were also apparent in the 1985 speech given by Lynn Shaw, the commander-in-chief of the SCV, at the Wirz memorial event. "Southerners today," Shaw lamented, "have lost sight of the contributions made by Southern men in the founding of our country before and after the War Between the States."[35] At a time when the South received so much negative attention, the positive atmosphere created by the combination of thousands of tourists and the congratulatory press coverage offered hope to Shaw, Maddox, and others that Andersonville, Wirz, and therefore the South as well, need apologize no longer for the southern past. Newspaper accounts of 1980s Wirz memorial ceremonies revealed that these events drew up to 200 attendees and culminated each year with a group of Confederate re-enactors who fired a volley in Wirz's memory.[36] But even the revived interest in the injustice done to Wirz soon declined. By the time Tony Horwitz, whose description of one of these memorial programs appears in *Confederates in the Attic,* attended the event in the mid-1990s, only forty "neo-Confederates" showed up to protect the "memory of the Confederacy and of hero-martyrs like Henry Wirz."[37]

The persistence of the small band of Wirz supporters—and the complex meaning(s) of heritage at Andersonville—reveals the ongoing paradox that many contemporary white southerners face as new generations, each more divorced from the actual events, come to terms with the embedded memories of the Civil War and its prisons. Although Andersonville residents like Sheppard continue to defend Wirz's innocence, the financial interest of the town depends on a muted portrayal of the prison controversy. The resulting presentation of the town's history is artificial, but understandably so. Today's

Andersonville residents have little or no personal connection to the horrors of 1864 except to recognize that that history represents a viable commercial asset. The community benefits far more from the yearly visits of the tens of thousands of casually interested tourists, many of whom know nothing about what happened at Andersonville Prison and have little personal stake in dwelling on the old wounds, than from the gatherings of the pro-Confederate diehards. For most participants in the Historic Fair, enjoyment of the rustic Civil War town's appearance is all that matters. While the reputation of Andersonville sparks interest, the design of the town and its annual celebrations acknowledges the controversy but refuses to risk alienating potential visitors. Andersonville thus offers its history on two levels—the general ambiance of the Civil War era, intended to charm the crowds of infrequent tourists, and the opportunity to learn of Wirz's unjust execution, targeted at southerners more deeply interested in the subject of Civil War prisons. Andersonville introduces many visitors to the controversy over Civil War prisons but, upon arrival, those same tourists encounter an idealized rather than actual history. As the emphasis on general ambiance continues, the influence and numbers of Wirz supporters correspondingly decline. Although a few white southerners cling to the heritage of their Confederate ancestors and make their token appearance to honor Wirz every November, the waning intensity of the devotion suggests that memories of Civil War prisons now provoke mere curiosity instead of inspiring cause.

Through the formalized nature of their tribute, white Andersonville residents and Wirz defenders also indicate the diluted power of Confederate heritage in the contemporary South. The sense of urgency and the need to protect southern honor that once inspired the pen of Jefferson Davis or even Mildred Rutherford dissipated long ago. Although the declining intensity of the sectional bitterness emerged as a natural consequence of the passage of time, the commercialization of the prison controversy also explains why the pro-Confederate voices of today lack the conviction of the past. While contemporary publications outlining the old southern deflective memory of Civil War prisons still appear, the old goal, to present true history and convert new disciples, has faded. Articles in *Blue and Gray* and the *United Daughters of the Confederacy Magazine,* or in books like *Andersonville: The Southern Perspective,* seem calculated for a core audience already initiated into the circle of southern apologists.[38] Current devotees who remember their Confederate heritage expect a little protest against the injustices of history, not because they still believe that the South will rise at any moment, but because previous generations of white southerners fought the same rhetorical war as well. Flashing the scars of defeat, in contrast to the disappearance of the old northern divisive memory in recent years, keeps a fading identity alive. While northerners, who, as the victors, can afford to relinquish their virtuous memory of the prison controversy, Confederate heritage groups cannot because the stain of defeat, and years of accusations concerning Civil War prisons, still require refutation. As a result, the halfhearted recycling of bitter memories reflects a sense of obligation to the past rather than actual optimism that Wirz or the Confederacy will at this late date find their reputations restored. The personal stake in the past that once infused the Lost Cause with energy has been replaced by attempts to cash in on its corpse. As long as a few white southerners continue to show up in Andersonville each November, subscribe to Civil War magazines, and buy copies of pro-Confederate books, the defense of Wirz and the Confederate prison system will persist—not, as many insist, out of a devotion to history but rather because of the opportunity of profit and the stubbornness of identity that derives from memory.

But the final, and perhaps most compelling, reason for the declining support among white southerners for the defense of Wirz and the Confederate prison system hinges on the fact that the traditional sectional memories, at least in the perception of most observers of Civil War prisons, seem increasingly superfluous in light of the ever-growing acceptance of the objective interpretation of the prison controversy. Over the last few decades, an avalanche of printed materials have appeared in response to the challenge of meeting "the need," in the phrase of historians James M. McPherson and William J. Cooper, Jr., for a deeper understanding of Civil War prisons. Built on the edifice of the objective approach of Hesseltine, these studies collectively reinforce the idea that the story of Civil War prisons was a national tragedy with roots in both the Union and Confederacy and, in the process, drown out the voices of southern protesters.[39]

In the early 1960s, two works in particular reinforced the prevailing objective memory of Civil War prisons. The first was the 1961 edition of James G. Randall and David Donald's *The Civil War and Reconstruction*. The second was a 1962 issue of *Civil War History*, guest edited by Hesseltine, devoted entirely to the prison controversy. "The fair-minded observer," according to Randall and Donald, "will be likely to discountenance any sweeping reproach by one side upon the other." "Whatever be the message of the dead at Andersonville and Rock Island," they concluded, "that message is not to be read as a mandate for the perpetuation of sectional blame and censure."[40] And while Hesseltine acknowledged "that the custodians were hardly a loveable lot" and deserved the criticism they received, he also declared that the prison controversy revealed "that the atrocities of the prison camps were only phases of the greater atrocity of war itself."[41] The real point of studying Civil War prisons, these scholars concluded, was that it was less critical to measure the exact amounts of sectional responsibility, as had been the goal for so many decades after the war, than to push instead for a recognition of the horrors of modern war to ensure that history would not repeat itself in the future. By 1988, when James M. McPherson published his bestselling *Battle Cry of Freedom*, the idea that responsibility was even worth arguing seemed increasingly outdated. "The treatment of prisoners during the Civil War," McPherson stated, "was something that neither side could be proud of."[42] Left unsaid, but strongly implied, was an acceptance that modern war, and not individual human choices and actions, inevitably caused such disasters.

Other historians, most notably Reid Mitchell, turned to a comparative methodology in their investigation of Civil War prisons with the specific hope of answering the destructive questions posed by modern war. In a 1997 essay published in *On the Road to Total War: The American Civil War and the German Wars of Unification, 1861–1871*, Mitchell commented on the inherent difficulty of placing the atrocities of any war in proper perspective. "The relationship of Civil War prisons to the evolution of total war is a historical problem," Mitchell argued, a conundrum complicated by his belief that "the concept of total war itself is problematic." After all, he asked, "where do we look for our model of total war?" Identifying the Civil War as a total war and equating Andersonville and Elmira with the Holocaust or the Bataan Death March, in Mitchell's opinion, "trivializes the horrors that the twentieth century concocted." Despite the inherent uncertainties and value judgments that inevitably color historical analysis of cruelties committed in any war, one truism, according to Mitchell, remained constant. "Modern wars," he concluded, "are detestably cruel to prisoners."[43] On that point at least, no matter the difference of opinion as to which historical atrocities represent the nadir of modern civilization, few could disagree.

Mitchell's attempt to reconcile the atrocities of Civil War prisons with those committed in World War II followed a tradition that dated to James Bonner, MacKinlay Kantor, and Saul Levitt. But by the 1970s, the controversy over the Vietnam War and how its prisoners of war fared provided scholars with yet another comparative model. In 1974, the Institute for World Order, an international organization devoted to world peace, released *War Criminals, War Victims: Andersonville, Nuremberg, Hiroshima, My Lai*. As part of a series of books called "Crises in World Order," *War Criminals, War Victims* presented the view that these four symbols of the destructive nature of modern warfare shared common origins. The juxtaposition of these four case studies of atrocity was intentionally calculated to force readers to address what the editors called the "central" question provoked by the recurrence of atrocities with each successive modern war. Their assessment of the relationship between "law," "morality," and "individual conscience" and how those abstract concepts applied to the problem of "individual responsibility in time of war" anticipated Mitchell's findings. The most troubling aspect about the stubborn appearance of atrocities over the course of a century involved humanity's inability (or unwillingness) to learn from the miseries of past conflicts. When Lieutenant William Calley stated, "I am hopeful that My Lai will bring the meaning of war to the surface not only to our nation but to all nations," the irony lay in the fact that if the knowledge of the horrors of Andersonville, the Holocaust, and Hiroshima combined failed to drive home "the meaning of war," discussion of the My Lai massacre had little chance to accomplish that idealistic goal.[44]

For historians Eric T. Dean and Robert C. Doyle, Vietnam also served as a lens through which to better understand the nature of the prisoner-of-war experience in all modern wars. Dean's *Shook over Hell: Post-Traumatic Stress, Vietnam, and the Civil War* focused on the effects of combat on soldiers in both wars and argued that Civil War prisoners exhibited similar symptoms to those of Vietnam veterans in their postwar lives.[45] Doyle's *Voices from Captivity* examined the remarkable consistency of prisoner-of-war accounts regardless of the conflict they described. "Although the technology of warfare has changed," Doyle pointed out, "the fearful horrors of captivity have not." The common themes of food, escape, boredom, exchange, or release dominated prisoner narratives regardless of the particular war.[46] By echoing Hesseltine's statement of "the greater atrocity of war itself," Doyle thus simultaneously confirmed the objective interpretation of Civil War prisons as well as the unsettling suspicions of Dean, Mitchell, and the Institute of World Order that the cycle of atrocity might be endless. Such sentiments made sense in the depressing aftermath of the

Vietnam War and showed why an understanding of Civil War prisons remained important—remembering that such atrocities occurred in the Civil War was useful in a time of questioning America's national character, as the persistence of similar atrocities throughout the twentieth century revealed that our sense of morality had not improved.

But for all the continued attention paid to Civil War prisons by professional scholars over the last few decades, with objectivity secured and responsibility evenly dispersed, once again the sanitized memories of the wartime prisons surfaced most frequently, and profitably, in popular culture.[47] Amateur historians in particular, drawn to the subject by the dramatic tales of suffering, responded to a gap in the historiography of Civil War prisons by publishing histories of the specific events that transpired at almost every individual prison camp during the war. A glance at such titles as *Andersonville: The Last Depot* and *To Die in Chicago* shows the purpose of many of these scholars.[48] These works were not monolithic in their intent. Some authors, like Michael Horigan, author of *Elmira: Death Camp of the North,* revived the old southern deflective accusations of deliberate northern cruelty, while Benton McAdams's *Rebels at Rock Island* depicted Rock Island, in keeping with the objective tradition, as a place merely typical of the cruelties of war. But the overall trend of these prison histories was clear. The objective removal of responsibility for the suffering exhaustively detailed in these accounts encouraged these repetitive depictions of human misery. A similar motivation appeared in the work of Lonnie Speer, whose 1997 *Portals to Hell* marked the first attempt at a full overview of Civil War prisons since the 1930s. The reason that so much time passed between Hesseltine's and Speer's work manifests itself in how completely Speer accepted his predecessor's objective interpretation. The singular strength of Speer's book lay in its attention to detail—whereas Hesseltine's 1930 *Civil War Prisons* explained the story of what happened in the prison controversy, Speer provides a summary of each individual prison and what took place inside its walls.[49] Although these works together produce a more complete depiction of the Civil War prison experience, their common argument that the fortunes of war doomed Civil War prisoners to their fate solidified the already dominant objective appraisal.

At the beginning of the twenty-first century, some authors make even less of an attempt to hide their hopes of cashing in on the desire to remember Civil War prisons. Books like *Best Little Stories from the Civil War, The*

Amazing Civil War and *Blood: Stories of Life and Death from the Civil War*
contain sensationalistic excerpts of prisoner suffering or great escapes de-
void of any historical context.[50] Although they offer no interpretation of
substance, such opportunism testifies to the ongoing financial profitability
of the Civil War legacy. Crass profiteering aside, the booming interest in
Civil War prisons among amateur historians also influences contemporary
regimental and state histories, as well as more general studies of soldiering
during the Civil War.[51] The cumulative impact of these efforts to apply the
objective memory of Civil War prisons in discussions of individual prisons,
prisoners, regiments, states, or Civil War soldiers in general adds an important dimension to the understanding of the subject. As these histories pile
up, they represent a growing recognition of the centrality of the prison experience to the overall story of the Civil War and collectively cement the
widespread acceptance of the prisons as a product of national rather than
sectional responsibility.

With the shift in contemporary interest away from exploring the apparently resolved question of responsibility in favor of investigating the daily
reality of being imprisoned, Civil War prisoner accounts also returned to
the spotlight and the cottage industry of reprinting these memoirs resumed.
One critical difference, however, distinguished the volumes of post-1960s
prisoner narratives from past editions. When first published between the
1860s and 1930s, the accounts, almost always dominated by divisive memory,
represented an obvious attempt to add evidence to one side or the other of
the debate over whether the Union or Confederacy bore more responsibility for or committed greater crimes in Civil War prisons. Today, whether
in new editions of old accounts or previously unprinted diaries or memoirs, editors now justify the recycling of these arguments with claims of
their redeeming educational or entertaining qualities. According to editor
Steve Meyer, the 1995 version of Benjamin Booth's *Dark Days of the Rebellion,* originally published in 1897, instead of inciting sectional discord, provides a "microcosm of the great conflict which refined and defined our great
nation during its trial from 1861 to 1865."[52] Newcomers to the 1998 copy of
J. V. Hadley's *Seven Months a Prisoner,* which dated to 1898, were encouraged by editor Libbe Hughes to enjoy "a story of imprisonment and escape,
adventure and suspense."[53] Through these introductions, editors of prison
narratives downplay the sectional hatred inspired by memories of the war
and attempt to divorce these accounts from their original, now unseemly

theme that Yankees or Rebels intentionally committed atrocities. To appeal to an audience that often views the Civil War as a fascinating story and the Union and Confederacy as quintessential American protagonists, the calculated goal of softening the strident rhetoric of the prison accounts ensures a wider audience. The irony is that the same accusations that once perpetuated sectional division while turning a profit now serve the cause of reconciliation even as the quest to cash in on the prison controversy continues. The popularity of current editions of prison narratives depends more on being a good yarn than a window into the angry emotions stirred by memories of the real war.

But as the example of the overt commercialization of the town of Andersonville indicates, history often is not left to historians, either professional or amateur. Contemporary conceptions of Civil War prisons are shaped as much if not more by movies, novels, and even folk rock songs as the industry of American popular culture continues to churn out prison-related products.[54] As the 2008 appearance of actor Gene Hackman's novel *Escape from Andersonville* reveals, even 150 years after these tragic events it seems that we are no nearer to escaping from the constant presence of Civil War prisons as commodity.[55] One of the best examples of the resulting incongruities that occur when history and popular culture collide involved the 1996 TNT movie *Andersonville*. Intended as homage to the sufferings of the prisoners, *Andersonville* focused on the deprivation of the Union POWs who maintain an unbroken spirit despite facing constant misery and death. The Wirz depicted in the movie resembles the old caricature, a less-than-human figure ultimately responsible for the thousands of fatalities as he berates helpless prisoners and callously disregards men dying in his stocks. During the final scene, a camera slowly pans backward to reveal the 13,000 white headstones that mark the national cemetery. As the screen fades to black, the final words pronounce the familiar judgment of Wirz: "After the war, Wirz was hanged, the only soldier to be tried and executed for war crimes committed during the civil war."[56] But the central concept behind the movie was not to revive the old demonized image of Wirz. Instead *Andersonville,* like all forms of popular culture, simply played on the stereotypes available to it—in this case the infamous reputation of Wirz and Andersonville—in order to be easily digested by the public. And while Andersonville remains the only Civil War prison deemed worthy of its own movie, a portrayal of Elmira as "hell" appeared in a brief scene in the 1982 miniseries *The Blue and the Gray.*[57] These visual depictions of Union and Confederate prisoners and the hardships they endured do not, nor do they intend to, challenge the dominance of objective memory. Instead, they exist as products designed to appeal to the timeless desire to reflect on the horrors of war. There is—and always will be—a grim fascination with the misery inflicted by fate on others and not on ourselves. Confirmation of the dread symbolic power that the name of Andersonville still conjures up comes from author Sarah Vowell, who wrote in 2002's *The Partly Cloudy Patriot*, "In my self-help universe, when things go wrong I whisper mantras to myself, mantras like 'Andersonville.'" "Andersonville,'" she explained, "is a code word for 'you could be one of the prisoners of war dying of disease and malnutrition in the worst Confederate prison, so just calm down about the movie you wanted to go to being sold out.'"[58] Whether we derive entertainment from the memories of Civil War prisons, or like Vowell, use them to remind ourselves of our good fortune, their relevance compels us to inquire about, and thus consume, those remembrances.

The fact that we cannot escape from the subject of Civil War prisons should not be construed as entirely negative. It is clear that neither the divisive nor objective memories of the prison controversy—the emancipationist memory, as connected to prisons, remains largely ignored—satisfy our need to better comprehend the wartime prisons. Even the white noise created by the proliferation and consumption of prison materials in the name of profit cannot prevent the eventual emergence of new strands of prison memory. There are signs, most notably the recent work of historians Charles Sanders, Jr., whose *While in the Hands of the Enemy: Military Prisons of the Civil War* is an unflinching look at the immoral choices made by the officials who operated the Union and Confederate prison systems, and James Gillispie, whose *Andersonvilles of the North: The Myths and Realities of Northern Treatment of Civil War Confederate Prisoners* details the unavoidable impact of disease on Civil War prisoners, that the long obfuscation of the reality of Civil War prisons may no longer satisfy the cultural needs of America. Although Sanders and Gillispie disagree in their emphasis—Sanders prefers to focus on the moral questions raised by the deliberate manipulation of Civil War prisoners according to political convenience, while Gillispie confronts the reality of how those prisoners died—they share a common desire to challenge the pervasive myths deeply rooted in the American memory of the prison controversy. Perhaps the yearning to more honestly and accurately assess the prison tragedy may yet lead to a more precise, fuller understanding of the elusive questions of responsibility for the failures of the past.[59] But there is also the danger that Americans, in learning of the brutality inflicted on Civil War prisoners, may continue to favor the seductive blamelessness of objective memory and categorize such cruelties as further evidence of equalized, and therefore meaningless, guilt. The pattern of avoidance and the preference for more comforting interpretations will be difficult to break.

Along with the tentative steps to more accurately reassess the problem of responsibility, the persistence in popular culture of the perception of Andersonville as a place of exceptional cruelty indicates that the memory of Civil War prisons, despite the widespread acceptance of the objective interpretation, is still contested even in the early twenty-first century. But the terms of the contest have not changed. The malleable nature of Civil War prison memory ensures that it serves, as it always has before, the interests of those who manipulate it in the name of inspiring patriotism, promoting tourism, rallying Confederate heritage, exploring the meaning of history, seeking the essence of modern war, or simply cashing in on various products. The enduring fascination with the horrors of Civil War prisons has and will continue to spread, promulgated by its commercialization and the resulting unsatisfied itch of curiosity, because we are convinced that there remains a useful lesson in the story, if it is possible to learn.

"The Task of History Is Never Done"

ANDERSONVILLE NATIONAL HISTORIC SITE, THE NATIONAL POW
MUSEUM, AND THE TRIUMPH OF PATRIOTIC MEMORY

A
s a result of its brief but devastating existence during the Civil
War, Andersonville became and remains a term synonymous
with atrocity. Despite the emergence of the objective memory of
Civil War prisons during the twentieth century, the stigma of past bitterness refuses to fade completely. The focal point of that remaining acrimony,
the ground zero of Civil War prisons, is located at the same spot as in
1865—Andersonville National Cemetery, resting place for 13,000 dead prisoners, and the adjacent prison grounds. Throughout the years Andersonville
became increasingly and naturally central in the public perception of Civil
War prisons for several reasons. Its casualties represented nearly one-fourth
of all the prisoners who died in the Civil War, and its 29-percent mortality
rate made it the deadliest prison on a comparative basis as well. The execution of Henry Wirz as solely responsible for the camp's deplorable conditions further marked Andersonville as the singularly important Civil War
prison. While survivors of other prison facilities wrote memoirs and discussed the horrors they experienced, as the largest prison Andersonville
inspired the most narratives and monuments, including the controversial
Wirz memorial. Artists and writers from Thomas Nast to MacKinlay Kantor exploited and explored the image of Andersonville as the primary symbol of Civil War prisons. Andersonville also claimed one other advantage in
the postwar contest for public attention—as a result of the federal government's establishment of Andersonville National Cemetery in 1865 and assumption of ownership of the prison grounds in 1910, by the late twentieth
century it was the only major Civil War prison site left largely intact.

Across Highway 49, the town of Andersonville attempted to shed the
guilt of the past and embraced the commercial possibilities of remembering,

in calculated form, its Civil War history. The care of the actual location where some of the worst Civil War atrocities occurred, however, required a more delicate touch.[1] In the last half of the twentieth century, the national government, after years of passive oversight, became interested in developing the Andersonville site. Along with the process of preservation came the recognition that success in this undertaking depended on the creation of a usable interpretation out of the contested memories of Andersonville.

Between 1910, when the national government accepted stewardship of the Andersonville prison grounds from the Women's Relief Corps, and the late 1950s, a calm settled over the location as the number of visitors and public interest in Civil War prisons waned.[2] Under the management of the Army, the minimal preservation efforts at Andersonville Prison Park and the national cemetery reflected not only the declining interest in the site after the deaths of both Civil War veterans and those who most staunchly vied to remember correctly the history of Civil War prisons but also the government's willingness to allow the once intense controversy over the sensitive subject to fade. With the exception of the efforts of Civilian Conservation Corps laborers during the 1930s, improvements took place only sporadically. But the peace and quiet at Andersonville dissipated with the 1955 publication of MacKinlay Kantor's *Andersonville*. By the late 1950s tourists started to overwhelm the limited Army staff, and the Civil War Centennial celebrations only heightened the curiosity about Andersonville. As early as 1959, Army officials recognized the impracticability of the current state of affairs and let it be known that "the operation and maintenance of the park" had become burdensome.[3]

As rumors of Andersonville's uncertain future swirled in the early 1960s, the question of what would happen to the site became paramount. With the growing acceptance of the objective memory of Civil War prisons and the rising tourist interest sparked by the combination of Kantor's novel and the Civil War Centennial, some Georgians saw dollar signs when they looked at the prison and began a campaign for "a properly developed and promoted Andersonville historical complex."[4] In early 1966, Georgia senator Richard B. Russell arranged a meeting between prominent Georgian supporters of the idea and Secretary of the Interior Stewart Udall. Along with Georgia's other senator, Herman Talmadge, state senator Jimmy Carter—the chairman of the West Central Georgia Area Planning and Development Commission—led the delegation, which requested Udall's support for a proposed "national historical memorial on the site of the Confeder-ate prison near Andersonville, Ga." Carter took pains to assure Udall that Georgians had no intent "to reconstruct a one-sided version of what took place at Andersonville" but rather preferred to focus on the "national sig-nificance" of Andersonville "as part of the nation's history." Udall, although noncommittal, indicated that the concept intrigued him. "I like the idea," Udall declared, because "that is the story of life." "History," he stated, "con-tains many things that are pleasant and unpleasant."[5] The meeting of these officials marked the beginning of the campaign to transform Anderson-ville into a national park. If properly presented, the history of Anderson-ville promised not only financial benefits but a chance to further defuse the sectional animosities of the past and, unfortunately, present. In the recent climate of the Civil Rights Movement, which once again pitted the South against the rest of the nation, the opportunity to recast a symbol of sec-tional bitterness as a healing memorial to all prisoners of war (one that, not coincidentally, avoided the peculiar and potentially inflammatory racial di-mensions of Civil War prisons) made both business and political sense. By the fall of 1966, a National Park Service planning study expressed increasing interest in assuming control of Andersonville and its unique legacy. "Since many people tend to think of the Civil War in terms of gallant charges and nostalgic battle songs, it is," the report concluded, "perhaps appropriate that they have an opportunity to see a side of the War that was only too familiar to the men who fought in it."[6]

Although many Georgians and National Park Service members saw the possibilities of Andersonville, the transition of the grounds from the De-partment of Defense to the Department of the Interior was no "easy task" because the creation of a national park required congressional approval.[7] In September 1970, Georgia congressman Jack Brinkley, sponsor of the bill to safeguard the prison location as a national park, addressed the House of Representatives to explain why the creation of an Andersonville National Historic Site was necessary. Andersonville "is the only Civil War prison site in the Nation physically in existence and still untouched by urban growth," Brinkley stated, and therefore its preservation was vital. But if the impor-tance of history failed to rally supporters to the cause, Brinkley also re-minded listeners that, as "an outstanding point of interest," Andersonville "will attract many, many thousands of visitors each year."[8]

Brinkley's persuasive case aside, an understated but critical source of motivation for the establishment of the Andersonville National Historic Site came from the contemporary events taking place in Vietnam. On October 7, 1970, the day the Senate passed Brinkley's bill, the Senate placed into the official record an excerpt from a statement advocating adoption of the measure. Not only would the creation of Andersonville National Historic Site pay tribute to the "painful sacrifices of those who preceded us," the report declared, but Andersonville would also serve "as a memorial" to "all Americans who have served their country, at home and abroad, and suffered the loneliness and anguish of captivity. It is the undaunted spirit of men such as these that keeps America the Nation that it is." The harsh lessons being learned once again in Vietnam about the suffering of prisoners of war prompted the Senate's understanding of Andersonville as an important opportunity to recognize permanently the "grim" reality of the "story of captivity."[9] Although Vietnam never received explicit mention, the universal language with which the Senate discussed the bill clearly reflected the impact of that terrible war and provided a powerful incentive to support the measure. The combination of Brinkley's pragmatic presentation and the desire to recognize the current prisoners of war won the day; the transfer of the grounds to the National Park Service became official. Andersonville National Cemetery and Andersonville Prison Park merged together to form Andersonville National Historic Site.

Although the successful creation of Andersonville National Historic Site helped inspire the "Andersonville Trail" and the Andersonville Guild's restoration of the town itself, not all Georgians viewed the government's plan to raise Andersonville's national profile as a positive step. Even as the bill emerged successfully from the labyrinth of Congress, the controversy over Andersonville flared once again in a debate over the appropriate role of the federal government in promoting "the interpretation of the life of a prisoner-of-war and the role of prison camps in history."[10] Leadership of the opposition to the new Andersonville National Historic Site came from the organization long distinguished by its devotion to righting the historical injustices committed against the South, the United Daughters of the Confederacy. J. G. Madry, chair of the UDC's Andersonville committee, explained that Brinkley in particular "got our dander up" because he "turned against the South."[11] In a time when the identity of white southerners was once again being challenged, the UDC feared that allowing the national government increased control over Andersonville would only further erode the proper memory of the Civil War. Motivated by the desire to protect southern memories of Civil War prisons, and as part of the larger struggle to preserve the Confederate heritage of the white South, the UDC actively campaigned to repeal the legislation designating Andersonville as a national park. Madry and the UDC resented that "this prison is being singled out," when "we feel that what happened to our Confederate soldiers in Northern prisons is as bad as what happened to Union soldiers at Andersonville." "Most tourists aren't historians," she exclaimed, and therefore, no matter how objective the presentation of history or strong the emphasis on the universal story of prisoner of war suffering, Madry feared that the site would only reconfirm the "malicious and libelous, insulting and injurious myth" of Andersonville's singular reputation for cruelty.[12]

Even if it could not stop the transformation of Andersonville into a national park, the UDC hoped to at least find a way to influence the process. In early 1972, UDC vice president Mildred Veasey outlined the terms that would ensure her organization's support for the Andersonville project in a letter to Jimmy Carter, then governor of Georgia. Although she could not resist "expressing resentment" over the travesty of "the so-called National Historic Site at Andersonville, Georgia," Veasey recognized that, thanks to the support of such a powerful alliance of Georgia politicians and businessmen behind the project, repeal of the law seemed unlikely. She hoped nevertheless that Carter would at least consider delaying any appropriations to Andersonville "unless and until" additional laws gave the UDC and the Sons of Confederate Veterans the means to prevent the "injurious myth" from spreading further. Veasey asked that the UDC be allowed to participate in the process of interpreting history at Andersonville by placing monuments "honoring Southern men who died in Northern prison camps," constructing markers "giving the South's historic position before the war," including "information about conditions and deaths in Northern prisoner-of-war camps" in "any exhibits, speeches, or recordings at the center," and appointing "representatives to serve on any historical committee."[13]

The demands of the UDC made little impact on Carter, whose staunch support for the Andersonville National Historic Site dated to the 1960s. Rather than allow the UDC to rehash old divisive memories, Carter ignored Veasey and Madry and instead embraced the concept of transforming Andersonville into a symbol of the common suffering endured by prisoners of war. As part of his efforts to turn division into unity, Carter appointed a Governor's Commission and charged it with the building of a Georgia monument at Andersonville National Historic Site. In 1973, the commission, led by Brinkley, selected University of Georgia sculptor William Thompson for the task of creating the Andersonville monument. The following year Thompson described his intentions for the Andersonville sculpture at a presentation of his proposed model. Thompson's statue consisted of three emaciated, wounded prisoners of war, each struggling to assist his comrades. The monument was designed to provoke the realization, Thompson explained, "that the conditions I am trying to depict are universal." The emotional scene, he hoped, conveyed the feelings of all prisoners, from the "combination of resignation to the tragedy of confinement and hope for freedom and a new life."[14] At a time when "prisoners of war from Viet Nam were returning," these broader feelings and lessons about the prisoner of war experience, for Thompson and Carter at least, comprised Andersonville's true legacy.[15] The amount earmarked for the project, $110,000, seemed a small price to pay for a monument designed to generate positive memories out of Andersonville's brutal past.

On Memorial Day, May 30, 1976, Thompson unveiled his finished tribute to all American prisoners of war.[16] As the *Americus Times-Recorder* noted, it was the "first of its kind erected."[17] Located at the entrance to Andersonville National Cemetery, the inscription on the base of the sculpture, in contrast to the old state monuments with their accusatory lists of casualties, took a passage from the book of Zechariah, "Turn ye to the stronghold, ye prisoners of hope." Speaker Brinkley reminded the crowd of about 1,500 that, in keeping with the spirit of Thompson's monument, "we should remember the most recent war when our soldiers fought without question." Vietnam veterans, especially former prisoners of war, Brinkley stated, "should be saluted and their families given deep gratitude."[18] The vision of Thompson, Brinkley, and Carter conflated the separate prisoner-of-war tragedies into one unifying presentation that acknowledged the sacrificing nature and heroic qualities displayed by POWs in all wars. Thompson's statue visually confirmed the growing acceptance of the objective memory of Civil War prisons as part of a larger pattern of modern war. It also—in its deliberate invocation of intangible, noncontroversial sentiments of freedom, hope, and nationalism—carefully avoided entangling the patriotism it evoked with the old memories of intentional evil or questions of race and, in doing so, set the tone for how the history of Civil War prisons would be remembered at Andersonville National Historic Site. Controversial conflicts such as the Civil War and Vietnam would be revisited based on a generalized interpretation that preferred to ignore the specific animosities generated by each particular war. Such a blurring of historical particularities continued to manifest itself during the 1980s, as new monuments joined the landscape of Andersonville's still active national cemetery, including displays honoring the World War II victims of the Bataan Death March and Stalag XVII-B. Recast as a shrine to the universal tragedy of war, Andersonville National Historic Site continued the paradoxical transformation of Civil War prisons from a symbol of shrill sectional division into a solemn and reassuring testament to the patriotism displayed by all American prisoners of war.

As the sizable gathering for the 1976 Memorial Day ceremony indicated, the reinvention of Andersonville as a national park also brought a renewed emphasis on the once popular Memorial Day tradition. Between World War II and the late 1960s, perhaps due to "white superiority" and "black backlash," the local tradition either ceased entirely or, if gatherings were held, was not covered by the local newspapers. Since 1970, however, the annual customs of speeches, grave decorations, and musical tributes have been fully revived as crowds yearly made (and still make) the pilgrimage to southwest Georgia. Although at first glance the contemporary Memorial Day programs seem to mirror those of the early 1900s, two noticeable changes distinguish the current celebrations from those of the past. Prior to World War II, local coverage of the festivities focused on the racial makeup (and behavior) of the participants, suggesting the importance of the ongoing competition between the bitter sectional memories and the emancipationist recollection of Andersonville and Civil War prisons. But over the last few decades, the diversity of the annual crowds goes unreported. This testifies to how powerfully the older memories of the Civil War have been overshadowed by and absorbed into the allure of Andersonville as a symbol of national identity. Also striking is the emphasis of the more recent Memorial Day tributes on latter-day wars, particularly Vietnam. On May 30, 1988, Vietnam widow Barbara Smith addressed the attendees, reminding them that Vietnam "is still being fought in our hearts and minds today, and I say to you that we are all still Prisoners of War." The yearly display of such emotions by Smith and former POWs revealed—quite legitimately—that Andersonville's tragic history did (and does) not matter nearly as much as the prison's redefined role as a national mourning ground for all American prisoners of war. And this preference for an Andersonville that comforted rather than challenged did not go unnoticed—or unrewarded.[19]

The annual Memorial Day services attracted the most attention to the park, but throughout the early years of Andersonville National Historic Site, National Park Service (NPS) officials daily faced a demanding task as they, in the words of current park superintendent Fred Boyles, "were busy in the 1970s telling the story of Andersonville."[20] The overall mission of the national park, according to the 1971 master plan for the location, centered on the "presentation of an effective interpretive story" of "life and death in military prisons throughout the ages of man." Making that ambition a reality at Andersonville would require years of work. Luckily, the years of care lavished on the site by the Women's Relief Corps and the maintenance of the area by the Army during the previous decades gave the NPS a firm foundation on which to build. The 1971 master plan for the national park testified to the already powerful appearance of the grounds, noting that "the unique value of Andersonville is that here the harshness of history is tempered by a landscape of beauty which raises hope that reason and harmony can still prevail in the affairs of man." Turning such a "landscape of beauty" into a finished presentation, however, still posed challenges. A new entrance to the park would be required, as would the construction and repaving of roads and parking lots to allow vehicles to circumnavigate the old prison stockade. Walking tours, following pathways that proceeded from the main parking lot into the national cemetery and prison grounds, also needed to be designed.[21] But the immediate priority, argued historian Edwin Bearss, had to be the preservation and interpretation of the "structural history of the prison." His 1970 "Historic Resource Study and Historical Base Map" created the framework for this initial goal.[22] The problem, as Bearss noted, and the 1971 master plan confirmed, was that while the national cemetery remained in attractive condition, "the stockades and various structures associated" with the actual prison "have not been restored." Other than the state monuments built at the location, little evidence of Andersonville Prison itself remained visible for potential visitors to inspect. The years of relative neglect needed to be overcome through "excavation" in order to convey the details of life at Andersonville.[23] Over the next few decades, replicas of prison walls and prisoners' shelters joined the "landscape of beauty" in order to better communicate the "harshness of history."

With restoration efforts underway at the prison site, the NPS continued to consider the problem of how to juxtapose the specific story of Civil
War Andersonville with the universal perspective of the common suffering
of all prisoners of war. The 1974 "Interpretive Prospectus" for Andersonville
National Historic Site acknowledged that the "touchy" subject of Andersonville made it essential that visitors to the park proceed through an "interpretive facility" before touring the prison and cemetery. A combination
of lobby, "mood room," and brief audiovisual presentation on the general
experience of prisoners of war would establish the broad context of what it
meant to be held as a POW. As tourists then viewed the specific story of
Andersonville, park officials hoped that the visitors would understand that,
as unpleasant as Andersonville had been, the suffering there was simply
one chapter in a larger, ongoing tale. "We would like visitors," the prospectus stated, "to leave the area with a feeling of antipathy for war, hope for
peace."[24] Due to limited budgets and the demands of getting the new unit
at Andersonville up to speed, however, expanding on the "little attention"
given to "the larger story of all POWs" remained difficult.[25] The NPS's 1979
"Environmental Assessment for General Management Plan/Developmental
Concept Plan" admitted that, after almost a decade of operations, the park
still failed to properly emphasize its desired theme. The "small" size of the
"visitor contact facility" prevented any substantial presentation of the larger
interpretation, while the "inadequate" and "hazardous" nature of the facilities and circular access route through the prison grounds further discouraged repeat visits.[26] As Andersonville National Historic Site entered its
second decade of existence, its core mission of crafting a more accessible
presentation of Andersonville's history remained only partially realized.

In the early 1980s, Boyles reported, Chief Ranger Alfredo Sanchez "recognized that the park was ignoring its larger mission of commemorating
all POWs." By now accustomed to budget shortages, Sanchez turned to a
private group, the American Ex-Prisoners of War (AXPOW), as a potential ally to help achieve that goal. By 1984, AXPOW agreed to support the
building of a museum "on site to tell the larger story." To fund the proposed
National Prisoner of War Museum, AXPOW created the Andersonville
Fund, a campaign that hoped to raise $2.5 million and thus offset any resid-
ual effects of the government's underfunding of the Andersonville National
Historic Site. Throughout the 1980s, Sanchez and then-superintendent
John Tucker continued to reach out to various POW organizations. Efforts

to expand the small visitor center to include "exhibits on recent wars," along with invitations to groups like AXPOW, the American League of Families for Ex-POWs and MIAs, and Nam-POWs to attend ceremonies at Andersonville, encouraged the growing visibility of the park among all veterans, not just prisoners of war.[27] New, "unbiased" NPS brochures also appeared in 1987, and the redesigned pamphlets offered comparative death rates of prisoners in the Civil War, World Wars I and II, Korea and Vietnam.[28] Slowly but surely the interpretation of the universal prisoner-of-war story started to come into focus.

Thanks to a congressional appropriation in the early 1990s, Boyles stated, planning for the National POW Museum "began in earnest." The alliance between the NPS and AXPOW led to the formation of the Andersonville Task Force Committee, a group comprised of ex-prisoners from World War II, Korea, and Vietnam who offered their input on the museum's design and presentation of the prisoner-of-war experience. The NPS also reached out to the local community, particularly Friends of Andersonville, a group, as Boyles noted, led by a former POW, Carl Runge. Runge spearheaded efforts to raise an additional $400,000 for the museum; led a successful campaign to have the government build a new park entrance road to the facility; and "developed national publicity for Andersonville and the museum" by getting Turner Productions interested in filming the TNT movie *Andersonville*.[29]

Despite the cooperation of the NPS, AXPOW, and Friends of Andersonville, according to Wayne Hitchcock, national commander of AXPOW, the original $2.5 million goal remained out of reach in the early 1990s. Although the government agreed to match the money privately raised with federal funds, the National POW Museum would remain in limbo unless an additional source of revenue could be found. In 1993, to secure the necessary funding for the project, Florida congressman Pete Peterson, a Vietnam POW, introduced a bill for the minting of a "Prisoner of War Commemorative Coin." On one side of the proposed $30 coin, an inscription read "freedom" next to the image of "a chained eagle" breaking through barbed wire, the remnants of the chain dangling from its leg. The opposite side of the coin featured a depiction of the hoped-for National POW Museum. By the end of 1993 Congress approved the coin, and the proceeds of the sales, although not as brisk as anticipated, helped raise the capital needed to continue.[30]

With the financial hurdles finally overcome, on July 15, 1996, the Mitch-ell Group, a Georgia company, received the nearly $4 million contract and began construction.[31] The National POW Museum was underway. As NPS architect Carla McConnell explained it, several considerations influenced the museum's location and design, but the overall purpose "has been to de-velop an architectural vocabulary which reinforces the stories related by all POWs." A new entry road funneled all visitors "directly to the Museum," she pointed out, and although the large museum needed to be "dramati-cally visible," the issue of the building's height initially proved troublesome. If too tall, the structure would detract "from the Andersonville prison site," McConnell pointed out, and so the finished product took the form of a "long, low solid dark-maroon brick building punctuated with three grey granite towers." The museum's appearance "is reminiscent of prisons," she argued, "and uses the thematic elements common to all POW stories: tow-ers, gates, confinement, water and light." The addition of the outdoor Com-memorative Courtyard behind the museum, an open space containing a "meandering stream" and sculptures provided a peaceful spot of contempla-tion as well as an opportunity to gather one's thoughts before proceeding on to the prison stockade or the national cemetery.[32]

Just as the outside of the National POW Museum invoked the univer-sal themes of prisons, the interior design was calculated to do the same. J. Scott Harmon, exhibit planner at the Harpers Ferry Center, described the collaborative process of his NPS unit with the Denver Service Center, AXPOW, and Barry Howard Associates, a California exhibit design com-pany, as based on "the guiding principle" that "we were to tell the story of all of America's prisoners of war, not just the Civil War story of Camp Sumter, or Andersonville." An initial proposal of a chronological design starting with the French and Indian War through the Persian Gulf War met with rejection due to too "much repetition." Instead, Harmon explained, the planners realized that the exhibits needed "to focus on those experiences that are common to all prisoners of war." Visitors would circulate through a series of exhibits, starting with "What is a POW?" followed by "Capture," "Living Conditions," "News and Communications," "Those Who Wait," "Privation," "Morale and Relationships," and "Escape and Freedom." The series of exhibits ended by depositing viewers in a central corridor that dis-played a "more specific interpretation" of Civil War prisons and Anderson-ville. Thus museum guests encountered the specific tragedy of Civil War prisons only after it had been placed in the larger context of the more general presentation of the experience of all prisoners of war.[33]

As visitors passed through the museum, the audiovisual presentation of prisoner interviews and footage of reunions, along with the introductory film, "Echoes of Captivity," narrated by General Colin Powell, drove home the point that while the uniforms and technology changed from war to war, the emotional and physical challenges that prisoners of war faced maintained an unfortunate consistency.[34] The juxtaposition of artifacts from the various wars also reinforced the overall interpretation. In the "Living Conditions" exhibit, canteens and utensils from Andersonville prisoners rested alongside the canteens and utensils of World War II and Korea POWs.[35] Lying side by side, these relics poignantly reminded viewers that the mutual suffering of all prisoners of war crossed historical boundaries. No matter when or where imprisonment occurred, deprivation invariably followed. The relentlessly emotional presentation served a clear purpose, one apparent upon entrance into the museum lobby. "The National Prisoner of War Museum," a dedication panel read, "is dedicated to the men and women of this country who suffered captivity so that others could remain free. Their story is one of sacrifice and courage; their legacy, the gift of liberty." This acknowledgment of sacrifice not only echoed the words found in the narratives of Civil War prison survivors but congratulated them on their patriotic achievement—the protection of freedom for subsequent generations of Americans, some of whom made the same sacrifices in later wars. Although the rhetoric emphasizing sacrifice hearkened back to the explanations of the past, the museum dedication served the needs of the present. Despite the inherently depressing subject material, the museum infused the tragedy of war with an optimistic meaning of redemption. The idealized dedication ignored the reality that Confederate prisons existed precisely to deny the "gift of liberty" to African Americans and suggested that the specific actions of the Confederacy no longer mattered. The torment experienced by all American prisoners of war, not just those of the Civil War, now took place for a reason. No matter how unspeakable each individual prisoner's ordeal, all Americans could recognize the heroic courage of prisoners of war, feel comfort in the meaning of each prisoner's sacrifice, and, as a result, remember their own patriotic responsibility to honor the ideal of freedom for which those captives suffered.

On April 9, 1998, the anniversary of the Bataan Death March (which, purely coincidentally—and for many attendees, irrelevantly—shared the date with Lee's surrender at Appomattox), the dedication ceremonies of the National POW Museum drew more than 3,000 observers, mostly ex-POWs, to Andersonville National Historic Site. Although President Clinton did not attend, he sent his blessing, thanking "these American heroes" for reminding us "that freedom does not come without a price."[36] The main speaker, Senator John McCain, himself a Vietnam POW, told the crowd that "all the Andersonvilles in our history" tell the "story of a struggle against daunting odds to choose their own way, to stay faithful to a shared cause."[37] Many former prisoners of war witnessed the ceremony and toured the exhibits in amazement, feeling overwhelmed by the nature of the tribute. Ohioan Harley Coon, a Korean War POW, exulted in the moment: "Americans need to realize the pain and suffering they went through to preserve our freedom." Even in captivity, Coon remembered, "every day we fought 'em, in any way we could. We disrupted anything we could. We fought with anything we could."[38] In the midst of the tears of memory, pride, and anguish, a sense of appreciation for the museum's purpose permeated the crowd. As a monument to American patriotism, the museum would remind current and future generations of the value of freedom. "That's what this is about," Georgia governor Zell Miller "said proudly," as he observed "a youngster watching a video in the museum."[39]

The emotional opening of the National POW Museum offers a valuable window of insight into the malleable nature of public memory and how the process of historical construction works. The parallels of the universal experience of prisoners of war did not stop after capture, imprisonment, and release. For decades, especially in their twilight years, Civil War prison survivors fought a rhetorical war in the form of monuments and testimonials to reassure themselves that their sacrifices meant something. The same historical concerns motivated the efforts of World War II, Korea, and Vietnam POWs to transform Andersonville into their monument too. It is an understandable pattern, and one that is hard not to view with sympathy. By the 1990s, as the World War II and Korean War generation of POWs faced the prospect of death, the campaign for the National POW Museum and the preservation of their story offered one final chance to feel appreciated and remind all Americans of the significance of their suffering. For Vietnam POWs, it represented yet another positive step back from the painful divisions of the past. In each Memorial Day ceremony, with each visitor inspired by the national park, Andersonville became (and becomes) the setting for a mystical transubstantiation, where the haunting memories of meaningless atrocity became (and becomes) a celebration of the triumph of patriotic sacrifice. History may not run in cycles, nor is it endlessly repetitive, but some human needs do and are.

On many levels, the National POW Museum qualified as a triumph for the National Park Service. Attendance at the park dipped to 129,316 in 1993, but by 1998, thanks to the interest in the museum, it nearly doubled, to 221,546. Although attendance slid until 2001, when 162,416 made their way to Andersonville, the events of September 11 prompted 190,001 visitors in 2002.[40] The comforting interpretation of atrocity as meaningful was lucrative as well as inspiring. The heightened volume of tourists translated into brisk sales of postcards, t-shirts, children's guides, Andersonville books, and prisoner narratives at the museum gift shop. To the delight of Lewis Easterlin and Peggy Sheppard, many also crossed Highway 49 to see the quaint little town of Andersonville. At the park, an ongoing effort to record the oral histories of American POWs reflected the continued dedication of the NPS to preserving and interpreting the universal story of prisoners of war.[41] Currently in the works, as part of the centennial celebration of the NPS in 2016, is the preparation, again based on the partnership between the NPS, Friends of Andersonville, and AXPOW, of a traveling exhibit, "Echoes of Captivity: A Moving Tribute to the American Prisoner of War Experience."[42] In this context the word moving has two meanings—not only will the display traverse the country but it will no doubt emphasize the emotional patriotism central to the interpretation of the National POW Museum. Secretary of the Interior Bruce Babbitt might well have had the example of Andersonville National Historic Site in mind when he wrote in 2000, "the task of history is never done." We "make our future better," he declared, "by understanding the past."[43]

The transformation of Andersonville from symbol of sectional division to a monument to American patriotism thus will continue for the foreseeable future. It is the logical consequence of our accepting the objective memory of Civil War prisons. And it is in part a positive development. The popularity of the universalist approach taken at Andersonville National Historic Site and the National POW Museum offers compelling evidence that, at long last, the sectional wounds of the Civil War prison tragedy can be considered almost fully healed. Reconciliation—except perhaps to the

UDC and a few other dissenters—seems essentially complete, although the scars will never fade.

But our contemporary memories of Civil War prisons also remain, sadly, unsatisfactory at best and misleading at worst. On the question of determining responsibility for the suffering of Civil War prisoners, Andersonville National Historic Site provided only an ambiguous response to the old debate. Although the juxtaposition of the national cemetery and stockade grounds with the context of the larger story of prisoners of war defused to some extent the traditional memories, it did so in large part by ignoring the critical realization that each war, no matter what general characteristics it shared with wars of other generations, also possessed unique qualities. Andersonville's individual history became dangerously irrelevant in this repackaged presentation. The National POW Museum's idealized interpretation of the experience of prisoners of war as a celebration of patriotism confuses the contemporary American memory of Civil War prisons in several important ways.

First, taking the long view of prisoners of war subtly excuses the suffering that transpires in each particular conflict. Each war requires that these patriotic martyrs endure hell as a sacrifice for an indefinite, but clearly precious, freedom. Instead of lamenting atrocity we rejoice in its ritualistic embrace. Since prisoners of war fare badly in all wars, low expectations for our standards of behavior in current and future conflicts remain acceptable.

Another obfuscation results from the fact that, in the Civil War, Americans committed these atrocities against each other. By conflating all modern wars, the NPS again excuses, or at least distracts attention from, the tortured morality of the deliberate nature of the policy choices made by, and thus the responsibility shared for, the Union and Confederacy in the tragedy of Civil War prisons. Although the ideal of freedom permeates Andersonville today, it has been stripped of its emancipationist connotations and thus, ironically, its essential meaning. Compelled by the desire for a larger narrative, Americans, through the selective nature of memory, celebrate an ahistorical, but emotionally powerful, spirit of American freedom. It is convenient (and profitable) to do so, but in a world where prison atrocities, along with racial inequalities, remain prevalent, it is also disingenuous.

In its enthusiasm for the patriotic memory of prisoners of war, the National POW Museum raises one additional point of concern—that in the attempt to find meaning in the brutality of the past, too much importance is placed on the shared sacrifice of all American POWs. Instead of expressing regret or fear about the terrible nature of war, the emphasis on sacrifice actually suggests that the experience of prisoners of war, and even war itself, serves as an opportunity to celebrate liberty and the price we are willing to pay for it. The NPS's presentation of war as positive and meaningful provides a troubling contrast to past scholarship on Civil War prisons and shows how, in the wrong hands, an objective memory that equalizes blame and deemphasizes consequence can become little more than propaganda. When Hesseltine and other scholars looked at the context of how prisoners fared in all modern wars, they did so in an attempt to show the pervasive evil of war, with the hopes of avoiding future horrors. Although perhaps naive, that goal should remain an aspiration, and, in its current incarnation, intentionally or not, the National POW Museum minimizes that important quest. That the NPS's agenda of promoting patriotism trumps the need for examining the nuances of morality reveals the danger of relying on government-sponsored history for our memories. At just over a decade old, the National POW Museum's impact on the memory of Civil War prisons remains uncertain. Given the current political climate of hyperpatriotism, the national park today exists as a lesson to the public about the important values of sacrifice and service in the face of terrible adversity, a message that resonates in a time of fear. But this interpretation too will change over time, because if any fundamental lesson of Andersonville exists, it is that people will see in its questions what they want to see.

Conclusion

From almost the outset of the Civil War down to the present, the controversy over the treatment of Civil War prisoners, and particularly the attempt to pinpoint responsibility for their suffering, captivated Americans struggling to understand first the meaning of the Civil War and later the meaning of modern war in general. For several decades, until the horrors of the world wars of the first half of the twentieth century, divisive memories dominated the perception of Civil War prisons. Although all agreed that atrocities had been perpetrated, sharp disagreement persisted as to the source of the prison suffering. Depending on sectional allegiance, the blame for the misery fell either on the ruthless, unfeeling policies of Abraham Lincoln's Union or the amoral, treasonous nature of Jefferson Davis's Confederacy. As representatives of the tragedy, individual Civil War officials, most notably Henry Wirz, were condemned as sadistic and demonic. Throughout these years, defenders of the Union and Confederate prison systems recycled the shrill arguments of the war, often for political gain, frequently to avoid the cause abandoned of racial equality, but always to confirm their sense of identity and to justify their understanding of what the Civil War really meant. Although northerners dominated and defined the terms of the debate over Civil War prisons, white southerners succeeded, as part of the Lost Cause mythology, in deflecting much of the enduring northern criticism and in muting the public visibility of African American celebrations of emancipation. The inherent hostility evoked by the competing sectional memories prolonged the intense rhetorical battle to shape the public remembrance of the Civil War and delayed the progression of reconciliation.

Although the old animosities over Civil War prisons faded by the midpoint of the twentieth century, in a curious twist on the process of reconciliation, the bitterness dissipated only as Americans recognized that, in the treatment of their prisoners, both Union and Confederacy deserved a generalized scorn. Reconciliation over the prison controversy became possible in the aftermath of World War I and II for two reasons. The deaths of the last Civil War prisoners and the staunchest sectional defenders coincided with the emergence of a more objective memory of Civil War prisons based on the depressing realization that the committing of atrocities against prisoners occurred, alarmingly, in all modern wars. The history of Civil War prisons became a warning, not of the deficiencies of the North or South, but of the need to be on guard against mankind's inherent potential for evil. Recasting the public memory of Civil War prisons helped inspire, at least in theory, that necessary vigilance at a time, not coincidentally, when America assumed a leadership role in world affairs. But in its focus on the patterns, and not the particulars, the relativity inherent in the objective memory also seduced Americans into believing that a closer examination of the peculiar immoralities of Civil War prisons was unnecessary. Reassuring memories are always the easiest to accept.

Over the last few decades, the objective redefinition of the Civil War prison legacy produced a curious paradox. Although a few diehards clung (and still cling) to the traditional divisive memories, events such as the Civil War Centennial—motivated by the lure of profit and the desire to celebrate American heritage—cemented the power of the objective prison memory in the American mind. Andersonville and its fellow Civil War prisons, once regarded solely as controversial symbols of sectional atrocity, now stood proudly as symbols of national unity. Andersonville itself was the epicenter of this reinvention, as the recasting of the town of Andersonville as a tourist-friendly Civil War village and the remaking of the old prison grounds and national cemetery into Andersonville National Historic Site revealed. The 1998 opening of the National Prisoner of War Museum further confirmed Andersonville's new identity as the national memorial ground for all American prisoners of war. The successful fusion of history, commemoration, and tourism at the transformed Andersonville National Historic Site and National POW Museum corresponded to the ongoing desire of Americans to patriotically remember, and admire, the sacrifices of past soldiers.

The widespread acceptance of the objective reimagination of the past testifies to the continued—and understandable—American attraction to the comforts of myth. But it must be recognized that that same preference inhibits a candid assessment of the evils committed during the Civil War. It seems that the attraction of the Civil War as a national fairy tale continues to overshadow the need to confront more honestly the tragedies of American history.

Although the currently dominant objective memory of Civil War prisons emphasizes a message of unity instead of division, the transformation of the prison controversy from national scar to usable past remains incomplete. The yearning for an idealized, ahistorical past unfortunately minimizes the most important legacy of Andersonville and Civil War prisons—the issue of responsibility for the humane treatment of POWs. Events of the early twenty-first century have shown that the lessons of the past have yet to inspire any fundamental change in our behavior toward prisoners of war. The outrage over the American torture of Al Qaeda suspects at Guantanamo Bay and Iraqi captives at Abu Ghraib testifies to the enduring importance of the issue of proper treatment of prisoners of war and reminds us that the historical example of Civil War prisons retains its relevance today. Although the Civil War and the war on terror share little in common, the shock and disgust Americans felt when the knowledge of recent atrocities surfaced echoed the emotions of outrage and disbelief felt in the Union and Confederacy during the Civil War when both sides learned about the scale of the suffering endured in captivity. As Americans, we asked ourselves, as our counterparts did in 1865, the old questions of responsibility and meaning, with one difference. Instead of inquiring how this could happen, we wonder how this could happen again. Part of the surprise in learning that our generation can commit similar inhumanities against our fellow human beings came from the shame that we should know better, given our awareness of the mistakes of the Civil War, World War II, and Vietnam, among many others. And yet, generation after generation, the deeply rooted faith in the identity of American exceptionalism persists. Our ability to idealize a carefully constructed past allows us to believe that America still leads the rest of the world down a path of Manifest Destiny to a mythical reality where such horrors no longer hold sway. There are, in short, consequences to the identities and illusions we create and cherish. That we still have the capacity to express disbelief at atrocities committed against prisoners of war after nearly 150 years of frequent brutality speaks to the equal influence of the positive trait of innate human optimism and the more negative human appetite for delusion. It also suggests that because of the fluidity of memory, there are limits on history's power to change human behavior.

NOTES

INTRODUCTION

1. Charles H. Metzger, *The Prisoner in the American Revolution* (Chicago: Loyola University Press, 1971); Larry G. Bowman, *Captive Americans: Prisoners during the American Revolution* (Athens: Ohio University Press, 1976); Donald R. Hickey, *The War of 1812: A Forgotten Conflict* (Urbana: University of Illinois Press, 1989), 176–81, 306–7; Charles W. Sanders, Jr., *While in the Hands of the Enemy: Military Prisons of the Civil War* (Baton Rouge: Louisiana State University Press, 2005), 7–24.

2. Edwin G. Burrows, "Patriots or Terrorists? The Lost Story of Revolutionary POWS," *American Heritage* 58 (Fall 2008): 57–60.

3. Charles Royster, *The Destructive War: William Tecumseh Sherman, Stonewall Jackson, and the Americans* (New York: Vintage, 1993), xi.

4. David W. Blight, *Race and Reunion: The Civil War in American Memory* (Cambridge, Mass.: Belknap Press of Harvard University Press, 2001), 152. See also Michael G. Kammen, *Mystic Chords of Memory: The Transformation of Tradition in American Culture* (New York: Vintage, 1991), 101.

5. Among the growing literature on the memory of the Civil War, these works remain essential: Blight, *Race and Reunion;* David W. Blight, *Beyond the Battlefield: Race, Memory, and the American Civil War* (Cambridge: University of Massachusetts Press, 2002); David R. Goldfield, *Still Fighting the Civil War: The American South and Southern History* (Baton Rouge: Louisiana State University Press, 2002); Kammen, *Mystic Chords of Memory;* Alice Fahs and Joan Waugh, eds., *The Memory of the Civil War in American Culture* (Chapel Hill: University of North Carolina Press, 2004); Jim Weeks, *Gettysburg: Memory, Market, and an American Shrine* (Princeton, N.J.: Princeton University Press, 2003).

6. Edward F. Roberts, *Andersonville Journey* (Shippensburg, Pa.: Burd Street, 1998); Douglas G. Gardner, "Andersonville and American Memory: Civil War Prisoners and Narratives of Suffering and Redemption" (Ph.D. diss., Miami University, 1998); Nancy A. Roberts, "The Afterlife of Civil War Prisons and Their Dead" (Ph.D. diss., University of Oregon, 1996).

CHAPTER ONE

1. *Charleston Mercury,* June 19, 1861, http://www.accessible.com (accessed February 8, 2003).

2. Eugene M. Thomas, III, "Prisoner of War Exchange during the American Civil War" (Ph.D. diss., Auburn University, 1976), 3–4. Along with Thomas, for the best discussion of the complexities surrounding the fluctuating process of exchange during the Civil War, see William B. Hesseltine, *Civil War Prisons: A Study in War Psychology* (1930; repr., Columbus: Ohio State University Press, 1998), chaps. 2, 5, and 10 as well as Charles W. Sanders, Jr., *While in the Hands of the Enemy: Military Prisons of the Civil War* (Baton Rouge: Louisiana State University Press, 2005), esp. chaps. 5 and 6.

3. Hesseltine, *Civil War Prisons*, 6.

4. Sanders, *While in the Hands of the Enemy*, 112–15.

5. Thomas, "Prisoner of War Exchange," 46–47.

6. U.S. War Department, *War of the Rebellion: A Compilation of the Official Records of the Union and Confederate Armies* (Washington, D.C.: Government Printing Office, 1894–1899), Series II, Vol. III, 157, hereafter referred to as *O.R.*, with all references to Series II unless otherwise noted.

7. Hesseltine, *Civil War Prisons*, 17–18.

8. Thomas, "Prisoner of War Exchange," 59, 87–88.

9. Hesseltine, *Civil War Prisons*, 26, 67–68.

10. *O.R.*, Vol. IV, 266–68. The cartel declared that a general-in-chief was worth 60 enlisted men, lieutenant general, 40; major general, 30; brigadier general, 20; colonel, 15; lieutenant colonel, 10; major, 8; captain, 6; lieutenant, 4; second lieutenant, 3; noncommissioned officers, 2.

11. Sanders, *While in the Hands of the Enemy*, 128–45; Thomas, "Prisoner of War Exchange," 104–25.

12. Hesseltine, *Civil War Prisons*, 103–11.

13. Gregory J. W. Urwin, ed., *Black Flag over Dixie: Racial Atrocities and Reprisals in the Civil War* (Carbondale: Southern Illinois University Press, 2004); George S. Burkhardt, *Confederate Rage, Yankee Wrath: No Quarter in the Civil War* (Carbondale: Southern Illinois University Press, 2007); John Cimprich, *Fort Pillow, a Civil War Massacre, and Public Memory* (Baton Rouge: Louisiana State University Press, 2005); Joseph T. Glaathaar, *Forged in Battle: The Civil War Alliance of Black Soldiers and White Officers* (New York: Free Press, 1990), 201–5.

14. Lonnie R. Speer, *Portals to Hell: Military Prisons of the Civil War* (Mechanicsburg, Pa.: Stackpole, 1997), 114.

15. William Marvel, *Andersonville: The Last Depot* (Chapel Hill: University of North Carolina Press, 1994), 154–55; Robert Scott Davis, "'Near Andersonville': An Historical Note on Civil War Legend and Reality," *Journal of African American History* 92 (Winter 2007): 101.

16. Thomas, "Prisoner of War Exchange," 297–99.

17. Edward Younger, ed., *Inside the Confederate Government: The Diary of Robert Garlick Hill Kean* (1957; repr., Baton Rouge: Louisiana State University Press, 1993), 102.

18. Hesseltine, *Civil War Prisons*, 214.

19. Grant's statements are quoted in James M. McPherson, *Battle Cry of Freedom* (New York: Ballantine, 1988), 799–800.

20. Arch Blakey, *General John H. Winder, C.S.A.* (Gainesville: University of Florida Press, 1990), 120–39.

21. Blakey, *General John H. Winder*, 158.

22. *O.R.*, VII: 1150.

23. Hesseltine, *Civil War Prisons*, 42–48.

24. Leslie G. Hunter, "Warden for the Union: General William Hoffman (1807–1884)" (Ph.D. diss., University of Arizona, 1971), 28, 43, 58–59.

25. William Hoffman to Edwin Stanton, September 19, 1863, Personal Papers of William Hoffman, entry 16, RG 249, National Archives.

26. *O.R.*, VIII: 997–1003.

27. James M. Gillispie, *Andersonvilles of the North: The Myths and Realities of Northern Treatment of Civil War Confederate Prisoners* (Denton: University of North Texas Press, 2008), 217–38.

28. Walt Whitman, *Memoranda during the War [&] Death of Abraham Lincoln*, ed. Roy P. Basler (1875; repr., Bloomington: Indiana University Press, 1962), 4.

29. James B. Murphy, ed., "A Confederate Soldier's View of Johnson's Island Prison," *Ohio History* 79 (Spring 1970): 109.

30. Ruth Woods Dayton, ed., *The Diary of a Confederate Soldier James E. Hall* (N.p.: privately printed, 1961), 92.

31. William Whatley Pierson, Jr., ed., *Whipt 'em Everytime: The Diary of Bartlett Yancey Malone* (Jackson, Tenn.: McCowat-Mercer, 1960), 93.

32. Walter L. Williams, "A Confederate View of Prison Life: A Virginian in Fort Delaware, 1863," *Delaware History* 18 (Fall–Winter 1979): 228, 232.

33. Robert Bingham, "Prison Experience," pp. 7–8, Robert Bingham Papers, Folder 2, Southern Historical Collection at the University of North Carolina at Chapel Hill.

34. L. Leon, *Diary of a Tar Heel Confederate Soldier* (Charlotte, N.C.: Stone, n.d.), 68–69.

35. Joseph M. Kern, "Diary and Scrapbook," p. 33, Joseph Mason Kern Papers, Folder 2, Southern Historical Collection at the University of North Carolina at Chapel Hill.

36. Joseph T. Durkin, ed., *John Dooley: Confederate Soldier* (Washington, D.C.: Georgetown University Press, 1945), 165.

37. Ted Genoways and Hugh H. Genoways, eds., *A Perfect Picture of Hell: Eyewitness Accounts by Civil War Prisoners from the 12th Iowa* (Iowa City: University of Iowa Press, 2001), 71, 78–79.

38. Genoways and Genoways, *A Perfect Picture of Hell*, 209, 212, 207, 213.

39. Samuel Fiske, *Dunn Browne in the Army* (Boston: Nichols & Noyes, 1865), 157.

40. John Quinn Imholte, "The Civil War Diary and Related Sources of Corporal Newell Burch 154th New York Volunteers Covering the Period August 25, 1862 to April 21, 1865," p. 108, Michael Winey Collection, United States Army Military History Institute.

41. Don Allison, ed., *Hell on Belle Isle: Diary of a Civil War POW* (Bryan, Ohio: Faded Banner, 1997), 57, 65, 81, 65, 82.

42. On other Confederate prisons in 1864–65, see Thomas M. Boaz, *Libby Prison & Beyond: A Union Staff Officer in the East, 1862–1865* (Shippensburg, Pa.: Burd Street, 1999); Philip N. Racine, ed., *"Unspoiled Heart": The Journal of Charles Mattocks of the 17th Maine* (Knoxville: University of Tennessee Press, 1994); Margaret W. Peelle, *Letters from Libby Prison* (New York: Greenwich, 1956); Joseph Ferguson, "Civil War Journal," Civil War Miscellaneous Collection, United States Colored Troops, United States Army Military History Institute.

43. Thomas Francis Galwey, *The Valiant Hours*, ed. W. S. Nye (Harrisburg, Pa.: Stackpole, 1961), 200.

44. John Sawyer Patch, "Diary of John Sawyer Patch," p. 17, Andersonville Subject Files, Andersonville National Historic Site.

45. Henry W. Tisdale, "Civil War Diary of Sergt. Henry W. Tisdale," p. 112, Civil War Prisoner of War Resource Files, Andersonville National Historic Site.

46. Wayne Mahood, ed., *Charlie Mosher's Civil War* (Hightstown, N.J.: Longstreet House, 1994), 240.

47. C. M. Destler, ed., "An Andersonville Prison Diary," *Georgia Historical Quarterly* 24 (March 1940): 65.

48. Paul C. Helmreich, "The Diary of Charles G. Lee in the Andersonville and Florence Prison Camps, 1864," *Connecticut Historical Society Bulletin* 41 (January 1976): 19.

49. Wayne Mahood, *Charlie Mosher's Civil War*, 220.

50. Francis M. Shaw, "Transcription of Diary," p. 12, Civil War Miscellaneous Collection, 3rd series, Box 5, Pennsylvania, United States Army Military History Institute.

51. Leon Basile, ed., *The Civil War Diary of Amos E. Stearns, a Prisoner at Andersonville* (London: Associated University Presses, 1981), 77.

52. George Foxcroft Read, "Transcription of Diary," pp. 16, 14, Civil War Miscellaneous Collection, 3rd series, *Civil War Times Illustrated* Collection, Box 1, Iowa, Kansas, Kentucky, Maine, Maryland, United States Army Military History Institute.

53. The Tritt and Umsted quotes come from Glenn M. Robins, "Race, Repatriation, and Galvanized Rebels: Union Prisoners and the Exchange Question in Deep South Prison Camps," *Civil War History* 53 (June 2007): 123–24.

54. Ibid., 132–35.

55. *New York Herald*, December 23, 1861, www.accessible.com (accessed February 9, 2003).

56. *Harper's Weekly*, August 30, 1862, www.harpweek.com (accessed March 3, 2003).

57. Charles Lanman, ed., *Journal of Alfred Ely: A Prisoner of War in Richmond* (New York: D. Appleton, 1862), 281–83.

58. For early Confederate prison accounts, see George A. Lawrence, *Border and Bastille* (New York: W. I. Pooley, 1863), and J. C. Poe, ed., *The Raving Foe* (Eastland, Tex.: Longhorn, 1967).

59. J. J. Geer, *Beyond the Lines; or, A Yankee Prisoner Loose in Dixie* (Philadelphia: J. W. Daughaday, 1863), 284.

60. Harold Earl Hammond, ed., *Diary of a Union Lady, 1861–1865* (New York: Funk & Wagnalls, 1962), 364.

61. Charles F. Larimer, ed., *Love and Valor: The Intimate Love Letters between Jacob and Emeline Ritner* (Western Springs, Ill.: Sigourney, 2000), 364.

62. Georgeanna Woolsey Bacon and Eliza Woolsey Howland, *My Heart towards Home: Letters of a Family during the Civil War*, ed. Daniel John Hoisington (Roseville, Minn.: Edinborough Press, 2001), 373–74.

63. G. Glenn Clift, ed., *The Private War of Lizzie Hardin* (Frankfort: Kentucky Historical Society, 1963), 224.

64. Charles East, ed., *The Civil War Diary of Sarah Morgan* (Athens: University of Georgia Press, 1991), 598.

65. Ernest M. Lander, Jr., and Charles M. McGee, Jr., eds., *A Rebel Came Home: The Diary and Letters of Floride Clemson, 1863–1866* (Columbia: University of South Carolina Press, 1961), 89.

66. Thomas J. Green to Hon. W. J. Greene, Fayetteville, NC, 15 or 20 (date unclear) August 1864, Thomas J. Green Papers, Folder 41, Southern Historical Collection at the University of North Carolina at Chapel Hill.

67. *Charleston Mercury*, February 18, 1864, www.accessible.com (accessed February 6, 2003).

68. *Macon Daily Telegraph*, June 11, 1864, Civil War Miscellany Papers, Box 1, Andersonville, Georgia, Military Prison Folder, Georgia State Archives.

69. The Manigault letter appears in an article edited by Spencer B. King, Jr., "Letter from an Eyewitness at Andersonville Prison, 1864," *Georgia Historical Quarterly* 38 (March 1954): 85.

70. Douglas G. Gardner, "Andersonville and American Memory: Civil War Prisoners and Narratives of Suffering and Redemption" (Ph.D. diss., Miami University, 1998), 180–96.

71. *Harper's Weekly,* January 9, 1864, www.harpweek.com (accessed March 9, 2003).

72. *New York Herald,* November 22, 1864, www.accessible.com (accessed February 6, 2003).

73. *Harper's Weekly,* December 5, 1863, March 5, 1864, December 10, 1864, January 14, 1865, www.harpweek.com (accessed March 1 and 9, 2003).

74. Ibid., April 15, 1865, www.harpweek.com (accessed March 3, 2003).

75. Kathleen Collins, "Living Skeletons; Carte-de-visite Propaganda in the American Civil War," *History of Photography* 12 (April–June 1988): 103.

76. Hesseltine, *Civil War Prisons,* 172–73.

77. U.S. Congress, House, Joint Committee on the Conduct of the War, *Returned Prisoners,* 38th Congress, 1st sess., 1864, Report No. 67, 1.

78. United States Sanitary Commission, *Narrative of Privations and Sufferings of United States Officers and Soldiers while Prisoners of War in the Hands of the Rebel Authorities, Being the Report of a Commission of Inquiry* (Philadelphia: King & Baird, 1864). See also William B. Hesseltine, "The Propaganda Literature of Confederate Prisons," *Journal of Southern History* 1 (February–November 1935): 60–61.

79. *O.R.,* VII: 618–19.

80. Robert S. Davis, *Ghosts and Shadows of Andersonville: Essays on the Secret Social Histories of America's Deadliest Prison* (Macon, Ga.: Mercer University Press, 2006), 153–61.

81. Charles Sumner, *Speech of Hon. Charles Sumner, in the Senate of the United States, January 29th, 1865, on the Resolution of the Committee on Military Affairs, Advising Retaliation in Kind for Rebel Cruelties to Prisoners* (New York: Young Men's Republican Union, 1865), 8.

82. Sanders, *While in the Hands of the Enemy,* 310–11.

83. Bruce Tap, "'These Devils Are not Fit to Live on God's Earth': War Crimes and the Committee on the Conduct of the War, 1864–1865," *Civil War History* 38 (June 1996): 125–31.

84. Sanders, *While in the Hands of the Enemy,* 312–16.

85. *O.R.,* VIII: 337–38, 347, 349.

86. Ibid., 350.

87. J. B. Jones, *A Rebel War Clerk's Diary,* ed. Howard Swiggett (New York: Old Hickory Bookshop, 1935), 340.

88. *O.R.,* VIII: 350.

89. Sanders, *While in the Hands of the Enemy,* 299–309.

CHAPTER TWO

1. U.S. Congress, House, Joint Committee on the Conduct of the War, *Report of the Joint Committee on the Conduct of the War,* 38th Congress, 2nd sess., 1865, House Executive Document No. 32, 54–77.

2. The controversial Wirz trial has been well documented. Accounts of significance include (but are not limited to) the following: William Hesseltine, *Civil War Prisons: A Study in War Psychology* (1930; repr., Columbus: Ohio State University Press, 1998), 237–47; Charles W. Sanders, Jr., *While in the Hands of the Enemy: Military Prisons of the Civil War* (Baton Rouge: Louisiana State University Press, 2005), 294–96; William Marvel, *Andersonville: The Last Depot* (Chapel Hill: University of North Carolina Press, 1994); Edward F. Roberts, *Andersonville Journey*

(Shippensburg, Pa.: Burd Street, 1998); Darrett B. Rutman, "The War Crimes and Trial of Henry Wirz," *Civil War History* 6 (June 1960): 117–33; Lewis L. Laska and James M. Smith, "'Hell and the Devil': Andersonville and the Trial of Captain Henry Wirz, C. S. A., 1865," *Military Law Review* 68 (1975): 77–132; Gayla Koerting, "The Trial of Henry Wirz and Nineteenth-Century Military Law" (Ph.D. diss., Kent State University, 1995); Robert E and Katharine M. Morseberger, "After Andersonville: The First War Crimes Trial," *Civil War Times Illustrated* 13 (July 1974): 30–40; James C. Bonner, "War Crimes Trials, 1865–1867," *Social Science* 22 (April 1947): 128–34.

3. *New York Times,* July 26, 1865.

4. *Harper's Weekly,* August 19, 1865, www.harpweek.com (accessed March 1, 2003).

5. Ibid., September 16, 1865, www.harpweek.com (accessed March 1, 2003).

6. *New York Times,* October 15, 1865.

7. Diary of Abram Varrick Parmenter, August 25, 26, and September 27, 1865, Abram Varrick Parmenter Papers, MMC 696, Library of Congress Manuscript Room.

8. Laska and Smith, "'Hell and the Devil,'" 100–102; Koerting, "The Trial of Henry Wirz," 69.

9. Hesseltine, *Civil War Prisons,* 239–42.

10. Laska and Smith, "'Hell and the Devil,'" 101.

11. U.S. Congress, House, *The Trial of Henry Wirz,* 40th Congress, 2nd sess., 1868, House Executive Document No. 23, 802, 777, 764, 756, 813–14.

12. Ella Lonn, *Foreigners in the Confederacy* (Chapel Hill: University of North Carolina Press, 1940), 273–75.

13. U.S. Congress, House, *Trial of Henry Wirz,* 814.

14. Koerting, "The Trial of Henry Wirz," 122.

15. Laska and Smith, "'Hell and the Devil,'" 106, 129; see also Rutman, "The War Crimes and Trial of Henry Wirz," 127–28.

16. Hesseltine, *Civil War Prisons,* 244.

17. William J. Cooper, Jr., *Jefferson Davis, American* (New York: Knopf, 2000), 540–41.

18. Morseberger, "After Andersonville," 37–40.

19. Edward Younger, *Inside the Confederate Government: The Diary of Robert Garlick Hill Kean* (1957; repr., Baton Rouge: Louisiana State University Press, 1993), 223, 230.

20. Randolph Stevenson, *The Southern Side; or, Andersonville Prison* (Baltimore: Turnbull Brothers, 1876), 133.

21. U.S. Congress, House, *Trial of Henry Wirz,* 704.

22. November 10, 1865, Parmenter Diary.

23. *Harper's Weekly,* November 25, 1865, www.harpweek.com (accessed March 3, 2003).

24. The post-trial publication of *The Demon of Andersonville; or, The Trial of Wirz, for the Cruel Treatment and Brutal Murder of Helpless Union Prisoners in his Hands. The Most Highly Exciting and Interesting Trial of the Present Century, his Life and Execution Containing also a History of Andersonville, with Illustrations, Truthfully Representing the Horrible Scenes of Cruelty Perpetuated by Him* (Philadelphia: Barclay, 1865) indicated how much Wirz was reviled in 1865.

25. Robert Penn Warren, *The Legacy of the Civil War* (1961; repr., Lincoln: University of Nebraska Press, 1998), 59–66.

26. David W. Blight, *Race and Reunion: The Civil War in American Memory* (Cambridge, Mass.: Belknap Press of Harvard University Press, 2001), 152.

27. Hans L. Trefousse, *Thaddeus Stevens: Nineteenth-Century Egalitarian* (Mechanicsburg, Pa.: Stackpole, 2001), 168.

28. U.S. Congress, House, Joint Committee on Reconstruction, *Report of the Joint Committee on Reconstruction*, 39th Congress, 1st sess., 1866, Report No. 30, x–xi, 278–87.

29. *Harper's Weekly*, June 30, 1866, www.harpweek.com (accessed March 3, 2003).

30. Ibid., March 23, 1867, www.harpweek.com (accessed March 3, 2003).

31. Ibid., July 21, 1866, www.harpweek.com (accessed March 3, 2003).

32. Nancy Roberts, "The Afterlife of Civil War Prisons and Their Dead" (Ph.D. diss., University of Oregon, 1996), 218–29.

33. Quartermaster General's Office, *The Martyrs Who, for Our Country, Gave up their Lives in the Prison Pens in Andersonville, GA.* (Washington, D.C.: Government Printing Office, 1866), 8.

34. Hesseltine, *Civil War Prisons*, 247–48.

35. Augustus C. Hamlin, *Martyria; or, Andersonville Prison* (Boston: Lee & Shepard, 1866); Robert H. Kellogg, *Life and Death in Rebel Prisons* (1865; repr., Freeport, N.Y.: Books for Libraries Press, 1971); Joseph Ferguson, *Life Struggles in Rebel Prisons: A Record of the Sufferings, Escapes, Adventures, and Starvation of the Union Prisoners* (Philadelphia: James A. Ferguson, 1865), 72–73.

36. William Burson, *A Race For Liberty, or My Capture, Imprisonment, and Escape* (Wellsville, Ohio: W. G. Foster, 1867), 41.

37. Albert D. Richardson, *The Secret Service, the Field, the Dungeon, and the Escape* (Hartford, Conn.: American Publishing, 1865), 417, 412.

38. Warren Lee Goss, *The Soldier's Story of His Captivity at Andersonville, Belle Isle, and other Rebel Prisons* (1866; repr., Scituate, Mass.: Digital Scanning, 2001), 257; Josiah C. Brownell, *At Andersonville. A Narrative of Personal Adventure at Andersonville, Florence and Charleston Rebel Prisons* (1867; repr., Glen Cove, N.Y.: Glen Cove Public Library, 1981), 7.

39. J. F. Brock, "The Personal Experience of J. F. Brock in the Rebel Prison Pens," p. 2, Civil War Miscellaneous Collection, 3rd series, Kansas City Civil War Round Table Collection, United States Army Military History Institute.

40. Decimus et Ultimus Barziza, *The Adventures of a Prisoner of War* (1865; repr., Austin: University of Texas Press, 1964), 103, 91.

41. A. M. Keiley, *In Vinculis; or, The Prisoner of War* (New York: Blelock, 1866), 5, 138–47, 141, 52.

42. L. M. Lewis, "Introduction," viii–ix, in W. A. Wash, *Camp, Field and Prison Life* (St. Louis: Southwestern, 1870).

43. Rutman, "The War Crimes and Trial of Henry Wirz," 133.

44. *Harper's Weekly*, November 9, 1867, July 4, 1868, July 11, 1868, www.harpweek.com (accessed March 3, 2003).

45. Ibid., October 3, 1868, October 24, 1868, www.harpweek.com (accessed March 3, 2003).

46. U.S. Congress, House, *Report on the Treatment of Prisoners of War by the Rebel Authorities*, 40th Congress, 3rd sess., 1869, Report No. 45, 6, 7.

47. Stuart McConnell, *Glorious Contentment: The Grand Army of the Republic, 1865–1900* (Chapel Hill: University of North Carolina Press, 1992), 94, 21, 28.

48. J. P. C. Shanks, *Speech of Gen. J. P. C. Shanks, of Indiana, on Treatment of Prisoners of War* (Washington D.C.: Judd & Detweiler, 1870), 3, 12; see also C. E. Reynolds, "Thirteen Months at Andersonville Prison and What I Saw There: A Paper Delivered before the N. L. Association, Napoleon, Ohio, April 24, 1869," *Northwest Ohio Quarterly* 27 (1955): 94–113.

49. Mary R. Dearing, *Veterans in Politics: The Story of the G. A. R.* (Baton Rouge: Louisiana State University Press, 1952), 203. Also see Reinhard H. Luthin, "Waving the Bloody Shirt:

Northern Political Tactics in Post-Civil War Times," *Georgia Review* 14 (Spring 1960): 64–71.

50. *Harper's Weekly,* September 21, 1872, www.harpweek.com (accessed March 3, 2003).

51. Gaines M. Foster, *Ghosts of the Confederacy: Defeat, the Lost Cause, and the Emergence of the New South 1865 to 1913* (New York: Oxford University Press, 1987), 22, 33.

52. Alexander H. Stephens, *Recollections of Alexander H. Stephens,* edited by Myrta Avary (1910; repr., Baton Rouge: Louisiana State University Press, 1998), 233–36.

53. John J. Craven, *Prison Life of Jefferson Davis* (New York: Carleton, 1866), 107–8.

54. The Louis Schade quotes come from an unknown newspaper dated April 4, 1867, Joseph Frederick Waring Papers, Folder 1, Southern Historical Collection at the University of North Carolina at Chapel Hill.

55. Blight, *Race and Reunion,* 2.

56. See William A. Blair, *Cities of the Dead: Contesting the Memory of the Civil War in the South, 1865–1914* (Chapel Hill: University of North Carolina Press, 2004); W. Fitzhugh Brundage, *The Southern Past: A Clash of Race and Memory* (Cambridge, Mass.: Belknap Press of Harvard University Press, 2005); Kathleen A. Clark, *Defining Moments: African American Commemoration and Political Culture in the South, 1863–1913* (Chapel Hill: University of North Carolina Press, 2005); Donald R. Shaffer, *After the Glory: The Struggles of Black Civil War Veterans* (Lawrence: University Press of Kansas, 2004).

57. Douglas G. Gardner, "Andersonville and American Memory: Civil War Prisoners and Narratives of Suffering and Redemption" (Ph.D. diss., Miami University, 1998), 61–69; Christopher Kent Wilson, "Winslow Homer's Images of Blacks: The Civil War and Reconstruction Years," *Journal of American History* 77 (June 1990): 247

58. Peggy Sheppard, *Andersonville Georgia USA* (1973, repr., Andersonville, Ga.: Sheppard, 2001), 66–68.

59. William B. Burnett, "Memorial Day through the Years," pp. 1–2, Andersonville Vertical Files, Andersonville National Historic Site. See also an unidentified newspaper clipping, dated June 3, 1870, in Andersonville Vertical Files, Andersonville National Historic Site.

60. Hill-Blaine Debate on Amnesty Bill, 44th Congress, 1st sess. *Congressional Record* 4 (January 10–14, 1876): H. 324.

61. E. Merton Coulter, "Amnesty for All except Jefferson Davis: The Hill-Blaine Debate of 1876," *Georgia Historical Quarterly* 56 (Winter 1972): 457; Roberts, "The Afterlife of Civil War Prisons," 41–49.

62. Hill-Blaine Debate on Amnesty Bill, *Congressional Record:* H. 345, 347, 351.

63. *Southern Historical Society Papers* 1 (January to June, 1876): 113. The full March 1876 issue on Civil War prisons runs from page 113 to 327.

CHAPTER THREE

1. Robert H. Wiebe, *The Search for Order 1877–1920* (New York: Hill & Wang, 1967); Nell Painter, *Standing at Armageddon: The United States 1877–1919* (New York: W. W. Norton, 1987); T. J. Jackson Lears, *No Place of Grace: Antimodernism and the Transformation of American Culture, 1880–1920* (Chicago: University of Chicago Press, 1983); Olivier Zunz, *Making America Corporate 1870–1920* (Chicago: University of Chicago Press, 1990).

2. James Garfield, "Speech of Gen. Garfield at the Andersonville Reunion at Toledo, Ohio, October 3, 1879," in Sergeant Oaks, *Prison Life in Dixie* (1880; repr., Scituate, Mass.: Digital Scanning, 1999), 204.

3. Reinhard H. Luthin, "Waving the Bloody Shirt: Northern Political Tactics in Post-Civil War Times," *Georgia Review* 14 (Spring 1960): 70.

4. James G. Blaine, *Political Discussions: Legislative, Diplomatic, and Popular* (Norwich, Conn.: Henry Bill, 1887), 160–61.

5. William Marvel, "Johnny Ransom's Imagination," *Civil War History* 41 (September 1995): 181–89; James M. Gillespie, "Postwar Mythmaking: The Case of the POWs," *North & South* 6 (April 2003): 40–49; and William Hesseltine, *Civil War Prisons: A Study in War Psychology* (1930; repr., Columbus: Ohio State University Press, 1998), 233–58.

6. Sergeant Oats, *Prison Life in Dixie (1880; repr., Scituate, Mass.: Digital Scanning, 1999)* 61, 60.

7. Willard Glazier, *Sword and Pen; or, Ventures and Adventures of Willard Glazier* (Philadelphia: P. W. Zeigler, 1881), i, 167, v. See also J. Madison Drake, *Fast and Loose in Dixie: An Unprejudiced Narrative of Personal Experience as a Prisoner of War at Libby, Macon, Savannah, and Charleston* (New York: Authors', 1880), 29; John W. Urban, *Battle Field and Prison Pen, or Through the War, and Thrice a Prisoner in Rebel Dungeons* (N.p.: Edgewood, 1882), viii; William B. Woolverton, "A Sketch of Prison Life at Andersonville," *Firelands Pioneer* 8 (January 1894): 65–68.

8. John McElroy, *Andersonville: A Story of Rebel Military Prisons* (1879; Greenwich, Conn.: Fawcett, 1962), 318, ix. Other important Union prisoner narratives of the period include, among others, Alonzo Cooper, *In and out of Rebel Prisons* (Oswego, N.Y.: R. J. Oliphant, 1888); William W. Day, *Fifteen Months in Dixie; or, My Personal Experience in Rebel Prisons* (Owatonna, Minn.: People's Press Print, 1889); S. S. Boggs, *Eighteen Months under the Rebel Flag* (Lovington, Ill.: privately printed, 1887); Thomas H. Mann, "A Yankee in Andersonville," *Century Illustrated Monthly Magazine* 40 (May–October 1890): 447–61, 606–22; Lessel Long, *Twelve Months in Andersonville* (Huntington, Ind.: Thad and Mark Butler, 1886).

9. John McElroy, *Andersonville*, 318, ix.

10. Herman Braun, *Andersonville: An Object Lesson on Protection* (Milwaukee: C. D. Fahsel, 1892), vi, 70, 98, 160–61.

11. Drew Gilpin Faust, *This Republic of Suffering: Death and the American Civil War* (New York: Knopf, 2008), xii.

12. Asa B. Isham, Henry M. Davidson, and Henry B. Furness, *Prisoners of War and Military Prisons* (Cincinnati, Ohio: Lyman & Cushing, 1890), 388.

13. Benjamin F. Booth and Steve Meyer, *Dark Days of the Rebellion: Life in Southern Military Prisons* (1897; repr., Garrison, Iowa: Meyer, 1996), xiii, xii.

14. Cooper, *In and Out of Rebel Prisons,* 46; Jesse Hawes, *Cahaba: A Story of Captive Boys in Blue* (New York: Burr, 1888), v.

15. James R. Compton, *Andersonville: The Story of Man's Inhumanity to Man* (Des Moines, Iowa: Iowa Printing, 1887), 2.

16. H. Clay Trumbull, *War Memories of a Union Chaplain* (New York: Charles Scribner's Sons, 1898), 278–79; Drake, *Fast and Loose in Dixie,* vi.

17. John V. Hadley, *Seven Months a Prisoner* (1898; repr., Hanover, Ind.: Nugget, 1998), 20.

18. Long, *Twelve Months in Andersonville,* 178.

19. McElroy, *Andersonville: A Story of Rebel Military Prisons,* 30.

20. William B. McCreery, "My Experience as a Prisoner of War and Escape from Libby Prison," in *War Papers Read before the Commandery of the State of Michigan: Military Order of the Loyal Legion of the United States* (Detroit: Winn & Hammond, 1893), 17.

21. *Famous Adventures and Prison Escapes of the Civil War* (New York: Century, 1893).

22. Douglas G. Gardner, "Andersonville and Historical Memory: Civil War Prisoners and Narratives of Suffering and Redemption" (Ph.D. diss., Miami University, 1998), 70.

23. Urban, *Battle Field and Prison Pen,* 484.

24. Booth and Meyer, *Dark Days of the Rebellion,* xiii.

25. Oats, *Prison Life in Dixie,* 5.

26. Jno. Robertson, *Michigan in the War* (Lansing, Mich.: W. S. George, 1882), 140–41.

27. W. T. Zeigler, *Half Hour with an Andersonville Prisoner. Delivered at the Reunion of Post 9, G. A. R., at Gettysburg, Pa, Jan. 8th, 1879* (N.p.: John M. Tate, 1879), 11.

28. William E. Chandler, *Decoration Day. Address of William E. Chandler, on Thursday, May 30, 1889, at Nashua, N. H., before John G. Foster Post No. 7, G. A. R.* (Concord, N.H.: Republican Press Association, 1889), 7.

29. Braun, *Andersonville,* 151.

30. Ann Fabian, *The Unvarnished Truth: Personal Narratives in Nineteenth-Century America* (Berkeley: University of California Press, 2000), 119, 118.

31. Gaines M. Foster, *Ghosts of the Confederacy: Defeat, the Lost Cause, and the Emergence of the New South, 1865–1913* (New York: Oxford University Press, 1987), 126.

32. Rufus B. Richardson, "The Prison Question Again," *Southern Historical Society Papers* 8 (January–December 1880): 569–70.

33. James T. Wells, "Prison Experience," *Southern Historical Society Papers* 7 (January–December 1879): 327–28, 489–90. Other examples of southern prison accounts in the *SHSP* include M. McNamara, "Lieutenant Charlie Pierce's Daring Attempts to Escape from Johnson's Island," *SHSP* 8 (January–December 1880): 61–67; T. D. Witherspoon, "Prison Life at Fort McHenry," *SHSP* 8 (January–December 1880): 111–19, 163–68; William G. Keady, "Incidents of Prison Life at Camp Douglas—Experience of Corporal J. G. Blanchard," *SHSP* 12 (January–December 1884): 269–73; Henry G. Damon, "A Florida Boy's Experience in Prison and Escaping," *SHSP* 12 (January–December 1884): 395–402.

34. Charles T. Loehr, "Point Lookout," *Southern Historical Society Papers* 18 (January–December 1890): 119–20.

35. George Wilson Booth, *A Maryland Boy in Lee's Army* (1898; repr., Lincoln: University of Nebraska Press, 2000), 164–66.

36. William Jones, "The Historical Register on our Papers," *Southern Historical Society Papers* 6 (July–December 1878): 238.

37. Jefferson Davis, *Andersonville and other War-Prisons* (New York: Belford, 1890), 161–62, 345–48.

38. N. P. Chipman, *The Horrors of Andersonville Prison* (San Francisco: Bancroft, 1891), 1, 3, 7, 79–80.

39. Thomas E. Spotswood, "Horrors of Camp Morton," *Southern Historical Society Papers* 19 (January–December 1891): 327–33; A. M. Keiley, "Prison-Pens North," *SHSP* 19 (January–December 1891): 333–40; T. E. Fell, "Escape of Prisoners from Johnson's Island," *SHSP* 19 (January–December 1891): 428–31; J. B. Traywick, "Prison Life at Point Lookout," *SHSP* 19 (January–December 1891): 431–35.

40. Spotswood, "Horrors of Camp Morton," 332.

41. Abram Fulkerson, "The Prison Experience of a Confederate Soldier," *Southern Historical Society Papers* 22 (January–December 1894): 127–46; Albert Caison, "Southern Soldiers in Northern Prisons," *SHSP* 23 (January–December 1895): 158–65; F. C. Barnes and R. E. Frayser, "Imprisoned Under Fire," *SHSP* 25 (January–December 1897): 365–77.

42. John Shirley Ward, "Responsibility for the Death of Prisoners," *Confederate Veteran* 4 (January 1896): 13.

43. Charles W. Frazier, "Prison Life on Johnson's Island," *Confederate Veteran* 2 (April 1894): 113–14; W. Gart Johnson, "Prison Life at Harper's Ferry and on Johnson's Island," *CV* 2 (August 1894): 242–43.

44. John R. Neff, *Honoring the Civil War Dead: Commemoration and the Problem of Reconciliation* (Lawrence: University Press of Kansas, 2005), 144–45; Nancy A. Roberts, "The Afterlife of Civil War Prisons and Their Dead" (Ph.D. diss., University of Oregon, 1996), 212–62.

45. "Confederate Dead at Indianapolis," *Confederate Veteran* 1 (January 1894): 18.

46. "Services at our Chicago Monument," *Confederate Veteran* 3 (July 1895): 209.

47. "Our Monument in Chicago," *Confederate Veteran* 3 (June 1895): 176.

48. "Camp Chase Confederate Dead," *Confederate Veteran* 4 (August 1896): 246–48.

49. "Camp Chase Confederate Graves," *Confederate Veteran* 5 (May 1897): 197.

50. Henry Howe Cook, "Story of the Six Hundred," *Confederate Veteran* 6 (March 1898): 120.

51. "Treatment of Prisoners," *Confederate Veteran* 3 (October 1895): 297.

52. "Andersonville," *American Missionary* XLV (September 1891): 318, http://cdl.library.cornell.edu/moa (accessed August 1, 2008).

53. "Letter from Andersonville, Ga," *The American Missionary* XLVI (March 1892): 93–94, http://cdl.library.cornell.edu/moa (accessed August 1, 2008).

54. Robert S. Davis, *Ghosts and Shadows of Andersonville: Essays on the Secret Social Histories of America's Deadliest Prison* (Macon, Ga.: Mercer University Press, 2006), 42–43.

55. *Americus Times-Recorder,* May 31, 1898, clipping in Andersonville Vertical Files, Andersonville National Historic Site.

56. Ibid., June 6, 1890, clipping in Andersonville Vertical Files, Andersonville National Historic Site.

57. Ibid., June 3, 1892, clipping in Andersonville Vertical Files, Andersonville National Historic Site.

58. Roberts, "The Afterlife of Civil War Prisons," 178–79.

59. *Americus Times-Recorder,* May 26, 1895, clipping in Andersonville Vertical Files, Andersonville National Historic Site.

60. Ibid., June 1, 1894, clipping in Andersonville Vertical Files, Andersonville National Historic Site.

61. Ibid., May 26, 1895, clipping in Andersonville Vertical Files, Andersonville National Historic Site.

62. *Loudoun Times Mirror,* February 16, 1888, clipping in Civil War Miscellaneous Collection, 3rd series, Confederate States Army Miscellaneous, United States Army Military History Institute. See also William B. Meyer, "The Selling of Libby Prison," *American Heritage* 45 (November 1994): 114–18.

63. Katherine W. Hannaford, "Culture versus Commerce: The Libby Prison Museum and the Image of Chicago, 1889–1899," *Ecumene* 8 (July 2001): 284–316.

64. *Libby Prison War Museum Catalogue and Program* (Chicago: Libby Prison War Museum Association, 1890).

65. Bruce Klee, "They Paid to Enter Libby Prison," *Civil War Times Illustrated* 37 (February 1999): 37.

66. *Thomasville Review,* March 7, 1893, clipping in Andersonville Vertical Files, Andersonville National Historic Site.

67. William Burnett, "The Woman's Relief Corps at Andersonville," Andersonville Vertical Files, Andersonville National Historic Site.

68. The newspaper headline comes from an unidentified, late 1890s newspaper clipping in the Civil War Miscellaneous Collection, Joseph Schubert Collection, United States Army Military History Institute.

69. Jim Weeks, *Gettysburg: Memory, Market, and an American Shrine* (Princeton, N.J.: Princeton University Press, 2003), 53.

70. John A Wyeth, "Prisoners North and South," *Southern Historical Society Papers* 20 (January–December 1892): 48, 51, 48. In keeping with the pattern of the Davis-Chipman exchange, Wyeth's statements unsurprisingly provoked a northern rebuttal. See James R. Carnahan, *Camp Morton* (N.p.: Baker-Randolph L. & E. Co., 1892).

71. Nathaniel Cheairs Hughes, Jr., *Sir Henry Morton Stanley, Confederate* (Baton Rouge: Louisiana State University Press, 2000), 146.

72. Herbert W. Collingwood, *Andersonville Violets: A Story of Northern and Southern Life* (1889; repr., Tuscaloosa: University of Alabama Press, 2000), xxxiii, 270.

CHAPTER FOUR

1. McKinley's comments are taken from Committee on Confederate Dead, Charles Broadway Rouss Camp No. 1191 United Confederate Veterans, *Report on the Re-burial of the Confederate Dead in Arlington Cemetery* (Washington, D.C., Judd & Detweiler, 1901), 10–11.

2. Gaines M. Foster, *Ghosts of the Confederacy: Defeat, the Lost Cause, and the Emergence of the New South 1865–1913* (New York: Oxford University Press, 1987), 145.

3. Gary Laderman, *The Sacred Remains: American Attitudes toward Death, 1799–1883* (New Haven, Conn.: Yale University Press, 1996); Edward T. Linenthal, *Sacred Ground: Americans and Their Battlefields* (Chicago: University of Illinois Press, 1991); Jim Weeks, *Gettysburg: Memory, Market, and an American Shrine* (Princeton, N.J.: Princeton University Press, 2003).

4. David Blight, *Race and Reunion: The Civil War in American Memory* (Cambridge, Mass.: Belknap Press of Harvard University Press, 2001); Cecilia E. O'Leary, "Blood Brotherhood: The Racialization of Patriotism, 1865–1918," in *Bonds of Affection: Americans Define their Patriotism*, ed. John Bodnar (Princeton, N.J.: Princeton University Press, 1996), 54; Stuart McConnell, *Glorious Contentment: The Grand Army of the Republic, 1865–1900* (Chapel Hill: University of North Carolina Press, 1992), 200.

5. Thomas J. Brown, *The Public Art of Civil War Commemoration* (New York: Bedford/St. Martin's, 2004), 6; Kirk Savage, *Standing Soldiers, Kneeling Slaves: Race, War and Monument in Nineteenth-Century America* (Princeton, N.J.: Princeton University Press, 1997), 209.

6. New Jersey Monument Commissioners, *Report of the New Jersey Andersonville Monument Commissioners* (Somerville, N.J.: Unionist-Gazette Association, 1899), 3, 7–8, 11.

7. *Report of the Maine Andersonville Monument Commissioners* (Augusta, Maine: Kennebec Journal, 1904); Commonwealth of Massachusetts, *Report of the Commission on Andersonville Monument* (Boston: Wright & Putter, 1902); *Report of the Joint Special Committee on Erection of Monument at Andersonville, Georgia* (Providence, R.I.: E. L. Freeman, 1903); *Dedication Connecticut Andersonville Monument: Dedication of the Monument at Andersonville, Georgia, October 23, 1907* (Hartford: Published by the State, 1908).

8. William Bennett, "Pennsylvania," in "Andersonville Monuments," p.1–2, Andersonville Vertical Files, Andersonville National Historic Site.

9. *Pennsylvania at Andersonville, Georgia, Ceremonies at the Dedication of the Memorial Erected by the Commonwealth of Pennsylvania in the National Cemetery at Andersonville, Georgia* (N.p.: C. E. Aughinbaugh, 1909), 16–17, 25–26, 28.

10. *Americus Times-Recorder,* December 8, 1905, clipping in Andersonville Vertical Files, Andersonville National Historic Site.

11. Ibid., September 13, 1907, clipping in Andersonville Vertical Files, Andersonville National Historic Site.

12. Ibid., September 28, 1911, clipping in Andersonville Vertical Files, Andersonville National Historic Site.

13. *Pennsylvania at Salisbury, North Carolina: Ceremonies at the Dedication of the Memorial Erected by the Commonwealth of Pennsylvania in the National Cemetery at Salisbury, North Carolina* (N.p.: C. E. Aughinbaugh, 1910).

14. *Report of the Maine Commissioners on the Monument Erected at Salisbury, N.C., 1908* (Waterville, Maine: Sentinel, 1908), 10, 13, 15, 19–20, 25.

15. Excerpts from the minutes of the 25th Women's Relief Corps National Convention, 231, the 27th Women's Relief Corps National Convention, 192, and the 28th Women's Relief Corps National Convention, 61–62, come from Andersonville Vertical Files, Andersonville National Historic Site.

16. John R. Neff, *Honoring the Civil War Dead: Commemoration and the Problem of Reconciliation* (Lawrence: University Press of Kansas, 2005).

17. Alonzo Abernethy, ed., *Dedication of Monuments Erected by the State of Iowa* (Des Moines, Iowa: Emory H. English, 1908), 99–100.

18. Ernest A. Sherman, *Dedicating in Dixie* (Cedar Rapids, Iowa: Press of the Record Printing Company, 1907), 45.

19. *Pennsylvania at Andersonville,* 47, 49.

20. Ralph O. Bates, *Billy and Dick from Andersonville Prison to the White House* (Santa Cruz, Calif.: Sentinel, 1910); William B. Clifton, *Libby and Andersonville Prisons: A True Sketch* (Indianapolis, Ind.: privately printed, 1910); James N. Miller, *The Story of Andersonville and Florence* (Des Moines, Iowa: Welch, The Printer, 1900); W. F. Lyon, *In and Out of Andersonville Prison* (Detroit: Geo. Harland, 1905); C. M. Prutsman, *A Soldier's Experience in Southern Prisons* (New York: Andrew H. Kellogg, 1901).

21. William H. Allen, "One Hundred and Ninety Days in Rebel Prisons," *Annals of Iowa* 38 (Winter 1966): 232, 234, 236.

22. John W. Northrop, *Chronicles from the Diary of a War Prisoner* (Wichita, Kans: privately printed, 1904), 195.

23. John Read, "Texas Prisons and a Comparison of Northern and Southern Prison Camps," in *Personal Recollections of the War of the Rebellion,* ed. A. Noel Blakeman (New York: G. P. Putnam's Sons, 1912), 249, 259.

24. Ezra H. Ripple, *Dancing along the Deadline, The Andersonville Memoir of a Prisoner of the Confederacy,* edited by Mark Snell (Novato, Calif.: Presidio Press, 1996), 5–6.

25. George H. Putnam, *A Prisoner of War in Virginia 1864–5* (New York: G. P. Putnam's Sons, 1912), 3.

26. Ripple, *Dancing Along the Deadline,* 1–2.

27. Thomas Sturgis, "Prisoners of War," in *Personal Recollections of the War of the Rebellion,* ed. A. Noel Blakeman (New York: G. P. Putnam's Sons, 1912), 270–71, 275, 305, 267.

28. Clay W. Holmes, *The Elmira Prison Camp* (New York: G. P. Putnam's Sons, 1912), v.

29. William H. Knauss, *The Story of Camp Chase* (1906; repr., Columbus, Ohio: The General's Books, 1994), xx.

30. Holland Thompson, ed., *Prisons and Hospitals, Vol. 7, The Photographic History of the Civil War in Ten Volumes,* ed. Francis Trevelyan Miller (New York: Review of Reviews Co., 1911), 18, 54, 136.

31. Sturgis, "Prisoners of War," 326–28.

32. *Minutes of the 8th Annual Meeting and Reunion of the United Confederate Veterans* (New Orleans: Hopkins' Printing Office, 1899), 70, 65–77; for similar sentiments, see *Minutes of the Tenth Annual Meeting and Reunion of the United Confederate Veterans* (New Orleans: Hopkins' Printing Office, 1902), 118–32, and George L. Christian, "The Confederate Cause and its Defenders," *Southern Historical Society Papers* 26 (January–December 1898): 323–47

33. James M. Page, *The True Story of Andersonville Prison* (1908, repr., Scituate, Mass.: Digital Scanning, 2000), 245–47.

34. Committee on Confederate Dead, *Report of Re-burial,* 3, 15–16.

35. Confederated Southern Memorial Association, *History of the Confederated Memorial Associations of the South* (New Orleans: Graham, 1904), 87–88.

36. Knauss, *The Story of Camp Chase,* xvii–xviii, 75, 73. See also "Camp Chase Memorial Association," *Confederate Veteran* 7 (July 1899): 305; *Minutes of the Eleventh Annual Meeting of the United Daughters of the Confederacy* (Nashville, Tenn.: Foster & Webb, 1905), 147–50.

37. Nancy A. Roberts, "The Afterlife of Civil War Prisons and Their Dead" (Ph.D. diss., University of Oregon, 1996), 238–47; "Monument to Confederate Dead of Fort Delaware," *Confederate Veteran* 22 (March 1914): 125.

38. Hunter McGuire, "School Histories in the South," *Confederate Veteran* 7 (November 1899): 500, 502.

39. A. W. Mangum, "History of the Salisbury, N. C., Confederate Prison," *Publications of the Southern History Association* 3 (1899): 336

40. See W. J. Bohon, "Rock Island Prison," *Confederate Veteran* 16 (July 1908): 346–47; George L. Christian, "Report of the History Committee," *Southern Historical Society Papers* 29 (January–December 1901): 99–131; George L. Christian, "Treatment and Exchange of Prisoners," *SHSP* 30 (January–December 1902): 77–104; R. A. Goodwin, "Memorial Sermon," *SHSP* 37 (January–December 1909): 338–47.

41. Marcus B. Toney, *Privations of a Private* (Nashville, Tenn.: privately printed, 1905); William A. Fletcher, *Rebel Private* (1908, repr., Austin: University of Texas Press, 1954); Alexander Hunter, *Johnny Reb and Billy Yank* (New York: Neale, 1905); Randolph H. McKim, *A Soldier's Recollections* (New York: Longmans, Green, 1911); John N. Opie, *A Rebel Cavalryman* (Chicago: W. B. Conkey, 1899); L. W. Hopkins, *From Bull Run to Appomattox* (Baltimore: Fleet-McGinley, 1908); I. Hermann, *Memoirs of a Veteran* (Atlanta: Byrd, 1911); Wayland F. Dunaway, *Reminiscences of a Rebel* (New York: Neale, 1913).

42. John H. King, *Three Hundred Days in a Yankee Prison* (1904, repr., Kennesaw, Ga.: Continental Book Company, 1959), 3, 84–85.

43. Confederated Southern Memorial Association, *History of the Confederated Memorial Associations of the South,* 31.

44. *Minutes of the Fifteenth Annual Meeting and Reunion of the United Confederate Veterans* (N.p.: privately printed, 1905), 30, 33.

45. McGuire, "School Histories in the South," 500. See also Karen L. Cox, *Dixie's Daughters:*

The United Daughters of the Confederacy and the Preservation of Confederate Culture (Gainesville, Fla.: University Press of Florida, 2003).

46. *Minutes of the Twelfth Annual Meeting of the United Daughters of the Confederacy* (Nashville, Tenn.: Foster, Webb & Parkes, 1906), 137–40.

47. L. G. Young, "Georgia U. D. C. to Honor Henry Wirz," *Confederate Veteran* 14 (April 1906): 181–82. See also James H. M'Neilly, "Andersonville and Maj. Henry Wirz," *CV* 15 (January 1907): 14–16; "Maj. Henry Wirz," *CV* 16 (May 1908): 199–200.

48. R. A. Brock, "Prisoners of War North and South," *Southern Historical Society Papers* 34 (January–December 1906): 69.

49. J. R. Gibbons, "The Monument to Henry Wirz," *Southern Historical Society Papers* 36 (January–December 1908): 226–36.

50. William Burnett, "The Wirz Monument at Andersonville," p. 5, Andersonville Vertical Files, Andersonville National Historic Site.

51. *Americus Times-Recorder,* January 28, 1908, clipping in Andersonville Vertical Files, Andersonville National Historic Site.

52. E. F. Andrews to Mr. Oglesby, Montgomery, Ala., April 29, 1907, Thaddeus Kosciuszko Papers, Box 2, Mss., Duke University, Durham, N.C. I am indebted to Gaines Foster for bringing this letter to my attention.

53. *Americus Times-Recorder,* March 22, 1908, clipping in Andersonville Vertical Files, Andersonville National Historic Site; Burnett, "The Wirz Monument at Andersonville," pp. 9–11.

54. Ibid., December 8, 1908, clipping in Andersonville Vertical Files, Andersonville National Historic Site.

55. Ibid., December 15, 1908, clipping in Andersonville Vertical Files, Andersonville National Historic Site.

56. Ibid., March 18, 1909, clipping in Andersonville Vertical Files, Andersonville National Historic Site.

57. William Burnett, "Memorial Day through the Years," pp. 5–6, Andersonville Vertical Files, Andersonville National Historic Site.

58. Burnett, "Memorial Day through the Years," p. 7.

59. Peggy Sheppard, *Andersonville Georgia USA* (1973, repr., Andersonville, Ga.: Sheppard, 2001), 59.

60. Burnett, "Memorial Day through the Years," pp. 8–9.

61. Sheppard, *Andersonville Georgia USA,* 59.

62. Abernethy, *Dedication of Monuments,* 103.

63. Sherman, *Dedicating in Dixie,* 53.

64. Burnett, "The Wirz Monument," pp. 8–9.

65. Gibbons, "The Monument to Captain Henry Wirz," 226, 233–34.

66. "Maj. Henry Wirz," *Confederate Veteran* 16 (May 1908): 199.

67. *The Trial and Death of Henry Wirz* (Raleigh, N.C.: E. M. Uzzell, 1908).

68. *Americus Times-Recorder,* May 13, 1909, clipping in Andersonville Vertical Files, Andersonville National Historic Site.

69. Burnett, "The Wirz Monument," p. 11. See also William Mickle, "General Orders," 22 May 1909 in Augustus W. Graham Papers, Series 2.6, Folder 251, 1909–1913, Southern Historical Collection at the University of North Carolina, Chapel Hill.

70. Burnett, "The Wirz Monument," p. 12.

71. John H. Stibbs, "Andersonville and the Trial of Henry Wirz," *Iowa Journal of History and Politics* 9 (1911): 34, 53.

72. Sturgis, "Prisoners of War," 311.

73. J. W. Elarton, *Andersonville* (Aurora, Neb.: privately printed, 1913).

CHAPTER FIVE

1. *A Pilgrimage to the Shrines of Patriotism* (Albany, N.Y.: J. B. Lyon, 1916), 25.

2. William Burnett, "Minnesota," in "Andersonville Monuments," pp. 1–2, Andersonville Vertical Files, Andersonville National Historic Site.

3. William Burnett, "Tennessee Monument," in "Andersonville Monuments," pp. 2–3, Andersonville Vertical Files, Andersonville National Historic Site.

4. William Burnett, "Clara Barton Monument," in "Andersonville Monuments," pp. 1–2, Andersonville Vertical Files, Andersonville National Historic Site. Other WRC-sponsored monuments included the "Our Lizabeth" monument," a 1908 tribute to former WRC president Elizabeth Turner; the "Providence Spring" monument, built in 1901; and a 1928 tribute to the Gettysburg Address.

5. William Burnett, "Sun Dial Monument," in "Andersonville Monuments," p. 1, Andersonville Vertical Files, Andersonville National Historic Site.

6. William Burnett, "8 State Monument," in "Andersonville Monuments," p. 1, Andersonville Vertical Files, Andersonville National Historic Site.

7. H. M .M. Richards, "In Rebel Prisons: A Tribute to Samuel B. Stafford," *Lebanon County Historical Society* 8 (1922): 275.

8. Peterson H. Cherry, *Prisoner in Blue: Memories of the Civil War after 70 Years* (Los Angeles: Wetzel, 1931), 70.

9. Charles A. Humphreys, *Field, Camp, Hospital and Prison in the Civil War, 1863–1865* (1918; repr., Freeport, N.Y.: Books for Libraries Press, 1971); A. L. Spencer, *Reminiscences of the Civil War and Andersonville Prison* (Ottawa, Kans.: Fulton, 1917); Daniel A. Langworthy, *Reminiscences of a Prisoner of War and His Escape* (Minneapolis, Minn.: Byron, 1915); Emogene Niver Marshall, *Reminiscences of the Civil War and Andersonville Prison* (Sandusky, Ohio: Krewson's, 1932); Walter R. Robbins, *War Record and Personal Experiences of Walter Raleigh Robbins* (N.p.: privately printed, 1923); David S. Whitenack, "Reminiscences of the Civil War: Andersonville," *Indiana Magazine of History* 11 (June 1915): 128–43; Henry Devillez, "Reminiscences of the Civil War: Andersonville," *Indiana Magazine of History* 11 (June 1915): 144–47.

10. See, e.g., C. M. Destler, "An Andersonville Prison Diary," *Georgia Historical Quarterly* 24 (March 1940): 56–76.

11. H. W. Graber, *The Life Record of H. W. Graber* (N.p.: privately printed, 1916), 136.

12. David E. Johnston, *The Story of a Confederate Boy in the Civil War* (Portland, Ore.: Glass & Prudhomme, 1914), 341.

13. John A. Wyeth, *With Sabre and Scalpel* (New York: Harper & Brothers, 1914); Jno B. Castleman, *Active Service* (Louisville, Ky.: Courier-Journal Job Printing, 1917); Absalom Grimes, *Confederate Mail Runner,* ed. M. M. Quaife (New Haven, Conn.: Yale University Press, 1926); John Dooley, *Confederate Soldier,* ed. Joseph T. Durkin (Ithaca, N.Y.: Cayuga, 1945).

14. R. T. Bean, "Seventeen Months in Camp Douglas," *Confederate Veteran* 22 (June 1914): 270.

15. Bennett H. Young, "Treatment of Prisoners of War," *Confederate Veteran* 26 (November 1918): 470, 501; "Prison Horrors Compared," *CV* 27 (November 1919): 410–11.

16. Gray Book Committee S. C. V., *The Gray Book* (N.p.: privately printed, 1920), 2–3.

17. "Major Henry Wirz," *William and Mary College Quarterly Historical Magazine* 27 (January 1919): 145.

18. Gray Book Committee, *The Gray Book,* 18–19.

19. A. T. Goodwyn, *Memorial Address* (Montgomery, Ala.: privately printed, 1926), 4.

20. Mildred L. Rutherford, *Wrongs of History Righted* (Savannah, Ga.: privately printed, 1914), 2–4.

21. *Americus Times-Recorder,* May 15, 1919, May 16, 1919, clippings in Andersonville Vertical Files, Andersonville National Historic Site.

22. Mildred L. Rutherford, *Facts and Figures vs. Myths and Misrepresentations: Henry Wirz and Andersonville Prison* (Athens, Ga.: privately printed, 1921), 52.

23. Sherwood Anderson, *Winesburg, Ohio,* ed. John H. Ferres (New York: Viking, 1966), 23.

24. The Margaret Mitchell quote comes from Edgar Stewart, review of *Camp Morton, 1861–1865: Indianapolis Prison Camp,* by Hattie Lou Winslow and Joseph R. H. Moore, *The American Historical Review* 47 (October 1941): 199.

25. *Minutes of the Forty-Fourth Annual Convention of the United Daughters of the Confederacy* (N.p.: privately printed, 1937), 185

26. Elizabeth L. Parker, "Henry Wirz, the Martyr," *United Daughters of the Confederacy Magazine* 12 (March 1949): 18. See also Elizabeth L. Parker, "The Civil War Career of Henry Wirz and Its Aftermath" (M.A. thesis, University of Georgia, 1948).

27. William Bennett, "Memorial Day through the Years," pp. 9–13, Andersonville Vertical Files, Andersonville National Historic Site.

28. Herbert C. Fooks, *Prisoners of War* (Federalsburg, Md.: J. W. Stowell, 1924), 263, 152, 156, 178–79, 184.

29. Fooks, *Prisoners of War,* 313.

30. William B. Hesseltine, *Civil War Prisons: A Study in War Psychology* (1930; repr., Columbus: Ohio State University Press, 1998), xxiii. On Hesseltine's background, training, and motivation, see William Blair, "Foreword," in *Civil War Prisons: A Study in War Psychology,* by William B. Hesseltine (Columbus: Ohio State University Press, 1998), ix–xx.

31. Charles W. Ramsdell, review of *Civil War Prisons: A Study in War Psychology,* by William B. Hesseltine, *Mississippi Valley Historical Review* 17 (December 1930): 481; Thomas Robson Hay, review of *Civil War Prisons: A Study in War Psychology,* by William B. Hesseltine, *The American Historical Review* 36 (January 1931): 455.

32. Hesseltine, *Civil War Prisons,* 113.

33. Ibid., 34, xxv.

34. Ibid., 133, 135.

35. Ibid., 254–56.

36. Peter Novick, *That Noble Dream: The "Objectivity Question" and the American Historical Profession* (New York: Cambridge University Press, 1988), 558.

37. Hesseltine, *Civil War Prisons,* 172, 177, 175–76.

38. William B. Hesseltine, "The Propaganda Literature of Confederate Prisons," *Journal of Southern History* 1 (February–November 1935): 56, 61.

39. Ella Lonn, *Foreigners in the Confederacy* (Chapel Hill: University of North Carolina Press, 1940), 275.

40. R. Walter Coakley, review of *Foreigners in the Confederacy,* by Ella Lonn, *William and Mary College Quarterly Historical Magazine* 22 (January 1942): 78.

41. William Q. Maxwell, *Lincoln's Fifth Wheel: The Political History of the United States Sanitary Commission* (New York: Longmans, Green, 1956), 308.

42. William F. Thompson, *The Image of War* (1959; repr., Baton Rouge: Louisiana State University Press, 1994), 92.

43. Reinhard H. Luthin, "Waving the Bloody Shirt: Northern Political Tactics in Post-Civil War Times," *Georgia Review* 14 (Spring 1960): 64, 67. See also Reinhard H. Luthin, "Some Demagogues in American History," *American Historical Review* 57 (October 1951): 40–41.

44. Frank L. Byrne, "Libby Prison: A Study in Emotions," *Journal of Southern History* 24 (November 1958): 444.

45. Richard F. Hemmerlein, *Prisons and Prisoners of the Civil War* (Boston: Christopher, 1934), 112.

46. Hattie Lou Winslow and Joseph R. H. Moore, *Camp Morton, 1861–1865: Indianapolis Prison Camp* (1940; repr., Indianapolis: Indiana Historical Society, 1995), 122.

47. Edgar Stewart, review of *Camp Morton, 1861–1865: Indianapolis Prison Camp,* by Hattie Lou Winslow and Joseph R. H. Moore, *American Historical Review* 47 (October 1941): 199; Oscar O. Winther, review of *Camp Morton, 1861–1865: Indianapolis Prison Camp,* by Hattie Lou Winslow and Joseph R. H. Moore, *Journal of Southern History* 7 (August 1941): 413.

48. James C. Bonner, "War Crimes Trials, 1865–1867," *Social Science* 22 (April 1947): 128, 130, 131, 134.

49. Bruce Catton, "Prison Camps of the Civil War," *American Heritage* 10 (August 1959): 97, 5.

50. *New York Times Book Review,* October 30, 1955.

51. Jeff Smithpeters, "'To the Latest Generation': Cold War and Post Cold War U.S. Civil War Novels in Their Social Contexts" (Ph.D. diss., Louisiana State University, 2005), 31, 58.

52. MacKinlay Kantor, *Andersonville* (1955; repr., New York: Plume, 1993), 761.

53. *New York Times Book Review,* October 30, 1955.

54. Lawrence S. Thompson, "The Civil War in Fiction," *Civil War History* 2 (March 1956): 93–94.

55. Kantor, *Andersonville,* 140, 142, 344, 168, 171, 739–40.

56. William B. Hesseltine, "Andersonville Revisited," *Georgia Review* 10 (Spring 1956): 97, 100, 99.

57. Smithpeters, "To the Latest Generation," 29.

58. Watt P. Marchman, ed., "The Journal of Sergt. Wm. J. McKell," *Civil War History* 3 (September 1957): 315–39; Donald F. Danker, ed., "Imprisoned at Andersonville: The Diary of Albert Harry Shatzell, May 5, 1864–September 12, 1864," *Nebraska History* 38 (June 1957): 81–124; J. B. Stamp, "Ten Months Experience in Northern Prisons," *Alabama Historical Quarterly* 18 (Winter 1956): 486–98.

59. Ovid Futch, "Andersonville Raiders," *Civil War History* 2 (December 1956): 47–60; Virgil C. Jones, "Libby Prison Break," *Civil War History* 4 (June 1958): 93–104.

60. Richard B. Harwell, *The Confederate Reader* (New York: Longmans, Green, 1957), and *The Union Reader* (New York: Longmans, Green, 1958).

61. Dumas Malone and Basil Rauch, *The New Nation, 1865–1917* (New York: Appleton-Century-Crofts, 1960), 5.

62. Kantor, *Andersonville,* 762.

63. John McElroy, *This Was Andersonville,* with an introduction by Roy Meredith (New York: Bonanza, 1957), xx–xxi.

64. *Atlanta Journal,* May 28, 1957, clipping in Civil War Miscellany Papers, Box 1, Andersonville, Georgia, Military Prison Folder, Georgia State Archives.

65. *Atlanta Constitution,* June 2, 1957, clipping in Civil War Miscellany Papers, Box 1, Andersonville, Georgia, Military Prison Folder, Georgia State Archives.

66. See ibid., October 6, 1957, June 29, 1958, October 29, 1958, April 22, 1959, August 30, 1959, September 1, 1959, September 5, 1959, September 22, 1959, November 22, 1959, December 1, 1959, and December 15, 1959, clippings in Civil War Miscellany Papers, Box 1, Andersonville, Georgia, Military Prison Folder, Georgia State Archives.

67. Ibid., September 2, 1959, clipping in Civil War Miscellany Papers, Box 1, Andersonville, Georgia, Military Prison Folder, Georgia State Archives.

68. *Atlanta Journal,* January 24, 1958, clipping in Civil War Miscellany Papers, Box 1, Andersonville, Georgia, Military Prison Folder, Georgia State Archives.

69. *Atlanta Constitution,* February 5, 1958 and February 6, 1958, clippings in Civil War Miscellany Papers, Box 1, Andersonville, Georgia, Military Prison Folder, Georgia State Archives.

70. Ibid., January 31, 1960, clipping in Civil War Miscellany Papers, Box 1, Andersonville, Georgia, Military Prison, Georgia State Archives.

71. Saul Levitt, *The Andersonville Trial* (New York: Random House, 1960), 13, 100, 105, 113, 120.

CHAPTER SIX

1. *Atlanta Constitution,* December 14, 1961, clipping in Civil War Miscellany Papers, Box 1, Andersonville, Georgia, Military Prison Folder, Georgia State Archives.

2. A. B. Moore, "Memorandum on the Potential Values of the National Centennial Commemoration of the Civil War," Georgia Civil War Centennial Commission Papers, Box 4, Reference Material for Speeches, Articles, etc., 1961, Georgia State Archives.

3. *Atlanta Constitution,* May 30, 1960, clipping in Civil War Miscellany Papers, Box 1, Andersonville, Georgia, Military Prison Folder, Georgia State Archives; Robert J. Cook, *Troubled Commemoration: The American Civil War Centennial Commission, 1961–1965* (Baton Rouge: Louisiana State University Press, 2007).

4. Bell I. Wiley, ed., "Report of the Activities Committee to the Civil War Centennial Commission," *Civil War History* 5 (December 1959): 374–81, 376.

5. Peter Z. Geer, "Untitled April 11, 1961 speech," pp. 1, 5, Georgia Civil War Centennial Commission Papers, Box 2, Civil War Centennial Commission 1959–65 Confederate States Civil War Centennial Commission Virginia Civil War Centennial Commission Folder, Georgia State Archives.

6. "Georgia Civil War Historical Sites," pp. 2–3, Georgia Civil War Centennial Commission Papers, Box 1, Monuments, Memorials & Commemorations Committee Civil War Centennial Commission 1959–60 Folder, Georgia State Archives; "Recapture History," p. 2, Georgia Civil War Centennial Commission Papers, Box 1, Correspondence of the Chairman Beverly M. DuBose, Jr. 1964 Folder, Georgia State Archives.

7. "Suggestions for Civil War Centennial Observances by Georgia Schools," pp. 1, 3, Georgia Civil War Centennial Commission Papers, Box 3, Education Outline 1961 Folder, Georgia State Archives.

8. "Georgia Association of Broadcasters Special Tourism Promotion February, 1964 Spots,"

p. 1, Georgia Historical Commission Papers, Box 3, Miscellaneous Folder, Georgia State Archives.

9. *Atlanta Journal,* July 30, 1959, clipping in Civil War Miscellany Papers, Box 1, Andersonville, Georgia, Military Prison Folder, Georgia State Archives.

10. Milt Berk to Peter Z. Geer, July 23, 1960, Georgia Civil War Centennial Commission Papers, Box 1, Official Souvenirs Committee Civil War Centennial Commission 1959–61 Folder, Georgia State Archives.

11. S. Ernest Vandiver to Eugene Cook, February 9, 1961, Georgia Civil War Centennial Commission Papers, Box 1, Souvenirs Folder, Georgia State Archives.

12. Walt Barber to Charles Stelling, June 10, 1960, Georgia Civil War Centennial Commission Papers, Box 1, Official Souvenirs Committee Civil War Centennial Commission 1959–61 Folder, Georgia State Archives.

13. *Atlanta Constitution,* April 21, 1960, clipping in Civil War Miscellany Papers, Box 1, Andersonville, Georgia, Military Prison Folder, Georgia State Archives.

14. *Atlanta Constitution,* February 23, 1964, clipping in Civil War Miscellany Papers, Box 1, Andersonville, Georgia, Military Prison Folder, Georgia State Archives.

15. "Reconciliation at Elmira," *New York State and the Civil War* 1 (July 1961): 13, article in Georgia Civil War Centennial Commission Papers, Box 1, New York State Civil War Centennial Folder, Georgia State Archives.

16. "The Civil War Prisoner," *Centennial News Letter* 5 (August 1963): 1–2, article in Georgia Civil War Centennial Commission Papers, Box 2, Virginia Civil War Centennial Commission Centennial Newsletters Folder, Georgia State Archives.

17. On state commission centennial histories, see Philip R. Shriver and Donald J. Breen, *Ohio's Military Prisons in the Civil War* (Columbus: Ohio State University Press, 1964); Victor Hicken, *Illinois in the Civil War* (Urbana: University of Illinois Press, 1966); William J. Petersen, ed., "Iowa at Andersonville," *Palimpsest* 42 (June 1961): 209–281; Harold R. Manakee, *Maryland in the Civil War* (Baltimore: Garamond, 1961). For individual prison accounts see John McElroy, *Andersonville: A Story of Rebel Military Prisons* (1879; New York: Fawcett, 1962); Decimus et Ultimus Barziza, *The Adventures of a Prisoner of War,* ed. R. Henderson Shuffler (1865; repr., Austin: University of Texas Press, 1964); Mary Lasswell, ed., *Rags and Hope* (New York: Van Rees, 1961); James Cooper Nisbet, *Four Years on the Firing Line,* ed. Bell I. Wiley (1914; Jackson, Tenn.: McCowat-Mercer, 1963); Thomas B. Turley, *A Narrative of His Capture and Imprisonment during the War between the States,* with an introduction by John H. Davis (Memphis, Tenn.: Southwestern at Memphis, 1961); Susan W. Benson, ed., *Berry Benson's Civil War Book* (Athens: University of Georgia Press, 1962).

18. "The Amazing Story of Pvt. Joe Shewmon," *Civil War Times Illustrated* 1 (April 1962): 45.

19. An extremely selective list of *Civil War Times Illustrated* articles on various aspects of Civil War prisons over the years includes James D. Jones, "A Guard at Andersonville—Eyewitness to History," *CWTI* 2 (February 1964): 24; Robert E. and Katharine Morseberger, "After Andersonville: The First War Crimes Trial," *CWTI* 13 (July 1974): 30; Tony Trimble, "A Quiet Sabbath: Reflections from Johnson's Island," *CWTI* 22 (January 1984): 20; Philip Rutherford, ed., "I Escaped from Andersonville," *CWTI* 27 (May 1988): 36.

20. Ovid L. Futch, *History of Andersonville Prison* (Indiantown: University of Florida Press, 1968).

21. Peggy Sheppard, *Andersonville Georgia USA* (1973; repr., Andersonville, Ga.: Sheppard, 2001), 79–80.

22. *Macon Telegraph,* September 3, 1971, clipping in Andersonville Vertical File, Andersonville National Historic Site.

23. Bobby L. Lowe to John D. Sewell, April 26, 1976, Georgia Department of Community Affairs Papers, Box 12, Andersonville Trail Study Folder, Georgia State Archives.

24. T. H. Watkins, "A Heritage Preserved," *American Heritage* 31 (April/May 1980): 101.

25. "Andersonville's Depot Part of Planned Tourist Boom," 1975 unidentified newspaper clipping in Andersonville Vertical File, Andersonville National Historic Site.

26. "Grant Application to Coastal Plains Regional Commission for Direct Grant (Andersonville Mall) by City of Andersonville November 1975," Georgia Department of Community Affairs Papers, Box 12, Andersonville Mall Folder, Georgia State Archives.

27. Zell Miller to Peter J. Novak, August 20, 1976, Georgia Lieutenant Governor's Office Papers, Box 2, 10/2/76 Andersonville Historic Fair Americus, GA Sumter Co. Folder, Georgia State Archives.

28. *Americus Times-Recorder,* October 7, 1985, April 8, 1985, clippings in Andersonville Vertical Files, Andersonville National Historic Site.

29. *Florida Times Union and Jacksonville Journal,* October 31, 1982, clipping in Andersonville Vertical Files, Andersonville National Historic Site.

30. Alan Patureau, "Old Andersonville Emerges without Shackles of Shame," undated *Atlanta Constitution* article, clipping in Andersonville Vertical Files, Andersonville National Historic Site.

31. Patureau, "Old Andersonville Emerges without Shackles of Shame," Andersonville Vertical File, Andersonville National Historic Site; see also Tony Horwitz, *Confederates in the Attic* (New York: Vintage, 1998), 312–335.

32. David Lowenthal, *Possessed by the Past: The Heritage Crusade and the Spoils of History* (New York: Free Press, 1996), 2.

33. *Rapid City Journal,* January 9, 1983, clipping in Andersonville Vertical Files, Andersonville National Historic Site.

34. *Americus Times-Recorder,* November 12, 1984, clipping in Andersonville Vertical Files, Andersonville National Historic Site.

35. *Americus Times-Recorder,* November 11, 1985, clipping in Andersonville Vertical Files, Andersonville National Historic Site.

36. *Americus Times-Recorder,* November 20, 1982, November 12, 1984, November 11, 1985, November 10, 1986, November 7, 1987, clippings in Andersonville Vertical Files, Andersonville National Historic Site.

37. Horwitz, *Confederates in the Attic,* 325–329.

38. James W. Thompson, "Southern Comment: Andersonville—Truth versus Falsehood," *Blue & Gray* 3 (December–January 1985–86): 28–35; Melanie Campbell, "Fort Delaware," *United Daughters of the Confederacy Magazine* 42 (November 1999): 36–37; J. H. Segars, ed., *Andersonville: The Southern Perspective* (Gretna, La.: Pelican, 2001).

39. James M. McPherson and William J. Cooper, Jr., eds., *Writing the Civil War: The Quest to Understand* (Columbia: University of South Carolina Press, 1998), 4.

40. James G. Randall and David Donald, *The Civil War and Reconstruction* (Boston: D. C. Heath, 1961), 339.

41. William B. Hesseltine, "Civil War Prisons—Introduction," in *Civil War Prisons* (1962; repr., Kent, Ohio: Kent State University Press, 1995), 6, 8.

42. James M. McPherson, *Battle Cry of Freedom* (New York: Ballantine, 1988), 802.

43. Reid Mitchell, "'Our Prison System, Supposing We Had Any': The Confederate and Union Prison Systems," in *On the Road to Total War: The American Civil War and the German Wars of Unification, 1861–1871*, ed. Stig Forster and Jorg Nagler (New York: Cambridge University Press, 1997), 584–85. A similar interpretation appears in Harry S. Stout, *Upon the Altar of the Nation* (New York: Penguin, 2006), 295–307.

44. Institute for World Order, *War Criminals, War Victims: Andersonville, Nuremberg, Hiroshima, My Lai* (New York: Random House, 1974), 1, 4, 48.

45. Eric T. Dean, *Shook over Hell: Post-Traumatic Stress, Vietnam, and the Civil War* (Cambridge, Mass.: Harvard University Press, 1997), 81–87.

46. Robert C. Doyle, *Voices from Captivity: Interpreting the American POW Narrative* (Lawrence: University Press of Kansas, 1994), 294–95.

47. Notable examples of such professional scholarship include David R. Bush, "Interpreting the Latrines of the Johnson's Island Civil War Military Prison," *Historical Archeology* 34, no. 1 (2000): 62; Joseph P. Cangemi and Casimir J. Kowalski, eds., *Andersonville Prison: Lessons in Organizational Failure* (Lanham, Md.: University Press of America, 1992); Robert S. Davis, *Ghosts and Shadows of Andersonville: Essays on the Secret Social Histories of America's Deadliest Prison* (Macon, Ga.: Mercer University Press, 2006); Leslie J. Gordon-Burr, "Storms of Indignation: The Art of Andersonville as Postwar Propaganda," *Georgia Historical Quarterly* 75 (Fall 1991): 587–600; Michael P. Gray, *The Business of Captivity: Elmira and Its Civil War Prison* (Kent, Ohio: Kent State University Press, 2001).

48. William Marvel, *Andersonville: The Last Depot* (Chapel Hill: University of North Carolina Press, 1994); George Levy, *To Die in Chicago: Confederate Prisoners at Camp Douglas 1862–1865* (Gretna, La.: Pelican, 1999). See also Michael Horigan, *Elmira: Death Camp of the North* (Mechanicsburg, Pa.: Stackpole, 2002); Benton McAdams, *Rebels at Rock Island* (DeKalb: Northern Illinois University Press, 2000); Dale Fetzer and Bruce Mowday, *Unlikely Allies: Fort Delaware's Prison Community in the Civil War* (Mechanicsburg, Pa.: Stackpole, 2000); Edwin Beitzell, *Point Lookout Prison Camp for Confederates* (N.p.: privately printed, 1972); Sandra V. Parker, *Richmond's Civil War Prisons* (Lynchburg, Va.: H. E. Howard, 1990); William O. Bryant, *Cahaba Prison and the Sultana Disaster* (Tuscaloosa: University of Alabama Press, 1990); Louis A. Brown, *The Salisbury Prison: A Case Study of Confederate Military Prisons 1861–1865* (Wilmington, N.C.: Broadfoot, 1992).

49. Lonnie R. Speer, *Portals to Hell: Military Prisons of the Civil War* (Mechanicsburg, Pa.: Stackpole, 1997).

50. C. Bryan Kelly, *Best Little Stories from the Civil War* (1994; repr., Nashville, Tenn.: Cumberland House, 1998); Webb Garrison, *The Amazing Civil War* (Nashville, Tenn.: Rutledge Hill, 1998); Peter Kadzis, ed., *Blood: Stories of Life and Death from the Civil War* (New York: Thunder's Mouth Press and Balliett & Fitzgerald, 2000).

51. Joseph Gibbs, *Three Years in the Bloody Eleventh* (University Park: Pennsylvania State University Press, 2002); Raymond J. Herek, *These Men Have Seen Hard Service* (Detroit: Wayne State University Press, 1998; William J. Jackson, *New Jerseyans in the Civil War* (New Brunswick, N.J.: Rutgers University Press, 2000); Alan A. Siegel, *Beneath the Starry Flag: New Jersey's Civil War Experience* (New Brunswick, N.J.: Rutgers University Press, 2001); David Madden, ed., *Beyond the Battlefield: The Ordinary Life and Extraordinary Times of the Civil War Soldier* (New York: Simon & Schuster, 2000); Ray M. Carson, *The Civil War Soldier* (Mechanicsburg, Pa.: Stackpole, 2000).

52. Benjamin F. Booth and Steve Meyer, *Dark Days of the Rebellion* (1897; repr., Garrison, Iowa: Meyer, 1996), vii.

53. J. V. Hadley, *Seven Months a Prisoner* (1898; repr., Hanover, Ind.: Nugget, 1998), I.

54. One folk rock song is Vigilantes of Love's "Andersonville."

55. Gene Hackman and Daniel Lenihan, *Escape from Andersonville* (New York: St. Martin's Press, 2008). Other recent novels involving Andersonville include Robert D. Dean, *Echoes of Andersonville* (Franklin, Tenn: Heritage, 1999); David Madden, *Sharpshooter* (Knoxville: University of Tennessee Press, 1996); Robert Vaughan, *Andersonville* (New York: Boulevard, 1996).

56. *Andersonville*, VHS, produced and directed by John Frankenheimer and David Rintels, Turner Pictures, 1996.

57. *The Blue and the Grey*, VHS, directed by Andrew V. McLaglen, Columbia Pictures Television, 1982.

58. Sarah Vowell, *The Partly Cloudy Patriot* (New York: Simon & Schuster, 2002), 40.

59. Charles W. Sanders, Jr., *While in the Hands of the Enemy: Military Prisons of the Civil War* (Baton Rouge: Louisiana State University Press, 2005); James M. Gillispie, *Andersonvilles of the North: The Myths and Realities of Northern Treatment of Civil War Confederate Prisoners* (Denton: University of North Texas Press, 2008).

CHAPTER SEVEN

1. Gregory Ashworth and Rudi Hartmann, eds., *Horror and Human Tragedy Revisited: The Management of Sites of Atrocities for Tourism* (Elmsford, N.Y.: Cognizant Communication, 2005).

2. Fred Boyles, "The Evolution of the National Prisoner of War Museum," in *National Prisoner of War Museum Andersonville, Georgia Dedication April 9, 1998* (N.p.: privately printed, 1998), 7.

3. Robert J. Hill and William B. Keeling, *Preliminary Development Study Andersonville Historical Complex* (Athens, Ga.: Bureau of Business and Economic Research and Institute of Community and Area Development, University of Georgia, 1965), 1.

4. Hill and Keeling, *Preliminary Development Study Andersonville Historical Complex*, 36.

5. *Atlanta Constitution*, March 25, 1966, clipping in Civil War Miscellany Papers, Box 1, Andersonville, Georgia, Military Prison Folder, Georgia State Archives.

6. *Planning Study Report Andersonville Prison Park Georgia* (Washington, D.C.: U.S. Department of the Interior, National Park Service, 1966), 13.

7. Boyles, "The Evolution of the National Prisoner of War Museum," 7.

8. Congressman Brinkley of Georgia speaking for Authorizing the Establishment of the Andersonville National Historic Site, Ga., 91st Congress, 2nd sess., *Congressional Record* 116, pt. 23 (September 14, 1970): H 31454.

9. Andersonville National Historic Site, Ga., 91st Congress, 2nd sess., *Congressional Record* 116, pt. 26 (October 7, 1970): S 35403.

10. Ibid.

11. *Atlanta Constitution*, November 12, 1971, clipping from Andersonville Vertical Files, Andersonville National Historic Site.

12. Ibid.

13. Mildred Veasey to Jimmy Carter, February 16, 1972, Georgia Governor's Office Papers, Box 12, Andersonville National Park Governor's Commission Folder, Georgia State Archives.

14. *Atlanta Constitution,* October 11, 1974, clipping in Georgia Governor's Office Papers, Box 12, Andersonville National Park Governor's Commission Folder, Georgia State Archives.

15. William J. Thompson, "Prisoners of War Memorial Georgia Memorial Andersonville, Georgia," undated statement in Andersonville Vertical Files, Andersonville National Historic Site.

16. For an analysis of the Thompson sculpture, see Michaela Oberlaender, "William J. Thompson's *Andersonville Memorial:* Historical Precedents and Contemporary Context" (M.A. thesis, University of Georgia, 1993).

17. *Americus Times-Recorder,* May 31, 1976, clipping in Andersonville Vertical Files, Andersonville National Historic Site.

18. William Burnett, "Memorial Day through the Years," p. 18, Andersonville Vertical Files, Andersonville National Historic Site.

19. William Burnett, "Memorial Day through the Years," pp. 15–25, Andersonville Vertical Files, Andersonville National Historic Site.

20. Boyles, "The Evolution of the National Prisoner of War Museum," 8.

21. *Master Plan* (Washington, D.C.: U,S. Department of the Interior, National Park Service, 1971), iii, 16, 31–33.

22. Edwin C. Bearss, *Andersonville National Historic Site Historic Resource Study and Historical Base Map* (Washington, D.C.: U.S. Department of the Interior, National Park Service, 1970), I.

23. *Master Plan,* 1971,16.

24. John E. Jensen, *Interpretative Prospectus* (Denver: U.S. Department of the Interior, National Park Service, 1974), 3–5, 19.

25. Boyles, "The Evolution of the National Prisoner of War Museum," 8.

26. Denver Service Center, *Environmental Assessment for General Management Plan/ Development Concept Plan, Andersonville National Historic Site, Georgia* (Washington, D.C.: U.S. Department of the Interior, National Park Service, 1979), 3.

27. Boyles, "The Evolution of the National Prisoner of War Museum," 8. See also *Americus Times-Recorder,* April 30, 1984, May 31, 1984, November 9, 1987, clippings in Andersonville Vertical Files, Andersonville National Historic Site.

28. *Citizen & Georgian,* February 18, 1987, clipping in Andersonville Vertical Files, Andersonville National Historic Site.

29. Boyles, "The Evolution of the National Prisoner of War Museum," 8–10.

30. Wayne Hitchcock, "The Coin That Made the Museum Possible," in *National Prisoner of War Museum Andersonville, Georgia Dedication April 9, 1998* (N.p.: privately printed, 1998), 15–16.

31. Leonard Simpson, "Construction of the National Prisoner of War Museum," in *National Prisoner of War Museum Andersonville, Georgia Dedication April 9, 1998* (N.p.: privately printed, 1998), 11.

32. Carla McConnell, "The Architecture of the National Prisoner of War Museum," in *National Prisoner of War Museum Andersonville, Georgia Dedication April 9, 1998* (N.p.: privately printed, 1998), 13–14.

33. J. Scott Harmon, "Evolution of an Exhibition," in *National Prisoner of War Museum Andersonville, Georgia Dedication April 9, 1998* (N.p.: privately printed, 1998), 18–20.

34. Tim Radford, "The Visual Story," in *National Prisoner of War Museum Andersonville, Georgia Dedication April 9, 1998* (N.p.: privately printed, 1998), 22–24; Polly Weister, "Echoes

of 'Echoes': Reflections on the Making of 'Echoes in Captivity,'" in *National Prisoner of War Museum Andersonville, Georgia Dedication April 9, 1998* (N.p.: privately printed, 1998), 25–26.

35. Barry Howard Limited, "First Draft Exhibit Notebook, National Prisoner of War Museum Book One," April 9, 1993, 5. 19. T1–5. 21. A1., in possession of the author, Andersonville National Historic Site.

36. *National Prisoner of War Museum Andersonville, Georgia Dedication April 9, 1998* (N.p.: privately printed, 1998), 1.

37. *Atlanta Journal and Constitution,* April 10, 1998, accessed through LexisNexis Academic, April 13, 2003.

38. *New York Times,* April 10, 1998, accessed through LexisNexis Academic, April 13, 2003.

39. *Cleveland Plain Dealer,* April 10, 1998, accessed through LexisNexis Academic, April 13, 2003.

40. "Andersonville Annual Visitation (1992–2002)," in possession of the author, Andersonville National Historic Site.

41. Fred Sanchez, "Andersonville Prisoner of War Oral History Institute: To Preserve the Legacy," in *National Prisoner of War Museum Andersonville, Georgia Dedication April 9, 1998* (N.p.: privately printed, 1998), 31–33.

42. "First Annual Centennial Strategy for Andersonville National Historic Site August 2007," http://www.nps.gov/ande/parkmgmt/centennial-initiative-2016.htm (accessed July 15, 2008).

43. Bruce Babbitt, "Foreword," in *Rally on the High Ground: The National Park Service Symposium on the Civil War,* ed. Robert K. Sutton (New York: Eastern National, 2001), vii.

WORKS CONSULTED

PRIMARY SOURCES

Manuscript Collections

Andersonville National Historic Site, Andersonville, Ga.
  Andersonville Annual Visitation 1992–2002 (in possession of the author)
  Andersonville Subject Files
  Andersonville Vertical Files
  Civil War Prisoner of War Resources Files
  First Draft Exhibit Notebook, National Prisoner of War Museum
    (in possession of the author)

Manuscript Department, William R. Perkins Library, Duke University,
    Durham, N.C.
  Thaddeus Kosciuszko Papers

Georgia State Archives, Morrow, Ga.
  Civil War Miscellany Papers
  Georgia Civil War Centennial Commission Papers
  Georgia Department of Community Affairs Papers
  Georgia Department of Natural Resources Papers
  Georgia Governor's Office Papers
  Georgia Historical Commission Papers
  Georgia Lieutenant Governor's Office Papers
  Parks and Historic Sites Division (of the Georgia Department of Natural
    Resources) Papers

Library of Congress, Washington, D.C.
  Abram Varrick Parmenter Papers
  John S. Swann Papers

The National Archives, Washington, D.C.
    Records of the Commissary General of Prisoners, Record Group 249,
        Entry 16, Personal Papers of General William Hoffman, 1863–1865

Southern Historical Collection, University of North Carolina Library,
    Chapel Hill, N.C.
        Robert Bingham Papers
        Francis A. Boyle Papers
        Anne Barbour Brown Papers
        Julian Shakespeare Carr Papers
        Robert Drummond Papers
        Augustus W. Graham Papers
        Thomas J. Green Papers
        Leeland Hathaway Papers
        Joseph Mason Kern Papers
        Elvira E. Moffitt Papers
        Julius Frederic Ramsdell Papers
        Joseph Frederick Waring Papers

Military History Institute Manuscript Collection, United States Army Military
    History Institute, Carlisle Barracks, Pa.
        Civil War Miscellaneous Collection
        Civil War Times Illustrated Collection
        Harrisburg Civil War Round Table Collection
        James Hutson Papers
        Kansas City Civil War Round Table Collection
        Joseph Schubert Collection
        Michael Winey Collection

Government Documents (Published)

Quartermaster General's Office. *The Martyrs Who, for Our Country, Gave up their
    Lives in the Prison Pens in Andersonville, GA.* Washington, D.C.: Government
    Printing Office, 1866.
U. S. Congress. *Congressional Record.* 44th Congress, 1st sess., 1876. Vol. 4.
———. *Congressional Record.* 91st Congress, 2nd sess., 1970. Vol. 116, pt. 23.
———. *Congressional Record.* 91st Congress, 2nd sess., 1970. Vol. 116, pt. 26.
———. House. Joint Committee on the Conduct of the War. *Returned Prisoners.*
    38th Congress, 1st sess., 1864, Report No. 67.
———. House. Joint Committee on the Conduct of the War. *Report of the Joint
    Committee on the Conduct of the War.* 38th Congress, 2nd sess., 1865, House Exe-
    cutive Document No. 32.

———. House. Joint Committee on Reconstruction. *Report of the Joint Committee on Reconstruction.* 39th Congress, 1st sess., 1866, Report No. 30.

———. House. *Trial of Henry Wirz.* 40th Congress, 2nd sess., 1868, House Executive Document No. 23.

———. House. Committee on the Treatment of Prisoners of War and Union Citizens. *Report on the Treatment of Prisoners of War by the Rebel Authorities.* 40th Congress, 3rd sess., 1869, Report No. 45.

United States War Department. *War of the Rebellion: A Compilation of the Official Records of the Union and Confederate Armies,* 70 vols., 130 books. Washington, D.C.: Government Printing Office, 1880–1901.

Newspapers

Atlanta Journal and Constitution, April 10, 1998, LexisNexis Academic (accessed April 13, 2003).

Charleston Mercury, June 19, 1861, February 18, 1864, www.accessible.com (accessed February 6 and 8, 2003).

Cleveland Plain Dealer, April 10, 1998, LexisNexis Academic (accessed April 13, 2003).

Harper's Weekly, August 30, 1862, December 5, 1863, January 9, March 5, December 10, 1864, January 14, April 15, August 19, September 16, November 25, 1865, June 30, July 21, 1866, March 23, November 9, 1867, July 4, July 11, October 3, October 24, 1868, September 21, 1872, www.harpweek.com (accessed March 1, 3, and 9, 2003).

National Observer, November 8, 1965.

New York Herald, December 23, 1861, November 22, 1864, www.accessible.com (accessed February 6 and 9, 2003).

New York Times, July 26 and October 15, 1865. April 10, 1998, LexisNexis Academic (accessed April 13, 2003).

New York Times Book Review, October 30, 1955.

Periodicals

American Missionary, 1891–92, http://cdl.library.cornell.edu/moa (accessed August 1, 2008).

Civil War Times Illustrated, 1962–2002.

Confederate Veteran, 1894–1931.

Minutes of the Annual Meetings and Reunions of the United Confederate Veterans, 1898, 1902, 1905, 1910, 1912.

Minutes of the Annual Meetings of the United Daughters of the Confederacy, 1904–5, 1910, 1913, 1921, 1924, 1926–27, 1933, 1937, 1939, 1940, 1942, 1948, 1952, 1954, 1956, 1959, 1961, 1971–72.

Minutes of the Annual Meetings of the United Sons of Confederate Veterans, 1906.

Southern Historical Society Papers, 1876–1930, 1941, 1943, 1953, 1958–59.

United Daughters of the Confederacy Magazine, 1947, 1949–50, 1960–62, 1971, 1986–87, 1989–95, 1998–99, 2001–2

Prison Narratives

Abbott, Horace R. *My Escape From Belle Isle*. Detroit: Winn & Hammond, 1889.

Allen, William H. "One Hundred and Ninety Days in Rebel Prisons." *Annals of Iowa* 38 (Winter 1966): 222–38.

Allison, Don, ed. *Hell on Belle Isle: Diary of a Civil War POW*. Bryan, Ohio: Faded Banner, 1997.

Alstrand, Gustaf. *The Story of a Private in the Civil War*. Fort Dodge, Iowa: *Evening Messenger*, 1970.

Andersonville: Giving up the Ghost, A Collection of Prisoners' Diaries, Letters & Memoirs. Kearny, N.J.: Belle Grove, 1996.

Andrews, Samuel J. M. *Sufferings of Union Soldiers in Southern Prisons*. Effingham, Ill.: Register Print, 1870.

Barbiere, Joe. *Scraps from the Prison Table at Camp Chase and Johnson's Island*. Doylestown, Pa.: W. W. H. Davis, 1868.

Barrett, John G., ed. *Yankee Rebel: The Civil War Journal of Edmund DeWitt Patterson*. Chapel Hill: University of North Carolina Press, 1966.

Barziza, Decimus et Ultimus. *The Adventures of a Prisoner of War*. Edited by R. Henderson Shuffler. Houston: News Job Office, 1865. Reprint, Austin: University of Texas Press, 1964.

Basile, Leon, ed. *The Civil War Diary of Amos E. Stearns, a Prisoner at Andersonville*. London: Associated University Presses, 1981.

Bates, Ralph O. *Billy and Dick from Andersonville Prison to the White House*. Santa Cruz, Calif.: Sentinel, 1910.

Benson, Susan W., ed. *Berry Benson's Civil War Book*. Athens: University of Georgia Press, 1962.

Berry, Chester D. *Loss of the Sultana and Reminiscences of Survivors*. Lansing, Mich.: Darius D. Thorp, 1892.

Beszedits, Stephen. *The Libby Prison Diary of Colonel Emeric Szabad*. Toronto: B & L Information Services, 1999.

Boaz, Thomas M. *Libby Prison & Beyond: A Union Staff Officer in the East, 1862–1865*. Shippensburg, Pa.: Burd Street, 1999.

Boggs, S. S. *Eighteen Months under the Rebel Flag*. Lovington, Ill.: privately printed, 1887.

Booth, Benjamin F., and Steve Meyer. *Dark Days of the Rebellion: Life in Southern Military Prisons*. 1897. Reprint, Garrison, Iowa: Meyer, 1996.

Booth, George Wilson. *A Maryland Boy in Lee's Army.* Baltimore: privately published, 1898. Reprint, Lincoln: University of Nebraska Press, 2000.

Braun, Herman. *Andersonville: An Object Lesson on Protection.* Milwaukee: C. D. Fahsel, 1892.

Brownell, Josiah C. *At Andersonville. A Narrative of Personal Adventure at Andersonville, Florence and Charleston Rebel Prisons.* Glen Cove, N.Y.: Gazette Book and Job Office, 1867. Reprint, Glen Cove, N.Y.: Glen Cove Public Library, 1981.

Burson, William. *A Race For Liberty, or My Capture, Imprisonment, and Escape.* Wellsville, Ohio: W. G. Foster, 1867.

Byers, S. H. M. *With Fire and Sword.* New York: Neale, 1911.

Camden, Thomas Bland. *My Recollections and Experiences of the Civil War.* Edited by Kathy Whelan. Parsons, W. Va.: McClain, 2000.

Casler, John O. *Four Years in the Stonewall Brigade.* Girard, Kans.: Appeal, 1906. Reprint, Marietta, Ga.: Continental, 1951.

Castleman, Jno. B. *Active Service.* Louisville, Ky.: Courier-Journal Job Printing 1917.

Cherry, Peterson H. *Prisoner in Blue: Memories of the Civil War after 70 Years.* Los Angeles: Wetzel, 1931.

Clark, Walter, ed. *Histories of the Several Regiments and Battalions from North Carolina in the Great War 1861–'65. Volume 4.* Goldsboro, N.C.: Nash Brothers, 1901.

Clark, Willene B., ed. *Valleys of the Shadow.* Knoxville: University of Tennessee Press, 1994.

Clifton, William B. *Libby and Andersonville Prisons: A True Sketch.* Indianapolis, Ind.: privately printed, 1910.

Collins, R. M. *Chapters from the Unwritten History of the War Between the States.* St. Louis: Nixon-Jones, 1893.

Committee on Publications, Massachusetts Commandery of the Military Order of the Loyal Legion. *Civil War Papers, Vols. I & II.* Boston: F. H. Gilson, 1900.

Compton, James R. *Andersonville: The Story of Man's Inhumanity to Man.* Des Moines, Iowa: Iowa Printing, 1887.

Cooper, Alonzo. *In and out of Rebel Prisons.* Oswego, N.Y.: R. J. Oliphant, 1888.

Cooper, Robert. *The Prison Pens of the South.* Brooklyn, N.Y.: Press of J. W. Chalmers, 1896.

Danker, Donald F., ed. "Imprisoned at Andersonville: The Diary of Albert Harry Shatzel, May 5, 1864—September 12, 1864." *Nebraska History* 38 (June 1957): 81–125.

Darsey, B. W. *A War Story, or, My Experience in a Yankee Prison.* 1901. Reprint, Statesboro, Ga.: News Print, 1968.

Davis, Washington. *Camp-Fire Chats of the Civil War.* Chicago: W. H. Ives, 1889.

Dawson, Francis W. *Reminiscences of Confederate Service 1861–1865.* Edited by Bell I. Wiley. Charleston, S.C.: News and Courier Book Presses, 1882. Reprint, Baton Rouge: Louisiana State University Press, 1993.

Day, William W. *Fifteen Months in Dixie; or, My Personal Experience in Rebel Prisons.* Owatonna, Minn.: People's Press Print, 1889.

Dayton, Ruth Woods, ed. *The Diary of a Confederate Soldier James E. Hall.* N.p.: privately printed, 1961.

Destler, C. M., ed. "An Andersonville Prison Diary." *Georgia Historical Quarterly* 24 (March 1940): 56–76.

Devillez, Henry. "Reminiscences of the Civil War: Andersonville." *Indiana Magazine of History* 11 (June 1915): 144–47.

Domschcke, Bernhard. *Twenty Months in Captivity.* Edited and translated by Frederic Trautmann. Milwaukee, Wisc.: W. W. Coleman, 1865. Reprint, London: Associated University Presses, 1987.

Dooley, John. *Confederate Soldier.* Edited by Joseph T. Durkin. Ithaca, N.Y.: Cayuga, 1945.

Drake, J. Madison. *Fast and Loose in Dixie: An Unprejudiced Narrative of Personal Experience as a Prisoner of War at Libby, Macon, Savannah, and Charleston.* New York: Authors' Publishing, 1880.

Dunaway, Wayland F. *Reminiscences of a Rebel.* New York: Neale, 1913.

Durkin, Joseph T., ed. *John Dooley: Confederate Soldier.* Washington, D.C.: Georgetown University Press, 1945.

Empson, W. H. *A Story of Rebel Military Prisons.* Lockport, N.Y.: Press of Roberts Brothers, n.d.

Fairchild, C. B., ed. *History of the 27th Regiment N. Y. Vols.* Binghamton, N.Y.: Carl & Matthews, 1888.

Famous Adventures and Prison Escapes of the Civil War. New York: Century, 1893.

Ferguson, Joseph. *Life Struggles in Rebel Prisons: A Record of the Sufferings, Escapes, Adventures, and Starvation of the Union Prisoners.* Philadelphia: James A. Ferguson, 1865.

Fiske, Samuel. *Dunn Browne in the Army.* Boston: Nichols & Noyes, 1865.

Fletcher, William A. *Rebel Private.* Beaumont, Tex.: Greer Press, 1908. Reprint, Austin: University of Texas Press, 1954.

Fort-La-Fayette Life. London: Simpkin, Marshall, 1865.

Fosdick, Charles. *Five Hundred Days in Rebel Prisons.* N.p.: privately printed, 1887.

Futch, Ovid M., ed. "The Andersonville Journal of Sergeant J. M. Burdick." *Georgia Historical Quarterly* 45 (September 1961): 287–94.

Galwey, Thomas Francis. *The Valiant Hours.* Edited by W. S. Nye. Harrisburg, Pa.: Stackpole, 1961.

Geer, J. J. *Beyond the Lines; or, A Yankee Prisoner Loose in Dixie.* Philadelphia: J. W. Daughaday, 1863.

Genoways, Ted, and Hugh H. Genoways, eds. *A Perfect Picture of Hell: Eyewitness Accounts by Civil War Prisoners from the 12th Iowa.* Iowa City: University of Iowa Press, 2001.

Glazier, Willard. *Sword and Pen; or, Ventures and Adventures of Willard Glazier.* Philadelphia: P. W. Zeigler, 1881.

Goss, Warren Lee. *The Soldier's Story of His Captivity at Andersonville, Belle Isle, and other Rebel Prisons.* Boston: Lee & Shepard, 1866. Reprint, Scituate, Mass.: Digital Scanning, 2001.

Graber, H. W. *The Life Record of H. W. Graber.* N.p.: Privately printed, 1916.

Grimes, Absalom. *Confederate Mail Runner.* Edited by M. M. Quaife. New Haven, Conn.: Yale University Press, 1926.

Hadley, John V. *Seven Months a Prisoner.* New York: Charles Scribner's Sons, 1898. Reprint, Hanover, Ind.: Nugget, 1998.

Hamlin, Augustus C. *Martyria; or, Andersonville Prison.* Boston: Lee & Shepard, 1866.

Hammer, Jefferson J., ed. *Frederic Augustus James's Civil War Diary.* Rutherford, N.J.: Fairleigh Dickinson University Press, 1973.

Harrold, John. *Libby, Andersonville, Florence. The Capture, Imprisonment, Escape and Rescue of John Harrold.* Atlantic City, N.J.: Daily Union, 1892.

Hawes, Jesse. *Cahaba: A Story of Captive Boys in Blue.* New York: Burr, 1888.

Helmreich, Paul C. "The Diary of Charles G. Lee in the Andersonville and Florence Prison Camps, 1864." *Connecticut Historical Society Bulletin* 41 (January 1976): 1–28.

Hermann, I. *Memoirs of a Veteran.* Atlanta: Byrd, 1911.

Hernbaker, Henry, Jr., and John Lynch. *True History. Jefferson Davis Answered. The Horrors of the Andersonville Prison Pen.* Philadelphia: Merrihew, 1876.

Hopkins, L. W. *From Bull Run to Appomattox.* Baltimore: Fleet-McGinley, 1908.

Houghton, W. R., and M. B. Houghton. *Two Boys in the Civil War and After.* Montgomery, Ala.: Paragon, 1912.

Huffman, James. *Ups and Downs of A Confederate Soldier.* New York: William E. Rudge's Sons, 1940.

Humphreys, Charles A. *Field, Camp, Hospital and Prison in the Civil War, 1863–1865.* 1918. Reprint, Freeport, N.Y.: Books for Libraries Press, 1971.

Hundley, D. R. *Prison Echoes of the Great Rebellion.* New York: S. W. Green, 1874.

Hunter, Alexander. *Johnny Reb and Billy Yank.* New York: Neale, 1905.

Isham, Asa B., Henry M. Davidson, and Henry B. Furness. *Prisoners of War and Military Prisons.* Cincinnati, Ohio: Lyman & Cushing, 1890.

Jeffery, William H. *Richmond Prisons 1861–1862.* St. Johnsbury, Vt.: Republican Press, 1893.

Jervey, Edward D., ed. *Prison Life among the Rebels: Recollections of a Union Chaplain.* Kent, Ohio: Kent State University Press, 1990.

Johnston, David E. *The Story of a Confederate Boy in the Civil War.* Portland, Ore.: Glass & Prudhomme, 1914.

Kakuske, Herbert P. *A Civil War Drama: The Adventures of a Union Soldier in Southern Imprisonment.* New York: Carlton, 1970.

Keiley, A. M. *In Vinculis; or, The Prisoner of War.* New York: Blelock, 1866.

Kellogg, John A. *Capture and Escape: A Narrative of Army and Prison Life.* N.p.: Wisconsin History Commission, 1908.

Kellogg, Robert. *Life and Death in Rebel Prisons.* Hartford, Conn.: L. Stebbins, 1865. Reprint, Freeport, N.Y.: Books for Libraries Press, 1971.

King, John H. *Three Hundred Days in a Yankee Prison.* Atlanta: Jas. P. Davies, 1904. Reprint, Kennesaw, Ga.: Continental, 1959.

King, Spencer B., Jr. "Letter from an Eyewitness at Andersonville Prison, 1864." *Georgia Historical Quarterly* 38 (March 1954): 82–85.

Kirke, Edmund. *Adrift in Dixie; or, A Yankee Officer among the Rebels.* New York: Carleton, 1866.

Langworthy, Daniel A. *Reminiscences of a Prisoner of War and His Escape.* Minneapolis, Minn.: Byron, 1915.

Lanman, Charles, ed. *Journal of Alfred Ely: A Prisoner of War in Richmond.* New York: D. Appleton, 1862.

Lasswell, Mary, ed. *Rags and Hope.* New York: Van Rees, 1961.

Lawrence, George A. *Border and Bastille.* New York: W. I. Pooley, 1863.

Leon, L. *Diary of a Tar Heel Confederate Soldier.* Charlotte, N.C.: Stone, n.d.

Lewis, L. M. "Introduction." In W. A. Wash, *Camp, Field and Prison Life,* v–x. St. Louis: Southwestern, 1870.

Long, Lessel. *Twelve Months in Andersonville.* Huntington, Ind.: Thad and Mark Butler, 1886.

Lyon, W. F. *In and Out of Andersonville Prison.* Detroit: Geo. Harland, 1905.

Mahood, Wayne, ed. *Charlie Mosher's Civil War.* Hightstown, N.J.: Longstreet House, 1994.

Mann, Thomas H. "A Yankee in Andersonville." *Century Illustrated Monthly Magazine* 40 (May–October 1890): 447–61, 606–22.

Marchman, Watt P., ed. "The Journal of Sergt. Wm. J. McKell." *Civil War History* 3 (September 1957): 315–39.

Marshall, Emogene Niver. *Reminiscences of the Civil War and Andersonville Prison.* Sandusky, Ohio: Krewson's, 1932.

McCreery, William B. "My Experience as a Prisoner of War and Escape from Libby Prison." In *War Papers Read before the Commandery of the State of Michigan: Military Order of the Loyal Legion of the United States,* 3–29. Detroit: Winn & Hammond, 1893.

McElroy, John. *Andersonville: A Story of Rebel Military Prisons.* With an introduction by Philip Van Doren Stern. 1879. Reprint, New York: Fawcett, 1962.

———. *This Was Andersonville.* With an introduction by Roy Meredith. New York: Bonanza, 1957.

McKim, Randolph H. *A Soldier's Recollections.* New York: Longmans, Green, 1911.

Miller, James N. *The Story of Andersonville and Florence.* Des Moines, Iowa: Welch, The Printer, 1900.

Moore, Frank, ed. *Anecdotes, Poetry and Incidents of the War: North and South. 1860–1865.* New York: privately printed, 1866.

Morgan, W. H. *Personal Reminiscences of the War of 1861–65.* Lynchburg, Va.: J. P. Bell, 1911.

Morton, Joseph, Jr. *Sparks from the Camp Fire.* Philadelphia: Keystone, 1891.

Murphy, James B., ed. "A Confederate Soldier's View of Johnson's Island Prison." *Ohio History* 79 (Spring 1970): 101–11.

Murray, George W. *A History of George W. Murray.* Northampton, Mass.: Trumbull & Gere, 1865.

Nisbet, James Cooper. *Four Years on the Firing Line.* Edited by Bell I. Wiley. Chattanooga, Tenn.: Imperial Press, 1914. Reprint, Jackson, Tenn.: McCowat-Mercer, 1963.

Northrop, John W. *Chronicles from the Diary of a War Prisoner.* Wichita, Kans: privately printed, 1904.

Nott, Charles C. *Sketches of the War.* New York: Anson D. F. Randolph, 1865.

Oats, Sergeant. *Prison Life in Dixie.* Chicago: Central Book Concern, 1880. Reprint, Scituate, Mass.: Digital Scanning, 1999.

Opie, John N. *A Rebel Cavalryman.* Chicago: W. B. Conkey, 1899.

Page, James M. *The True Story of Andersonville Prison.* New York: Neale, 1908. Reprint, Scituate, Mass.: Digital Scanning, 2000.

Peelle, Margaret W. *Letters from Libby Prison.* New York: Greenwich, 1956.

Pierson, William Whatley, Jr., ed. *Whipt 'em Everytime: The Diary of Bartlett Yancey Malone.* Jackson, Tenn.: McCowat-Mercer, 1960.

Poe, J. C., ed., *The Raving Foe: A Civil War Diary and List of Prisoners.* Eastland, Tex.: Longhorn, 1967.

Prutsman, C. M. *A Soldier's Experience in Southern Prisons.* New York: Andrew H. Kellogg, 1901.

Putnam, George H. *A Prisoner of War in Virginia 1864–5.* New York: G. P. Putnam's Sons, 1912.

Quincy, Samuel M. *History of the Second Massachusetts Regiment of Infantry. A Prisoner's Diary. A Paper Read at the Officers' Reunion in Boston, May 11, 1877.* Boston: George H. Ellis, 1882.

Racine, Philip N., ed. *"Unspoiled Heart": The Journal of Charles Mattocks of the 17th Maine.* Knoxville: University of Tennessee Press, 1994.

Ransom, John. *John Ransom's Andersonville Diary.* Philadelphia: Douglass Brothers, 1883. Reprint, New York: Berkley, 1994.

Ray, J. P., ed. *The Diary of a Dead Man.* New York: Eastern National, 2002.

Read, John. "Texas Prisons and a Comparison of Northern and Southern Prison Camps." In *Personal Recollections of the War of the Rebellion,* edited by A. Noel Blakeman, 249–59. New York: G. P. Putnam's Sons, 1912.

Reynolds, C. E. "Thirteen Months at Andersonville Prison and What I Saw There: A Paper Delivered before the N. L. Association, Napoleon, Ohio, April 24, 1869." *Northwest Ohio Quarterly* 27 (1955): 94–113.

Richards, H. M. M. "In Rebel Prisons: A Tribute to Samuel B. Trafford." *Lebanon County Historical Society* 8 (1922): 254–76.

Richardson, Albert D. *The Secret Service, the Field, the Dungeon, and the Escape.* Hartford, Conn.: American Publishing, 1865.

Ripple, Ezra. *Dancing along the Deadline: The Andersonville Memoir of a Prisoner of the Confederacy.* Edited by Mark Snell. Novato, Calif.: Presidio, 1996.

Robbins, Walter R. *War Record and Personal Experiences of Walter Raleigh Robbins.* N.p.: privately printed, 1923.

Sammons, John H. *Personal Recollections of the Civil War.* Greensburg, Ind.: Montgomery & Son, n.d.

Small, Abner R. *The Road to Richmond.* Berkeley: University of California Press, 1957.

Smedley, Charles. *A Pennsylvania Quaker in Andersonville.* With a foreword by James Durkin. Glenside, Pa.: J. Michael Santarelli, 1995.

Smith, Charles M. *From Andersonville to Freedom.* Providence: Rhode Island Soldiers and Sailors Historical Society, 1894.

Sneden, Robert. *Eye of the Storm: A Civil War Odyssey.* Edited by Charles Bryan, Jr., and Nelson Lankford. New York: Free Press, 2000.

Spencer, A. L. *Reminiscences of the Civil War and Andersonville Prison.* Ottawa, Kans.: Fulton, 1917.

Stamp, J. B. "Ten Months Experience in Northern Prisons." *Alabama Historical Quarterly* 18 (Winter 1956): 486–98.

Straubing, Harold Elk. *Civil War Eyewitness Reports.* Hamden, Conn.: Archon, 1985.

Sturgis, Thomas. "Prisoners of War." In *Personal Recollections of the War of the Rebellion,* edited by A. Noel Blakeman, 266–328. New York: G. P. Putnam's Sons, 1912.

Styple, William B., ed. *Death before Dishonor: The Andersonville Diary of Eugene Forbes.* Kearny, N.J.: Belle Grove, 1995.

Swift, F. W. "My Experiences as a Prisoner of War." In *War Papers Read before the Commandery of the State of Michigan: Military Order of the Loyal Legion of the United States.,* 3–24. Detroit: Wm. S. Ostler, 1888.

Toney, Marcus B. *Privations of a Private.* Nashville, Tenn.: privately printed, 1905.

Trumbull, H. Clay. *War Memories of a Union Chaplain.* New York: Charles Scribner's Sons, 1898.

Turley, Thomas B. *A Narrative of His Capture and Imprisonment during the War between the States.* With an introduction by John H. Davis. Memphis, Tenn.: Southwestern at Memphis, 1961.

Urban, John W. *Battle Field and Prison Pen, or Through the War, and Thrice a Prisoner in Rebel Dungeons.* N. p.: Edgewood, 1882.

Waters, Thad. *The Terrors of Rebel Prisons.* N.p.: privately printed, 1868.

Wells, James M. *With Touch of Elbow or Death Before Dishonor.* Chicago: John C. Winston, 1909.

Whitenack, David S. "Reminiscences of the Civil War: Andersonville." *Indiana Magazine of History* 11 (June 1915): 128–43.

Wiley, Bell I., ed. *Four Years on the Firing Line.* Jackson, Tenn.: McCowat-Mercer, 1963.

Wilkeson, Frank. *Recollections of a Private Soldier in the Army of the Potomac.* New York: G. P. Putnam's Sons, 1887.

Williams, Walter L. "A Confederate View of Prison Life: A Virginian in Fort Delaware, 1863." *Delaware History* 18 (Fall–Winter 1979): 226–35.

Woolverton, William B. "A Sketch of Prison Life at Andersonville." *Firelands Pioneer* 8 (January 1894): 63–71.

Wyeth, John A. *With Sabre and Scalpel.* New York: Harper & Brothers, 1914.

Zeigler, W. T. *Half Hour with an Andersonville Prisoner. Delivered at the Reunion of Post 9, G. A. R., at Gettysburg, Pa, Jan. 8th, 1879.* N.p.: John M. Tate, 1879.

Memoirs and Letters

Andrews, Eliza Frances. *The War-Time Journal of a Georgia Girl, 1864–1865.* Edited by Spencer Bidwell King, Jr. Macon, Ga.: Ardivan, 1960.

Bacon, Georgeanna Woolsey, and Eliza Woolsey Howland. *My Heart towards Home: Letters of a Family during the Civil War.* Edited by Daniel John Hoisington. Roseville, Minn.: Edinborough, 2001.

Clift, Glenn G, ed. *The Private War of Lizzie Hardin.* Frankfort: Kentucky Historical Society, 1963.

Cox, Jacob D. *Military Reminiscences of the Civil War. Volume II. November 1863–June 1865.* New York: Charles Scribner's Sons, 1900.

Crotty, D. G. *Four years Campaigning in the Army of the Potomac.* Grand Rapids, Mich.: Dygert Bros., 1874.

Dennis, Frank Allen, ed. *Kemper County Rebel: The Civil War Diary of Robert Masten Holmes, C.S.A.* Jackson: University and College Press of Mississippi, 1973.

East, Charles, ed. *The Civil War Diary of Sarah Morgan.* Athens: University of Georgia Press, 1991.

Hammond, Harold E., ed. *Diary of a Union Lady, 1861–1865.* New York: Funk & Wagnalls, 1962.

Hatley, Joe M., and Linda B. Huffman, eds. *Letters of William F. Wagner: Confederate Soldier.* Wendell, N.C.: Broadfoot's Bookmark, 1983.

Heller, J. Roderick, III, and Carolynn Ayres Heller, eds. *The Confederacy is on her way up the Spout.* Athens: University of Georgia Press, 1992.

Hennessy, John J., ed. *Fighting with the Eighteenth Massachusetts.* Baton Rouge: Louisiana State University Press, 2000.

Holstein, Mrs. *Three Years in Field Hospitals of the Army of the Potomac.* Philadelphia: J. B. Lippincott, 1867.

Jones, J. B. *A Rebel War Clerk's Diary.* Edited by Howard Swiggett. New York: Old Hickory Bookshop, 1935.

Jones, Terry L., ed. *Campbell Brown's Civil War.* Baton Rouge: Louisiana State University Press, 2001.

Lander, Ernest M., Jr., and Charles M. McGee, Jr., eds. *A Rebel Came Home: The Diary and Letters of Floride Clemson, 1863–1866.* Columbia: University of South Carolina Press, 1961.

Larimer, Charles, ed. *Love and Valor: The Intimate Love Letters between Jacob and Emeline Ritner.* Western Springs, Ill.: Sigourney, 2000.

Livermore, Mary A. *My Story of the War: A Woman's Narrative.* Hartford, Conn.: A. D. Worthington, 1889.

Osborne, Frederick M. *Private Osborne.* Gretna, La.: Pelican, 2002.

Pember, Phoebe Yates. *A Southern Woman's Story: Life in Confederate Richmond.* Edited by Bell I. Wiley. Jackson, Tenn.: McCowat-Mercer, 1959.

Stephens, Alexander H. *Recollections of Alexander H. Stephens.* Edited by Myrta Avary. New York: Doubleday, Page, 1910. Reprint, Baton Rouge: Louisiana State University Press, 1998.

Younger, Edward, ed. *Inside the Confederate Government: The Diary of Robert Garlick Hill Kean.* New York: Oxford University Press, 1957. Reprint, Baton Rouge: Louisiana State University Press, 1993.

Volumes on Monuments and Parks

Abernethy, Alonzo, ed. *Dedication of Monuments Erected by the State of Iowa.* Des Moines, Iowa: Emory H. English, 1908.

Appeal for Pecuniary Aid to Care for and Monument the Remains of the Confederate Dead Buried on Johnson's Island and at Columbus, Ohio. Cincinnati, Ohio: Cohen, 1892.

Averill, James P., ed. *Andersonville Prison Park. Report of its Purchase and Improvement.* Atlanta: Byrd, n.d.

Bearss, Edwin C. *Andersonville National Historic Site Historic Resource Study and Historical Base Map.* Washington, D.C.: U.S. Department of the Interior, National Park Service, 1970.

Committee on Confederate Dead, Charles Broadway Rouss Camp No. 1191 United Confederate Veterans. *Report on the Re-burial of the Confederate Dead in Arlington Cemetery.* Washington, D.C., Judd & Detweiler, 1901.

Commonwealth of Massachusetts. *Report of the Commission on Andersonville Monument.* Boston: Wright & Putter, 1902.

Confederated Southern Memorial Association. *History of the Confederated Memorial Associations of the South.* New Orleans: Graham, 1904.

Dedication Connecticut Andersonville Monument: Dedication of the Monument at Andersonville, Georgia, October 23, 1907. Hartford: Published by the State, 1908.

Denver Service Center. *Environmental Assessment for General Management Plan/ Development Concept Plan, Andersonville National Historic Site, Georgia.* Denver: U.S. Department of the Interior, National Park Service, 1979.

"First Annual Centennial Strategy for Andersonville National Historic Site August 2007." http://www.nps.gov/ande/parkmgmt/centennial-initiative-2016.htm (accessed July 15, 2008).

General Management Plan/Development Concept Plan/Environmental Assessment: Andersonville National Historic Site, Georgia. N.p.: Southeast Regional Office, U.S. Department of the Interior, National Park Service, 1988.

Hanly, Frank J. *Andersonville.* New York: Eaton & Mains, 1912.

Hill, Robert J., and William B. Keeling. *Preliminary Development Study Andersonville Historical Complex.* Athens, Ga.: Bureau of Business and Economic Research and Institute of Community and Area Development, University of Georgia, 1965.

Jensen, John E. *Interpretative Prospectus.* Denver: U.S. Department of the Interior, National Park Service, 1974.

Libby Prison War Museum Catalogue and Program. Chicago: Libby Prison War Museum Association, 1890.

Master Plan: Andersonville National Historic Site, Georgia. Washington, D.C.: U.S. Department of the Interior, National Park Service, 1968.

Master Plan: Andersonville National Historic Site, Georgia. Washington, D.C.: U.S. Department of the Interior, National Park Service, 1971.

National Prisoner of War Museum Andersonville, Georgia Dedication April 9, 1998. N.p.: privately printed, 1998.

New Jersey Monument Commissioners. *Report of the New Jersey Andersonville Monument Commissioners.* Somerville, N.J.: Unionist-Gazette Association, 1899.

Pennsylvania at Andersonville, Georgia, Ceremonies at the Dedication of the Memorial Erected by the Commonwealth of Pennsylvania in the National Cemetery at Andersonville, Georgia. N.p.: C. E. Aughinbaugh, 1909.

Pennsylvania at Salisbury, North Carolina: Ceremonies at the Dedication of the Memorial Erected by the Commonwealth of Pennsylvania in the National Cemetery at Salisbury, North Carolina. C. E. Aughinbaugh, 1910.

A Pilgrimage to the Shrines of Patriotism. Being the Report of the Commission to Dedicate the Monument Erected by the State of New York, in Andersonville, Georgia. Albany, N.Y.: J. B. Lyon, 1916.

Planning Study Report Andersonville Prison Park Georgia. Washington, D.C.: U.S. Department of the Interior, National Park Service, 1966.

Report of the Joint Special Committee on Erection of Monument at Andersonville, Georgia. Providence, R.I.: E. L. Freeman, 1903.

Report of the Maine Andersonville Monument Commissioners. Augusta, Maine: Kennebec Journal, 1904.

Report of the Maine Commissioners on the Monument Erected at Salisbury, N.C., 1908. Waterville, Maine: Sentinel, 1908.

Report of the Minnesota Commission Appointed to Erect Monuments to Soldiers in the National Military Cemeteries at Little Rock, Arkansas, Memphis, TN, Andersonville, GA. N.p.: 1916.

Robert and Company Associates, Architects, Engineers, Planners. *Master Development Plan May 1974 Prepared for the Middle Flint Area Planning and Development Commission.* Atlanta: privately printed, 1974.

Roster, the National Society of Andersonville Survivors 1912. New York: McConnell, 1912.

Sherman, Ernest A. *Dedicating in Dixie.* Cedar Rapids, Iowa: Press of the Record Printing Company, 1907.

Other Primary Sources

Bell, Landon C. *An Address at Johnson's Island.* N.p.: privately printed, 1929.

Blaine, James G. *Political Discussions: Legislative, Diplomatic, and Popular.* Norwich, Conn.: Henry Bill, 1887.

Board of Commissioners. *Minnesota in the Civil and Indian Wars 1861–1865.* St. Paul, Minn.: Pioneer, 1891.

Byers, S. H. M. *Iowa in War Times.* Des Moines, Iowa: W. D. Condit, 1888.

Carnahan, James R. *Camp Morton.* N.p.: Baker-Randolph L. & E. Co., 1892.

Chandler, William E. *Decoration Day. Address of William E. Chandler, on Thursday, May 30, 1889, at Nashua, N. H., before John G. Foster Post No. 7, G. A. R.* Concord, N.H.: Republican Press Association, 1889.

Chipman, N. P. *The Horrors of Andersonville Prison.* San Francisco: Bancroft, 1891.

Collingwood, Herbert W. *Andersonville Violets: A Story of Northern and Southern Life.* N.p.: Lee & Shepard, 1889. Reprint, Tuscaloosa: University of Alabama Press, 2000.

Craven, John J. *Prison Life of Jefferson Davis.* New York: Carleton, 1866.

Davis, Jefferson. *Andersonville and other War-Prisons.* New York: Belford, 1890.

The Demon of Andersonville; or, The Trial of Wirz, for the Cruel Treatment and Brutal Murder of Helpless Union Prisoners in his Hands. The Most Highly Exciting and Interesting Trial of the Present Century, his Life and Execution Containing also a History of Andersonville, with Illustrations, Truthfully Representing the Horrible Scenes of Cruelty Perpetuated by Him. Philadelphia: Barclay, 1865.

Elarton, J. W. *Andersonville.* Aurora, Neb.: privately printed, 1913.

Goodwyn, A. T. *Memorial Address.* Montgomery, Ala.: privately printed, 1926.

Gray Book Committee S. C. V. *The Gray Book.* N.p.: Privately printed, 1920.

Holmes, Clay W. *The Elmira Prison Camp.* New York: G. P. Putnam's Sons, 1912.

———. "The Elmira Prison Camp. Read by Clay W. Holmes of Elmira, Companion by Inheritance, February 7, 1912." In *Personal Recollections of the War of the*

Rebellion, edited by A. Noel Blakeman, 351–72. New York: G. P. Putnam's Sons, 1912.

Indiana Historical Collections. *Indiana in the War of the Rebellion: Report of the Adjutant General: A Reprint of Volume 1 of the Eight Volume Report Prepared by W. H. H. Terrill and Published in 1869.* N.p.: Indiana Historical Bureau, 1960.

Knauss, William H. *The Story of Camp Chase.* Nashville, Tenn.: Publishing House of the Methodist Episcopal Church, South, Smith & Lamar, Agents, 1906. Reprint, Columbus, Ohio; The General's Books, 1994.

Philadelphia *Weekly Times. The Annals of the War.* Philadelphia: Times Publishing, 1879.

Robertson, Jno. *Michigan in the War.* Lansing, Mich.: W. S. George, 1882.

Rutherford, Mildred L. *Address Delivered by Miss Mildred Lewis Rutherford, Historian General, United Daughters of the Confederacy: Wrongs of History Righted. Savannah, Georgia, Friday, Nov. 13, 1914.* Savannah, Ga.: privately printed, 1914.

———. *Facts and Figures vs. Myths and Misrepresentations: Henry Wirz and Andersonville Prison.* Athens, Ga.: privately printed, 1921.

Shanks, J. P. C. *Speech of Gen. J. P. C. Shanks, of Indiana, on Treatment of Prisoners of War.* Washington D.C.: Judd & Detweiler, 1870.

Stevenson, Randolph. *The Southern Side; or, Andersonville Prison.* Baltimore: Turnbull Brothers, 1876.

Stille, Charles J. *History of the United States Sanitary Commission: Being the General Report of its Work during the War of the Rebellion.* Philadelphia: J. B. Lippincott, 1866.

Sumner, Charles. *Speech of Hon. Charles Sumner, in the Senate of the United States, January 29th, 1865, on the Resolution of the Committee on Military Affairs, Advising Retaliation in Kind for Rebel Cruelties to Prisoners.* New York: Young Men's Republican Union, 1865.

Thirkield, Wilbur P. *Union, Peace, Fraternity: A Decoration Day Address by the Rev. Wilbur P. Thirkield, D. D. Delivered at the National Cemetery, Marietta, May 30, 1896.* Atlanta,: Published by the O. M. Mitchell Post, 1896.

Thompson, Holland, ed. *Prisons and Hospitals, Vol. 7, The Photographic History of the Civil War in Ten Volumes.* Edited by Francis Trevelyan Miller. New York: Review of Reviews Co., 1911.

The Trial and Death of Henry Wirz. Raleigh, N.C.: E. M. Uzzell, 1908.

United States Sanitary Commission. *Narrative of Privations and Sufferings of United States Officers and Soldiers while Prisoners of War in the Hands of the Rebel Authorities, Being the Report of a Commission of Inquiry.* Philadelphia, King & Baird, 1864.

Waite, Otis F. R. *Vermont in the Great Rebellion.* Claremont, N.H.: Tracy, Chase, 1869.

Whitman, Walt. *Memoranda during the War [&] Death of Abraham Lincoln.* Edited by Roy P. Basler. Camden, N.J.: privately printed, 1875. Reprint, Bloomington: Indiana University Press, 1962.

SECONDARY SOURCES

Books

Anderson, Sherwood. *Winesburg, Ohio.* Edited by John H. Ferres. New York: Viking, 1966.

Ashworth, Gregory, and Rudi Hartmann, eds. *Horror and Human Tragedy Revisited: The Management of Sites of Atrocities for Tourism.* Elmsford, N.Y.: Cognizant Communication, 2005.

Baker, Raymond F. *Andersonville: The Story of a Civil War Prison Camp.* Washington, D.C.: Office of Publications, U. S. Department of the Interior, National Park Service, 1972.

Beitzell, Edwin. *Point Lookout Prison Camp for Confederates.* N.p.: privately printed, 1972.

———. *Point Lookout Prison Camp for Confederates Supplemental Data.* N.p.: privately printed, 1977.

Bensel, Richard. *Yankee Leviathan: The Origins of Central State Authority in America, 1859–1877.* Cambridge, Mass.: Cambridge University Press, 1990.

Black, Robert C., III. *The Railroads of the Confederacy.* Chapel Hill: University of North Carolina Press, 1952.

Blair, William A. *Cities of the Dead: Contesting the Memory of the Civil War in the South, 1865–1914.* Chapel Hill: University of North Carolina Press, 2004.

Blakey, Arch Frederic. *General John Winder, CSA.* Gainesville: University of Florida Press, 1990.

Blanton, DeAnne, and Lauren M. Cook. *They Fought Like Demons: Women Soldiers in the American Civil War.* Baton Rouge: Louisiana State University Press, 2002.

Blight, David W. *Beyond the Battlefield: Race, Memory, and the American Civil War.* Cambridge: University of Massachusetts Press, 2002.

———. *Race and Reunion: The Civil War in American Memory.* Cambridge, Mass.: Belknap Press of Harvard University Press, 2001.

Bowman, Larry G. *Captive Americans: Prisoners during the American Revolution.* Athens: Ohio University Press, 1976.

Brown, Louis A. *The Salisbury Prison: A Case Study of Confederate Military Prisons 1861–1865.* Wilmington, N.C.: Broadfoot, 1992.

Brown, Thomas J. *The Public Art of Civil War Commemoration.* New York: Bedford/St. Martin's, 2004.

Brundage, W. Fitzhugh. *The Southern Past: A Clash of Race and Memory.* Cambridge, Mass.: Belknap Press of Harvard University Press, 2005.

Bryant, William O. *Cahaba Prison and the Sultana Disaster.* Tuscaloosa: University of Alabama Press, 1990.

Buck, Paul A. *The Road to Reunion, 1865–1900.* Boston: Little, Brown, 1947.

Burkhardt, George S. *Confederate Rage, Yankee Wrath: No Quarter in the Civil War.* Carbondale: Southern Illinois University Press, 2007.

Burnett, William G. *The Prison Camp at Andersonville.* New York: Eastern National Park & Monument Association, 1995.

Cangemi, Joseph P., and Casimir J. Kowalski, eds. *Andersonville Prison: Lessons in Organizational Failure.* Lanham, Md.: University Press of America, 1992.

Carson, Ray M. *The Civil War Soldier.* Mechanicsburg, Pa.: Stackpole, 2000.

Carter, Dan T. *When the War Was Over: The Failure of Self-Reconstruction in the South, 1865–1867.* Baton Rouge: Louisiana State University Press, 1985.

Catton, Bruce. *Reflections on the Civil War.* Garden City, N.Y.: Doubleday, 1981.

Chadwick, Bruce. *The Reel Civil War.* New York: Knopf, 2001.

Cimprich, John. *Fort Pillow, a Civil War Massacre, and Public Memory.* Baton Rouge: Louisiana State University Press, 2005.

Civil War Journal. The Legacies. Nashville, Tenn.: Rutledge Hill, 1999.

Clark, Kathleen A. *Defining Moments: African American Commemoration and Political Culture in the South, 1863–1913.* Chapel Hill: University of North Carolina Press, 2005.

Confederate Soldiers, Sailors and Civilians Who Died as Prisoners of War at Camp Douglas, Chicago, Ill., 1862–1865. Kalamazoo, Mich.: Edgar Gray, n.d.

Cook, Robert J. *Troubled Commemoration: The American Civil War Centennial Commission, 1961–1965.* Baton Rouge: Louisiana State University Press, 2007.

Cooper, William J., Jr. *Jefferson Davis, American.* New York: Knopf, 2000.

Cox, Karen L. *Dixie's Daughters: The United Daughters of the Confederacy and the Preservation of Confederate Culture.* Gainesville: University Press of Florida, 2003.

Cunningham, H. H. *Doctors in Gray: The Confederate Medical Service.* Baton Rouge: Louisiana State University Press, 1958. Reprint, Baton Rouge: Louisiana State University Press, 1993.

Davis, Robert S. *Ghosts and Shadows of Andersonville: Essays on the Secret Social Histories of America's Deadliest Prison.* Macon, Ga.: Mercer University Press, 2006.

Dean, Eric T. *Shook over Hell: Post-Traumatic Stress, Vietnam, and the Civil War.* Cambridge, Mass.: Harvard University Press, 1997.

Dean, Robert D. *Echoes of Andersonville.* Franklin, Tenn.: Heritage, 1999.

Dearing, Mary R. *Veterans in Politics: The Story of the G.A.R.* Baton Rouge: Louisiana State University Press, 1952.

Doyle, Robert C. *Voices from Captivity: Interpreting the American POW Narrative.* Lawrence: University Press of Kansas, 1994.

Dunham, Chester Forrester. *The Attitude of the Northern Clergy toward the South.* Toledo, Ohio: Gray, 1942.

Encyclopedia of the Confederacy. Volume 3. Edited by Richard N. Current. New York: Simon & Schuster, 1993.

England, Otis B. *A Short History of the Rock Island Prison Barracks.* Rock Island, Ill.: Historical Office, U. S. Army Armament, Munitions, and Chemical Command, 1985.

Fabian, Ann. *The Unvarnished Truth: Personal Narratives in Nineteenth-Century America.* Berkeley: University of California Press, 2000.

Fahs, Alice, and Joan Waugh, eds. *The Memory of the Civil War in American Culture.* Chapel Hill: University of North Carolina Press, 2004.

Faust, Drew G. *This Republic of Suffering: Death and the American Civil War.* New York: Knopf, 2008.

Fetzer, Dale, and Bruce Mowday. *Unlikely Allies: Fort Delaware's Prison Community in the Civil War.* Mechanicsburg, Pa.: Stackpole, 2000.

Fooks, Herbert C. *Prisoners of War.* Federalsburg, Md.: J. W. Stowell, 1924.

Foote, Corydon E., and Olive Deane Hormel. *With Sherman to the Sea: A Drummer's Story of the Civil War.* New York: John Day, 1960.

Ford, Annette Gee, ed. *The Captive.* Salt Lake City, Utah: Utah Bookbinding, 2000.

Foster, Gaines M. *Ghosts of the Confederacy: Defeat, the Lost Cause, and the Emergence of the New South, 1865–1913.* New York: Oxford University Press, 1987.

Frohman, Charles E. *Rebels on Lake Erie.* Columbus: Ohio Historical Society, 1965.

Futch, Ovid L. *History of Andersonville Prison.* Indiantown: University of Florida Press, 1968.

Garrison, Webb. *The Amazing Civil War.* Nashville, Tenn.: Rutledge Hill, 1998.

———. *Civil War Hostages: Hostage Taking in the Civil War.* Shippensburg, Pa.: White Mane Books, 2000.

Geier, Clarence R., and Stephen R. Potter, eds. *Archeological Perspectives on the Civil War.* Gainesville: University Press of Florida, 2000.

Georgia Civil War Historical Markers. N.p.: Georgia Historical Commission, 1964. Reprint, n.p.: Georgia Historical Commission, 1982.

Gibbs, Joseph. *Three Years in the Bloody Eleventh.* University Park: Pennsylvania State University Press, 2002.

Gillispie, James M. *Andersonvilles of the North: The Myths and Realities of Northern Treatment of Civil War Confederate Prisoners.* Denton: University of North Texas Press, 2008.

Glaathaar, Joseph T. *Forged in Battle: The Civil War Alliance of Black Soldiers and White Officers.* New York: Free Press, 1990.

Goldfield, David R. *Still Fighting the Civil War: The American South and Southern History.* Baton Rouge: Louisiana State University Press, 2002.

Gray, Michael P. *The Business of Captivity: Elmira and Its Civil War Prison.* Kent, Ohio: Kent State University Press, 2001.

Hackman, Gene, and Daniel Lenihan. *Escape from Andersonville.* New York: St. Martin's, 2008.

Harwell, Richard B. *The Confederate Reader.* New York: Longmans, Green, 1957.

———. *The Union Reader.* New York: Longmans, Green, 1958.

Hemmerlein, Richard F. *Prisons and Prisoners of the Civil War.* Boston: Christopher, 1934.

Herek, Raymond J. *These Men Have Seen Hard Service.* Detroit: Wayne State University Press, 1998.

Hesseltine, William Best. *Civil War Prisons: A Study in War Psychology.* Columbus: Ohio State University Press, 1930. Reprint, Columbus: Ohio State University Press, 1998.

———, ed. *Civil War Prisons.* Kent, Ohio: Kent State University Press, 1962. Reprint, Kent, Ohio: Kent State University Press, 1995.

Hicken, Victor. *Illinois in the Civil War.* Urbana: University of Illinois Press, 1966.

Hickey, Donald R. *The War of 1812: A Forgotten Conflict.* Urbana: University of Illinois Press, 1989.

Horigan, Michael. *Elmira: Death Camp of the North.* Mechanicsburg, Pa.: Stackpole, 2002.

Horwitz, Tony. *Confederates in the Attic.* New York: Vintage, 1998.

Hughes, Nathaniel Cheairs, Jr. *Sir Henry Morton Stanley, Confederate.* Baton Rouge: Louisiana State University Press, 2000.

Institute for World Order. *War Criminals, War Victims: Andersonville, Nuremberg, Hiroshima, My Lai.* New York: Random House, 1974.

Jackson, William J. *New Jerseyans in the Civil War.* New Brunswick, N.J.: Rutgers University Press, 2000.

Joslyn, Mauriel. *The Biographical Roster of the Immortal 600.* Shippensburg, Pa.: White Mane, 1992.

Kadzis, Peter, ed. *Blood: Stories of Life and Death from the Civil War.* New York: Thunder's Mouth Press and Balliett & Fitzgerald, 2000.

Kammen, Michael. *Mystic Chords of Memory: The Transformation of Tradition in American Culture.* New York: Vintage, 1991.

Kantor, MacKinlay. *Andersonville.* New York: HarperCollins, 1955. Reprint, New York: Plume, 1993.

Kelly, C. Bryan. *Best Little Stories from the Civil War.* Charlottesville Va.: Montpelier, 1994. Reprint, Nashville, Tenn.: Cumberland House, 1998.

Kelly, Orr, and Mary Davies Kelly. *Dream's End: Two Iowa Brothers in the Civil War.* New York: Kodansha America, 1998.

Laderman, Gary. *The Sacred Remains: American Attitudes toward Death, 1799–1883.* New Haven, Conn.: Yale University Press, 1996.

Lears, T. J. Jackson. *No Place of Grace: Antimodernism and the Transformation of American Culture, 1880–1920.* Chicago: University of Chicago Press, 1983.

Levitt, Saul. *The Andersonville Trial.* New York: Random House, 1960.

Levy, George. *To Die in Chicago: Confederate Prisoners at Camp Douglas 1862–65.* Gretna, La.: Pelican, 1999.

Lewis, George G., and John Mewha. *History of Prisoner of War Utilization by the United States Army 1776–1945.* Washington, D.C.: Department of the Army, 1955.

Linenthal, Edward T. *Sacred Ground: Americans and Their Battlefields.* Chicago: University of Illinois Press, 1991.

Lonn, Ella. *Foreigners in the Confederacy.* Chapel Hill: University of North Carolina Press, 1940.

Lowenthal, David. *Possessed by the Past: The Heritage Crusade and the Spoils of History.* New York: Free Press, 1996.

Lynn, John W. *800 Paces to Hell: Andersonville.* Fredericksburg, Va.: Sergeant Kirkland's Museum and Historical Society, 1999.

Macdonald, Dwight. *The Responsibility of Peoples.* London: Gollancz, 1957.

Madden, David, ed. *Beyond the Battlefield: The Ordinary Life and Extraordinary Times of the Civil War Soldier.* New York: Simon & Schuster, 2000.

———. *Sharpshooter.* Knoxville: University of Tennessee Press, 1996.

Malone, Dumas, and Basil Rauch. *The New Nation, 1865–1917.* New York: Appleton-Century-Crofts, 1960.

Manakee, Harold R. *Maryland in the Civil War.* Baltimore: Garamond, 1961.

Marsh, Michael Alan. *Andersonville: The Story behind the Scenery.* N.p.: KC Publications, 2000.

Marvel, William. *Andersonville: The Last Depot.* Chapel Hill: University of North Carolina Press, 1994.

Maxwell, William Q. *Lincoln's Fifth Wheel: The Political History of the United States Sanitary Commission.* New York: Longmans, Green, 1956.

McAdams, Benton. *Rebels at Rock Island: The Story of a Civil War Prison.* Dekalb: Northern Illinois University Press, 2000.

McConnell, Stuart. *Glorious Contentment: The Grand Army of the Republic, 1865–1900.* Chapel Hill: University of North Carolina Press, 1992.

McPherson, James M. *Battle Cry of Freedom.* New York: Ballantine, 1988.

McPherson, James M., and William J. Cooper, Jr., eds. *Writing the Civil War: The Quest to Understand.* Columbia: University of South Carolina Press, 1998.

Metzger, Charles H. *The Prisoner in the American Revolution.* Chicago: Loyola University Press, 1971.

Mitchell, Reid. *Civil War Soldiers.* New York: Simon & Schuster, 1988.

Neff, John R. *Honoring the Civil War Dead: Commemoration and the Problem of Reconciliation.* Lawrence: University Press of Kansas, 2005.

Nelson, William E. *The Roots of American Bureaucracy, 1830–1900*. Cambridge, Mass.: Harvard University Press, 1982.

Nevins, Allan. *The War for the Union, Volume III: The Organized War, 1863–64*. New York: Charles Scribner's Sons, 1971.

Novick, Peter. *That Noble Dream: The "Objectivity Question" and the American Historical Profession*. New York: Cambridge University Press, 1988.

Oates, Stephen B. *A Woman of Valor: Clara Barton and the Civil War*. New York: Free Press, 1994.

Painter, Nell. *Standing at Armageddon: The United States 1877–1919*. New York: W. W. Norton, 1987.

Parker, Sandra V. *Richmond's Civil War Prisons*. Lynchburg, Va.: H. E. Howard, 1990.

Price, William H. *Civil War Handbook*. Fairfax, Va.: L. B. Prince, 1961.

Radley, Kenneth. *Rebel Watchdog: The Confederate States Army Provost Guard*. Baton Rouge: Louisiana State University Press, 1989.

Ramsdell, Charles. *Behind the Lines in the Southern Confederacy*. Baton Rouge: Louisiana State University Press, 1997.

Randall, J. G., and David Donald. *The Civil War and Reconstruction*. Boston: D. C. Heath, 1961.

Rhodes, James F. *History of the United States from the Compromise of 1850 to the Restoration of Home Rule in the South in 1877*. London: MacMillan, 1904.

Roberts, Edward F. *Andersonville Journey*. Shippensburg, Pa.: Burd Street, 1998.

Rolph, Daniel N. *My Brother's Keeper: Union and Confederate Soldiers' Acts of Mercy during the Civil War*. Mechanicsburg, Pa.: Stackpole, 2002.

Royster, Charles. *The Destructive War: William Tecumseh Sherman, Stonewall Jackson, and the Americans*. New York: Vintage, 1993.

Sanders, Charles W., Jr. *While in the Hands of the Enemy: Military Prisons of the Civil War*. Baton Rouge: Louisiana State University Press, 2005.

Savage, Douglas J. *Prison Camps of the Civil War*. Philadelphia: Chelsea House, 2000.

Savage, Kirk. *Standing Soldiers, Kneeling Slaves: Race, War, and Monument in Nineteenth-Century America*. Princeton, N.J.: Princeton University Press, 1997.

Segars, J. H., ed. *Andersonville: The Southern Perspective*. Gretna, La.: Pelican, 2001.

Shaffer, Donald R. *After the Glory: The Struggles of Black Civil War Veterans*. Lawrence: University Press of Kansas, 2004.

Sheppard, Peggy. *Andersonville Georgia USA*. N.p.: privately printed, 1973. Reprint, Andersonville, Ga.: Sheppard, 2001.

Shriver, Philip R., and Donald J. Breen. *Ohio's Military Prisons in the Civil War*. Columbus: Ohio State University Press, 1964.

Siegel, Alan A. *Beneath the Starry Flag: New Jersey's Civil War Experience*. New Brunswick, N.J.: Rutgers University Press, 2001.

Speer, Lonnie R. *Portals to Hell: Military Prisons of the Civil War.* Mechanicsburg, Pa.: Stackpole, 1997.

—————. *War of Vengeance: Acts of Retaliation against Civil War POWs.* Mechanicsburg, Pa.: Stackpole, 2002.

Stephens, Clifford W, ed. *Rock Island Confederate Prison Deaths.* Rock Island, Ill.: Blackhawk Genealogical Society, 1973.

Stout, Harry S. *Upon the Altar of the Nation.* New York: Penguin, 2006.

Thompson, William F. *The Image of War.* N.p.: A. S. Barnes and Company, 1959. Reprint, Baton Rouge: Louisiana State University Press, 1994.

Trefousse, Hans L. *Thaddeus Stevens: Nineteenth-Century Egalitarian.* Mechanicsburg, Pa.: Stackpole, 2001.

Urwin, Gregory J. W. *Black Flag over Dixie: Racial Atrocities and Reprisals in the Civil War.* Carbondale: Southern Illinois University Press, 2004.

Vaughan, Robert. *Andersonville.* New York: Boulevard, 1996.

Vowell, Sarah. *The Partly Cloudy Patriot.* New York: Simon & Schuster, 2002.

Warren, Robert Penn. *The Legacy of the Civil War.* New York: Random House, 1961.

Weber, Max. *Essays in Sociology.* Translated and edited by H. H. Gerth and C. Wright Mills. New York: Oxford University Press, 1946.

Weeks, Jim. *Gettysburg: Memory, Market, and an American Shrine.* Princeton, N.J.: Princeton University Press, 2003.

Wiebe, Robert H. *The Search for Order 1877–1920.* New York: Hill & Wang, 1967.

Winslow, Hattie Lou, and Joseph R. H. Moore. *Camp Morton, 1861–1865: Indianapolis Prison Camp.* Indianapolis: Indiana Historical Society, 1940. Reprint, Indianapolis: Indiana Historical Society, 1995.

Woodworth, Steven E., ed. *The Loyal, True, and Brave: America's Civil War Soldiers.* Wilmington, Del.: Scholarly Resources, 2002.

—————. *While God Is Marching On: The Religious World of Civil War Soldiers.* Lawrence: University Press of Kansas, 2001.

Zunz, Olivier. *Making America Corporate, 1870–1920.* Chicago: University of Chicago, 1990.

Articles, Book Chapters, and Book Reviews

Babbitt, Bruce. "Foreword." In *Rally on the High Ground: The National Park Service Symposium on the Civil War,* edited by Robert K. Sutton, v–vii. New York: Eastern National, 2001.

Blair, William. "Foreword." In *Civil War Prisons: A Study in War Psychology,* by William Hesseltine, ix–xxi. Columbus: Ohio State University Press, 1998.

Boney, F. N. Review of *Andersonville: The Last Depot,* by William Marvel. *Journal of American History* 82 (September 1995): 749–50.

Bonner, James C. "War Crimes Trials, 1865–1867." *Social Science* 22 (April 1947): 128–34.

Boyles, Fred. "The Evolution of the National Prisoner of War Museum." In *National Prisoner of War Museum Andersonville, Georgia Dedication April 9, 1998*, 7–10. N.p.: privately printed, 1998.

Breeden, James O. "A Medical History of the Later Stages of the Atlanta Campaign." *Journal of Southern History* 35 (February 1969): 31–59.

Burrows, Edwin G. "Patriots or Terrorists? The Lost Story of Revolutionary POWS." *American Heritage* 58 (Fall 2008): 54–62.

Bush, David R. "Interpreting the Latrines of the Johnson's Island Civil War Military Prison." *Historical Archeology* 34, no. 1 (2000): 62–78.

Byrne, Frank L. "Libby Prison: A Study in Emotions." *Journal of Southern History* 24 (November 1958): 430–44.

———. Review of *Andersonville: The Last Depot*, by William Marvel. *Civil War History* 41 (June 1995): 169–71.

Catton, Bruce. "Prison Camps of the Civil War." *American Heritage* 10 (August 1959): 4–13, 96–97.

Chesson, Michael B. Review of *General John H. Winder, C.S.A*, by Arch F. Blakey. *Journal of Southern History* 58 (August 1992): 543.

Coakley, R. Walter. Review of *Foreigners in the Confederacy*, by Ella Lonn. *William and Mary College Quarterly Historical Magazine* 22 (January 1942): 75–80.

Collins, Kathleen. "Living Skeletons; Carte-de-visite Propaganda in the American Civil War." *History of Photography* 12 (April–June 1988): 103–20.

Connelly, Thomas L. Review of *History of Andersonville Prison*, by Ovid Futch. *Journal of American History* 55 (March 1969): 870–71.

Coulter, E. Merton. "Amnesty for All except Jefferson Davis: The Hill-Blaine Debate of 1876." *Georgia Historical Quarterly* 56 (Winter 1972): 453–94.

———. "What the South Has Done about Its History." *Journal of Southern History* 2 (February 1936): 3–28.

Davis, Robert S. "'Near Andersonville': An Historical Note on Civil War Legend and Reality." *Journal of African American History* 92 (Winter 2007): 96–105.

———. Review of *A Perfect Picture of Hell*, by Ted Genoways and Hugh H. Genoways. *Journal of Military History* 66 (January 2002): 211.

Edgar, Walter B. Review of *Andersonville: The Last Depot*, by William Marvel. *Journal of Southern History* 62 (February 1996): 156–57.

Faust, Drew Gilpin. "The Civil War Soldier and the Art of Dying." *Journal of Southern History* 67 (February 2001): 3–38.

Friedel, Frank. "General Orders 100 and Military Government." *Mississippi Valley Historical Review* 32 (March 1946): 541–56.

Futch, Ovid. "Andersonville Raiders." *Civil War History* 2 (December 1956): 47–60.

Garfield, James. "Speech of Gen. Garfield at the Andersonville Reunion at To-
    ledo, Ohio, October 3, 1879." In Sergeant Oaks, *Prison Life in Dixie*, 199–205.
    Chicago: Central Book Concern, 1880. Reprint, Scituate, Mass.: Digital Scan-
    ning, 1999.

Gillespie, James M. "Postwar Mythmaking: The Case of the POWs." *North & South*
    6 (April 2003): 40–49.

Gordon-Burr, Leslie J. "Storms of Indignation: The Art of Andersonville as Post-
    war Propaganda." *Georgia Historical Quarterly* 75 (Fall 1991): 587–600.

Gray, Michael. "Elmira, a City on a Prison Camp Contract." *Civil War History* 45
    (Spring 2000): 322–38.

Hannaford, Katherine W. "Culture versus Commerce: The Libby Prison Museum
    and the Image of Chicago, 1889–1899." *Ecumene* 8 (July 2001): 284–316.

Harmon, J. Scott. "Evolution of an Exhibition." In *National Prisoner of War Museum
    Andersonville, Georgia Dedication April 9, 1998*, 18–21. N.p.: privately printed,
    1998.

Hart, Kerry M. "Andersonville: Lessons for Today's Managers." In *Andersonville
    Prison: Lessons in Organizational Failure*, edited by Joseph P. Cangemi and
    Casimir J. Kowalski, 63–80. Lanham, Md.: University Press of America, 1992.

Hassler, Warren W., Jr. Review of *History of Andersonville Prison*, by Ovid Futch.
    American Historical Review 74 (April 1969): 1374–75.

Haverlin, Carl. Review of *Andersonville*, by MacKinlay Kantor. *Civil War History* 1
    (December 1955): 431–34.

Hay, Thomas Robson. Review of *Civil War Prisons: A Study in War Psychology*, by
    William B. Hesseltine. *American Historical Review* 36 (January 1931): 455–56.

Hesseltine, William B. "Andersonville Revisited." *Georgia Review* 10 (Spring 1956):
    92–100.

———. "Civil War Prisons—Introduction." In *Civil War Prisons*, edited by William
    Hesseltine, 5–8. Kent, Ohio: Kent State University Press, 1962. Reprint, Kent,
    Ohio: Kent State University Press, 1995.

———. "The Propaganda Literature of Confederate Prisons." *Journal of Southern
    History* 1 (February–November 1935): 56–66.

Hitchcock, Wayne. "The Coin That Made the Museum Possible." In *National Pri-
    soner of War Museum Andersonville, Georgia Dedication April 9, 1998*, 15–16. N.p.:
    privately printed, 1998.

Hyman, Harold M. "Civil War Turncoats: A Commentary on a Military View of
    Lincoln's War Prisoner Utilization Program." *Military Affairs* 22 (Autumn 1958):
    134–38.

Jones, Virgil Carrington. "Libby Prison Break." *Civil War History* 4 (June 1958):
    93–104.

Keen, Nancy Travis. "Confederate Prisoners of War at Fort Delaware." *Delaware
    History* 13 (April 1968): 1–27.

Klee, Bruce. "They Paid to Enter Libby Prison." *Civil War Times Illustrated* 37 (February 1999): 32–38.

Laska, Lewis L., and James M. Smith. "'Hell and the Devil': Andersonville and the Trial of Captain Henry Wirz, C. S. A., 1865." *Military Law Review* 68 (1975): 77–132.

Linderman, Gerald F. "Battle in Two Wars: The Combat Soldier's Perspective." In *War Comes Again,* edited by Gabor Boritt, 83–99. New York: Oxford University Press, 1995.

Long, Roger. "Northern Comment: The Truth about Andersonville Prison." *Blue & Gray* 3 (December–January 1985–86): 22–28.

Luthin, Reinhard H. "Some Demagogues in American History." *American Historical Review* 57 (October 1951): 22–46.

———. "Waving the Bloody Shirt: Northern Political Tactics in Post-Civil War Times." *Georgia Review* 14 (Spring 1960): 64–71.

Mahood, Wayne. Review of *Andersonville: The Southern Perspective,* edited by J. H. Segars, and *Andersonville,* screenplay by David W. Rintels. *Civil War History* 42 (September 1996): 277–78.

"Major Henry Wirz." *William and Mary College Quarterly Historical Magazine* 27 (January 1919): 145–53.

Mangum, A. W. "History of the Salisbury, N. C., Confederate Prison." *Publications of the Southern History Association* 3 (1899): 307–36.

Marvel, William. "Johnny Ransom's Imagination." *Civil War History* 41 (September 1995): 181–89.

McConnell, Carla. "The Architecture of the National Prisoner of War Museum," in *National Prisoner of War Museum Andersonville, Georgia Dedication April 9, 1998,* 13–14. N.p.: privately printed, 1998.

McMurry, Richard M. Review of *Images from the Storm,* by Robert K. Sneden. *Journal of Military History* 66 (April 2002): 564–65.

Meyer, William B. "The Selling of Libby Prison." *American Heritage* 45 (November 1994): 114–18.

Miller, Robert E. "War within Walls: Camp Chase and the Search for Administrative Reform." *Ohio History* 96 (Winter–Spring 1987): 33–56.

Mitchell, Reid. "'Our Prison System, Supposing We Had Any': The Confederate and Union Prison Systems." In *On the Road to Total War: The American Civil War and the German Wars of Unification, 1861–1871,* edited by Stig Forster and Jorg Nagler, 565–85. New York: Cambridge University Press, 1997.

Morseberger, Robert E., and Katharine M. Morseberger. "After Andersonville: The First War Crimes Trial." *Civil War Times Illustrated* 13 (July 1974): 30–40.

O'Leary, Cecilia E. "Blood Brotherhood: The Racialization of Patriotism, 1865–1918." In *Bonds of Affection: Americans Define Their Patriotism,* edited by John Bodnar, 53–81. Princeton, N.J.: Princeton University Press, 1996.

Peoples, Morgan. "'The Scapegoat of Andersonville': Union Execution of Confederate Captain Henry Wirz." *North Louisiana Historical Association Journal* 11 (Fall 1980): 3–18.

Petersen, William J., ed. "Iowa at Andersonville." *Palimpsest* 42 (June 1961): 209–81.

Radford, Tim. "The Visual Story." In *National Prisoner of War Museum Andersonville, Georgia Dedication April 9, 1998*, 22–24. N.p.: privately printed, 1998.

Ramsdell, Charles W. Review of *Civil War Prisons: A Study in War Psychology*, by William B. Hesseltine. *Mississippi Valley Historical Review* 17 (December 1930): 480–81.

Robertson, James I., Jr. "Houses of Horror: Danville's Civil War Prisons." *Virginia Magazine of History and Biography* 69 (July 1961): 329–45.

———. "The Scourge of Elmira." In *Civil War Prisons*, ed. William B. Hesseltine, 80–97. Kent, Ohio: Kent State University Press, 1962. Reprint, Kent, Ohio: Kent State University Press, 1995.

Robins, Glenn M. "Race, Repatriation, and Galvanized Rebels: Union Prisoners and the Exchange Question in Deep South Prison Camps." *Civil War History* 53 (June 2007): 117–40.

Ruffin, Edmund. "Extracts from the Diary of Edmund Ruffin." *William and Mary College Quarterly Historical Magazine* 23 (July 1914): 31–45.

Rutman, Darrett B. "The War Crimes and Trial of Henry Wirz." *Civil War History* 6 (June 1960): 117–33.

Sanchez, Fred. "Andersonville Prisoner of War Oral History Institute: To Preserve the Legacy." In *National Prisoner of War Museum Andersonville, Georgia Dedication April 9, 1998*, 31–33. N.p.: privately printed, 1998.

Sanders, Charles W., Jr. Review of *800 Paces to Hell*, by John Lynn, and *To Die in Chicago*, by George Levy. *Journal of Southern History* 66 (November 2000): 880–81.

Scroggs, Jack B. Review of *History of Andersonville Prison*, by Ovid Futch. *Journal of Southern History* 35 (February 1969): 104–5.

Shriver, Phillip R. Review of *History of Andersonville Prison*, by Ovid Futch. *Civil War History* 15 (March 1969): 79–80.

Simpson, Leonard. "Construction of the National Prisoner of War Museum." In *National Prisoner of War Museum Andersonville, Georgia Dedication April 9, 1998*, 11. N.p.: privately printed, 1998.

Skolnick, Andrew. "Medicine and War: Recognizing Common Vulnerability of Friend and Foe." *Journal of the American Medical Association* 265 (February 20, 1991): 834, 837.

Steere, Edward. "Genesis of American Graves Registration." *Military Affairs* 12 (Autumn 1948): 149–61.

Stewart, Edgar. Review of *Camp Morton, 1861–1865: Indianapolis Prison Camp,* by Hattie Lou Winslow and Joseph R. H. Moore. *American Historical Review* 47 (October 1941): 198–99.

Stibbs, John H. "Andersonville and the Trial of Henry Wirz." *Iowa Journal of History and Politics* 9 (1911): 33–56.

Summers, Mark W. Review of *Andersonville,* produced by David W. Rintels. *Journal of American History* 83 (December 1996): 1119–20.

Tap, Bruce. "'These Devils Are not Fit to Live on God's Earth': War Crimes and the Committee on the Conduct of the War, 1864–1865." *Civil War History* 38 (June 1996): 116–32.

Thompson, James W. "Southern Comment: Andersonville—Truth versus Falsehood." *Blue & Gray* 3 (December–January 1985–86): 28–35.

Thompson, Lawrence S. "The Civil War in Fiction." *Civil War History* 2 (March 1956): 83–95.

Thompson, William Y. "The U. S. Sanitary Commission." *Civil War History* 2 (June 1956): 41–63.

Tucker, Gwynn A. "Andersonville Prison: What Happened?" In *Andersonville Prison: Lessons in Organizational Failure,* ed. Joseph P. Cangemi and Casimir J. Kowalski, 1–34. Lanham, Md.: University Press of America, 1992.

Ward, Nathan. "The Time Machine." *American Heritage* 41 (November 1990): 42–46.

Watkins, T. H. "A Heritage Preserved." *American Heritage* 31 (April/May 1980): 100–101.

Weister, Polly. "Echoes of 'Echoes': Reflections on the Making of 'Echoes in Captivity.'" In *National Prisoner of War Museum Andersonville, Georgia Dedication April 9, 1998,* 25–26. N.p.: privately printed, 1998.

Weitz, Mark A. "Preparing for the Prodigal Sons: The Development of the Union Desertion Policy during the Civil War." *Civil War History* 45 (June 1999): 99–125.

Wiley, Bell I., ed. "Report of the Activities Committee to the Civil War Centennial Commission." *Civil War History* 5 (December 1959): 374–81.

Williamson, Hugh P. "Military Prisons in the Civil War." *Bulletin* 16 (July 1960): 329–32.

Wilson, Christopher Kent. "Winslow Homer's Images of Blacks: The Civil War and Reconstruction Years." *Journal of American History* 77 (June 1990): 246–53.

Winther, Oscar O. Review of *Camp Morton, 1861–1865: Indianapolis Prison Camp,* by Hattie Lou Winslow and Joseph R. H. Moore. *Journal of Southern History* 7 (August 1941): 413.

Woodward, C. Vann. Review of *The Past Is a Foreign Country,* by David Lowenthal. *History and Theory* 26 (October 1987): 346–52.

Wubben, H. H. "American Prisoners of War in Korea: A Second Look at the 'Something New in History' Theme." *American Quarterly* 22 (Spring 1970): 3–19.

Audiovisual Sources

Andersonville. VHS. Produced and directed by John Frankenheimer and David Rintels. Turner Pictures, 1996.

Andersonville National Historic Site Self-Guided Tour CD. N.p., 2001.

The Andersonville Trial. VHS. Produced and directed by George C. Scott. KCET Los Angeles, 1970.

The Blue and the Gray. VHS. Directed by Andrew V. McLaglen. Columbia Pictures Television, 1982.

Center for Business and Economic Development. *Andersonville, Cotton, & Carter Country: CD Driving Tour.* Recorded at Captive Sound Inc., Atlanta, Ga., 1998.

Echoes of Captivity. VHS. Produced by Polly Weister. Friends of Andersonville, 1998.

Hutchison, D. L. & Associates. *The Prison Camp at Andersonville Interactive CD-ROM.* Fowlerville, Mich.: Hutchinson's Heritage Press, 1999.

National Prisoner of War Museum. VHS. Produced by Tim Radford. Friends of Andersonville, 1998.

Vigilantes of Love, "Andersonville," *Killing Floor.* 1992.

Unpublished Theses and Dissertations

Boyer, Nathan G. "Prisoners of War: Policy and Consequence in the American Civil War." M.A. thesis, California State University, Fresno, 2000.

Chappo, John F. "Into the Valley of the Shadow: Governmental Policy, Camp Life, and Postbellum Remembrance of the American Civil War Prisoner-of-War System." M.A. thesis, University of Southern Mississippi, 2000.

Cloyd, Benjamin. "Prisoners of a New Bureaucracy: Organizational Failure at Andersonville and Elmira Prisons during the Civil War." M.A. thesis, Louisiana State University, 2000.

Gardner, Douglas G. "Andersonville and American Memory: Civil War Prisoners and Narratives of Suffering and Redemption." Ph.D. diss., Miami University, 1998.

Hunter, Leslie G. "Warden for the Union: General William Hoffman (1807–1884)." Ph.D. diss., University of Arizona, 1971.

Klemm, Amy L. "A Shared Captivity: Inmates and Guards in the Texas Military Prison System, 1863–1865." M.A. thesis, University of Houston, 1997.

Koerting, Gayla. "The Trial of Henry Wirz and Nineteenth-Century Military Law." Ph.D. diss., Kent State University, 1995.

Kubalanza, Joan Marie G. "A Comparative Study of Conditions at Two Civil War Prison Camps: Camp Douglas, Chicago, Illinois and Camp Sumpter, Andersonville, Georgia." M.A. thesis, DePaul University, 1979.

Oberlaender, Michaela. "William J. Thompson's *Andersonville Memorial:* Historical Precedents and Contemporary Context." M.A. thesis, University of Georgia, 1993.

Panhorst, Michael W. "Lest We Forget: Monuments and Memorial Sculpture in National Military Parks on Civil War Battlefields, 1861–1917." Ph.D. diss., University of Delaware, 1988.

Parker, Elizabeth Leonard. "The Civil War Career of Henry Wirz and Its Aftermath." M.A. thesis, University of Georgia, 1948.

Roberts, Nancy A. "The Afterlife of Civil War Prisons and Their Dead." Ph.D. diss., University of Oregon, 1996.

Smithpeters, Jeff. "'To the Latest Generation': Cold War and Post Cold War U.S. Civil War Novels in Their Social Contexts." Ph.D. diss., Louisiana State University, 2005.

Thomas, Eugene M., III. "Prisoner of War Exchange during the American Civil War." Ph.D. diss., Auburn University, 1976.

INDEX

CPSIA information can be obtained
at www.ICGtesting.com
Printed in the USA
LVHW111826151019
634274LV00003B/311/P